# THE NEXT GREAT CLASH

# The Next Great Clash

## China and Russia vs.
## the United States

**Michael L. Levin**

PRAEGER SECURITY INTERNATIONAL
Westport, Connecticut · London

**Library of Congress Cataloging-in-Publication Data**

Levin, Michael L.
   The next great clash : China and Russia vs. the United States / Michael L. Levin.
     p. cm.
   Includes bibliographical references and index.
   ISBN-13: 978-0-313-34592-0 (alk. paper)
1. Balance of power—Forecasting. 2. China—Foreign relations—Russia (Federation) 3. Russia
(Federation)—Foreign relations—China. 4. China—Foreign relations—United States. 5. United States
—Foreign relations—China. 6. Russia (Federation)—Foreign relations—United States. 7. United States
—Foreign relations—Russia (Federation) I. Title.
JZ1313.L48 2008
327.51073—dc22     2007027855

British Library Cataloguing in Publication Data is available.

Library of Congress Catalog Card Number: 2007027855
ISBN-13: 978-0-313-34592-0

First published in 2008

Praeger Security International, 88 Post Road West, Westport, CT 06881
An imprint of Greenwood Publishing Group, Inc.
www.praeger.com

Printed in the United States of America

The paper used in this book complies with the
Permanent Paper Standard issued by the National
Information Standards Organization (Z39.48–1984).

10 9 8 7 6 5 4 3 2 1

**Copyright Acknowledgments**

Table 2.5 is adapted and expanded based on Table 2.1, "Imperial Phases," in David B. Abernethy, *The Dynamics of Global Dominance: European Overseas Empires 1415–1980* (New Haven, CT: Yale University Press, 2000), 24.

This book is dedicated to my parents and sisters.

# CONTENTS

# TABLES

# ACKNOWLEDGMENTS

I have been blessed with so many dedicated teachers, especially Kelly; Anne Freedman, Lily Rose, Leon Stein, and Frank Untermyer at Roosevelt University; Theodore Friedgut, Ezra Mendelsohn, and Ida Stein at Hebrew University; John and Margaretta Mathis at Thunderbird; and Fouad Ajami, Eliot Cohen, Charles Gati, Bruce Parrott, S. Frederick Starr, and Anne Thurston at Johns Hopkins School of Advanced International Studies (SAIS).

I am especially indebted to my language teachers, Nachman, Tamar, and Sandra; the indefatigable Mrs. Z. at Hebrew University; Ke Tai Tai and Guo Laoshi at Thunderbird; and Natasha Simes at SAIS. Each new language gave me a new life, a new culture, a clean slate, a chance to plumb my depths, and these teachers were the best of guides.

A special thanks to Adam, Bill, Boyong, Chuck, Daphne, David, Denise, DB, Frankie, Geoff, Janelle, Jeff, John, Jonathan, Judy, Mary Pat, Maureen, Natasha, Oliver, Peter, Scott, Sue, and Tina for reading and commenting on various parts of this manuscript, and encouraging me throughout. To Julia Lord, my agent, who took me in, cheered me on, and guided me through to publication, and to Hilary Claggett, my editor at Praeger, thank you for your faith in an unpublished author. Anne Beer, a meticulous and gracious copy editor, saved me from a great deal of embarrassment.

Most importantly, this book is a tribute to all my friends in foreign lands—especially Mike, Moshe, Shimon, Tsuri, Andrei, Garik, Oleg, Olga, Sasha, Valeri, Adith, Boyong, Jason, and Lucia. I wrote this book with them in mind, and hope that together we can avoid *The Next Great Clash*.

# ABBREVIATIONS

| | |
|---|---|
| ABC | American-born Chinese |
| ABM | Anti-Ballistic Missile |
| BAM | Baikal-Amur Railway |
| BPD | Barrels Per Day (of oil) |
| $C^3I$ | Command, Control, Communications, and Intelligence |
| CCP | Chinese Communist Party |
| CER | China Eastern Railway |
| CIA | Central Intelligence Agency |
| CNOOC | China National Offshore Oil Corporation |
| CNPC | China National Petroleum Corporation |
| CPSU | Communist Party of the Soviet Union |
| CSIS | Center for Strategic & International Studies (United States) |
| DPP | Democratic Progressive Party (Republic of China) |
| DPRK | Democratic People's Republic of Korea (North) |
| EIA | Energy Information Administration (United States) |
| ERRF | European Rapid Reaction Force |
| ESPO | Eastern Siberia Pacific Ocean Pipeline |
| EU | European Union |
| FMS | foreign military sales |
| FSB | Federalnaya Sluzhba Bezopasnosti (Federal Security Service—Russia) |
| GDP | Gross Domestic Product |
| GNPOC | Greater Nile Petroleum Operating Company (Sudan) |
| ICBM | Intercontinental Ballistic Missile |
| IDF | Indigenous Defense Force, Indigenous Defense Fighter (Taiwan) |
| IISS | International Institute of Strategic Studies |
| IMF | International Monetary Fund |
| ISI | Inter-Service Intelligence Agency (Pakistan) |
| K-waves | Kondratieff Waves |
| KFOR | Kosovo Force |

| KGB | Komitet Gosudarstvennoi Bezopasnosti (Committee for State Security—USSR) |
|---|---|
| KMT | Kuomintang, or Nationalist Party |
| LC | Long Cycle |
| LNG | Liquid Natural Gas |
| MFO | Multinational Force and Observers |
| MID | Militarized Interstate Dispute |
| MLSA | Mutual Logistics Support Agreement |
| NATO | North Atlantic Treaty Organization |
| NEC | Northeast China |
| NGO | Non-governmental Organization |
| NMD | National Missile Defense |
| NRI | Non-resident Indian |
| ONGC | Oil and Natural Gas Corporation (India) |
| OPEC | Organization of the Petroleum Exporting Countries |
| PAWS | Phased Array Warning System |
| PFP | People's First Party (Republic of China) |
| PIO | Person of Indian Origin |
| PLA | People's Liberation Army (China) |
| PLAAF | People's Liberation Army Air Force (China) |
| PRC | People's Republic of China |
| QDR | Quadrennial Defense Review (United States) |
| RAS | Replenishment-at-Sea |
| RFE | Russian Far East |
| ROC | Republic of China (Taiwan) |
| ROK | Republic of Korea (South) |
| RMA | Revolution in Military Affairs |
| SALT | Strategic Arms Limitation Treaty |
| SCO | Shanghai Cooperation Organization |
| SEATO | Southeast Asia Treaty Organization |
| SIPRI | Stockholm International Peace Research Institute |
| SLBM | Submarine-launched Ballistic Missile |
| SLOC | Sea Lines of Communication |
| SOE | State-owned Enterprise |
| SOFA | Status of Forces Agreement |
| TMD | Theater Missile Defense |
| TSU | Taiwan Solidarity Union |
| UES | United Energy Systems (Russia) |
| WTO | World Trade Organization |

# 1 ⸻

# INTRODUCTION

*The trick's to find something no one else knows.*

—Ward Just, *An Unfinished Season*

As a wild teen run amok, they banished me to an island for wayward youth where rule number one was: Out of sight is out of bounds. Privacy here was a privilege to be earned on our island Skinner Box. We humored ourselves by calling this place Alcatraz Junior and thought of ourselves as the baddest of the bad. Because of our isolation, the island had a certain *Lord of the Flies* quality, but here the adults were still firmly in control.

In a rather sadistic twist, the adults had once taken a group of us to see Kubrick's film, *A Clockwork Orange,* based on the Anthony Burgess novel studded with Nadsat, a language concocted from a mixture of Russian, English, and American slang. A nasty tale of Alex and his *droogs* and their night of carousing and ultra-violence, Alex landed in an experimental government program where he was conditioned to associate violence and sex with the classical music that he so passionately loved, which in turn triggered waves of nausea and vomiting.

I left the island more than two years later, only seventeen, with a suitcase and with the firm conviction that the more you have, the more they can take away. I also left with a fierce determination to become a writer. I plowed through all of the *Paris Review* interviews looking for secrets of the trade and fixed on Henry Miller's practical advice to go and do because they cannot take that away. I also developed a fascination with psychology because I wanted to understand how they had reshaped me and my *droogs.*

\*

By coincidence, just a few months after I left the island, Burgess gave a reading from *A Clockwork Orange* at a local college. He had written the book in a mere six weeks, he said, after doctors told him that he had a few more months to live because of an inoperable brain tumor; he died more than thirty years and more than thirty books later.

America was in the throes of Watergate, but I had been enthralled with President Nixon's trip to China and fascinated by the Moscow summits. More than anyone, Dr. Henry Kissinger, the son of German immigrants who had fled the Nazis and made good in America, captured my imagination. Solzhenitsyn's *The Gulag Archipelago,* smuggled out of the Soviet Union, appeared under the imprint of the YMCA Press in 1973; I immersed myself in the land of the Gulag and its *zeks*—Soviet prison camp inmates—and made a list of Gulag argot.

A mysterious illness struck me down and almost killed me when I was eighteen. Blood clots in my lungs paralyzed me with pain and I waited for intravenous morphine every four hours. My parents were put on notice and a priest came in my room; he asked if I wanted to take last rites—I refused and told him I was Jewish, so he sent the rabbi.

The doctors were never able to name my illness, and for several years, I lived with the fear that it might return at any time. I steeped myself in the literature of death, especially Solzhenitsyn's *Cancer Ward* and Tolstoy's *The Death of Ivan Ilyich.*

After my recovery, adrift and uncertain, I enrolled in college and began to take a hodge-podge of courses, while working at various odd jobs—from janitor in an apartment complex to manager of a flophouse to runner in a car park to bellhop, doorman and front desk clerk. I secured a spot on the door at one of Chicago's most prestigious hotels and settled into a routine of working forty hours from Friday afternoon to Sunday night; I spent the week in school. My formal education proceeded in fits and starts—no 4-year trajectory for me, a self-styled Augie March.

I gravitated toward the history department and my world was set ablaze when I enrolled in a course on the Holocaust. The professor delivered his lectures in a trance-like state; he often closed his eyes, tilted his head backwards, and moved his hands round and round as though searching on a Ouija board for the right words to use for this almost unspeakable subject; he seemed haunted, a prince of death. I devoured the Holocaust, and thanked God that the Nazis didn't have computers.

In a survey course on China, I discovered a minor historical figure, Mikhail Borodin, and typed out this quote on a file card: "The silence that Borodin maintained about himself facilitated the manufacture of such fables. But what could have been more unbelievable than the truth? The Chinese revolution was being piloted to victory by a Chicago school-master, born a *shtetl* Jew in the Tsar's Pale, and now in the service of international Communism."[1] I learned about the

Cultural Revolution and the mass hysteria that gripped millions of Chinese as the young were turned against their elders, as Red was turned against expert. The Party's ability to mobilize fascinated and horrified me, and I sought to identify the techniques that governments used to manipulate the masses so that I would know how to resist.

My path from the island had led to Germany, Russia, China, Hitler, Stalin, Mao, the concentration camps, the Gulag, and China's *laogai*.

As I slowly made my way in the academic world, I was forced to narrow the scope of my interests, and so began to settle on Russia as my subject. I soon completed all of the related course work offered at Roosevelt, a comparatively small, private college in downtown Chicago.

I knew of no Russian studies programs for undergraduates in the United States, but an adviser told me that in Israel students chose their specialty as an undergraduate and focused on it for a full three years, unlike America's 4-year liberal arts curriculum. He suggested I look into the Department of Russian and Slavic Studies at the Hebrew University of Jerusalem.

I had studied Hebrew in preparation for my bar mitzvah—but that consisted of memorizing and reciting passages from the Torah. So I enrolled in an intensive summer language course and studied Hebrew all day, while parking cars, tending door, and bellhopping evenings and nights—all the while hoarding my tips. Finally, true to Miller's dictum to go and do, I packed my trunk and flew to Israel not long after Prime Minister Menachem Begin of Israel and President Anwar Sadat of Egypt signed their historic peace accord in 1979.

*

On my first night in the Holy Land, I ended up in a cockroach-infested motel on Tel Aviv's Hayarkon Street and was befriended by several Russian women lollygagging about on a verandah that overlooked the Mediterranean Sea. I hardly slept that night—what with the oppressive heat, no air-conditioner, jet lag, bedbugs, and a bevy of fornicators shrieking all around me. I was hungry but everything was closed; one of the Russians offered me a cucumber and a shot of vodka.

The next morning I made my way over to the central kibbutz office and was interviewed by a woman dressed in an outlandish kaftan and turban who told me that her name was Queen Mal'cah and that I was to stand before her; I was petrified that she'd ask me to prove that I was Jewish. But without looking at me she rattled off a series of questions, filled in a form, and—with all of her massive weight—whacked the form with an official stamp and sent me on my way to a kibbutz in the Galilee, not far from Nazareth.

In exchange for work in the kibbutz factory, cafeteria, or orange groves, the kibbutz provided a five-month language *ulpan*—an intensive Hebrew course that met six days a week for three or four hours each day—with room and board included; we even earned a small allowance in the form of a credit in the kibbutz canteen. It slowly began to dawn on me that many of the kibbutz elders had those numbers tattooed on their forearms.

Our *ulpan* comprised about thirty volunteers from all over the world, but many of them could never return to their homelands. My roommate, Sharon, a young Iranian, had fled Tehran after Khomeini's shock troops tortured his brother, who had worked for Savak, the Shah's secret police. Sharon stuttered and would periodically succumb to an uncontrollable tic, throwing his right hand over his left shoulder, as if to engage in religious flagellation.[2] Since we had no choice, we began to communicate with each other in Hebrew.

In the meantime, I had applied to Hebrew University and was accepted into the Russian and Slavic Studies program for the following academic year, contingent upon completion of a six-month intensive language program.

From 1980 to the end of 1982, I lived in Jerusalem and studied on the Mount Scopus campus, with its panoramic view of the Old City and the Temple Mount. I rode my bicycle everywhere, careening up and down the city's hills; on a few occasions, if I failed to make it home before sunset on Friday, the Hasidim in the Mea Sharim quarter threw rocks at me as I raced through their neighborhood.

Mrs. Z., our Russian teacher, dominated my life; powerfully built and eccentric, she rarely spoke about herself. Sometimes I espied her from afar, as she walked across campus in her trademark sunglasses, her beret akimbo, furtively puffing away on a cigarette. On the first day of class, she told her new charges that she didn't care how many of us remained, she was paid the same thank-you-very-much, and so would only teach the most dedicated students; the class size dwindled from thirteen to five. I lived in fear of the nyets that Mrs. Z. hurled at me like thunderbolts and cherished her occasional smiles.

Although I was preoccupied with preparing for Mrs. Z.'s daily Russian-language drills, I also enrolled in a survey course on pre-Revolutionary Russian literature, and so plowed through the major works of Pushkin, Lermontov, Gogol, Turgenev, Dostoevsky and Tolstoy in a year. Courses on the history and politics of Russia and the Soviet Union rounded out the curriculum, and I spent a full year in a one-on-one tutorial that focused on the development and evolution of the Russian and Soviet intelligence services.

The country erupted in joy on June 7, 1981, when Israeli jets destroyed the Osirak nuclear reactor in Baghdad. A bit more than a year later, Israel became enmeshed in Lebanon and General Ariel Sharon resigned his government post over Sabra and Shatila. A classmate of mine who seemed destined to fame as a concert pianist left the Mount Scopus campus for Lebanon's Bekaa Valley; I pictured his delicate fingers gliding across the keyboard and then wrapped around the trigger of an Uzi submachine gun.

My teachers in Israel told me that in order to take my Russian language skills to the next level I had to study in the Soviet Union. Since Israel did not have diplomatic relations with the USSR in the early 1980s, they advised me to return to America and provided me with reference letters.

\*

At the time, two organizations—with about two hundred slots to fill annually—controlled U.S.-USSR educational exchanges. Competition was fierce and the first time around I didn't make the cut; I reapplied and was accepted for the spring semester in 1984. These seemed to be the darkest of days in relations between the United States and the Soviet Union: Yuri Andropov, the former KGB Chairman, was ruling from a hospital bed as his kidneys failed; and in America, President Reagan's "Evil Empire" Speech was followed by the Soviet downing of KAL 007. All of this took place during the largest U.S. military buildup in peacetime. Andropov died and the ailing septuagenarian, Konstantin Chernenko, shuffled in to take his place.

In preparation for my journey to Moscow, I had contacted a local organization that lobbied on behalf of *refuseniks*—Soviet Jews whose applications to emigrate to Israel had been denied by the government. Some of the *refuseniks* had been imprisoned on trumped-up charges, several staged hunger strikes, many lost their jobs. I spent hours poring over their biographies and memorizing addresses, phone numbers, and public transportation routes. I was given a large suitcase filled with prescription drugs and instructed to deliver it to one of two primary contacts in Moscow. I was told to apply for a credit card and informed that my contacts would periodically give me lists of goods to purchase in Moscow's *beriozhkas*—special shops stocked with foreign goods that only accepted foreign currency; most Soviets were barred from these shops since they did not have foreign currency. I was assured that I would be reimbursed for all *beriozhka* purchases.

While in the Soviet Union, I was never to mention the names of my contacts in Chicago or the names of other families I met with in Moscow; however, the primary contacts could refer me to other families and ask me to make deliveries to them. I was reminded to avoid using public phones close to the institute where I'd be studying in Moscow, and I was issued one of those "Magic Writing Boards" where whatever has been written disappears by lifting the cover, a transparent page. I read all of the western journalists' accounts of life in Moscow and catalogued local lore; I immersed myself in spy novels, compiling lists of tradecraft.

The program director called me two days before our departure and told me that the Soviets did not issue my visa. He said there'd be a spot for me in the next group, and so I waited, my life in limbo, hoping, ironically, that the Soviets would let me in while the *refuseniks* clamored to get out.

\*

In early September, my group flew to Helsinki, transferred to the railway station, and boarded an overnight train for Moscow; foreigners had to travel in darkness.

I remember that night in 1984 because of the intensity of my fear as Soviet border guards stormed onto the train to inspect our documents. We had just crossed over from Finland and stopped at the Vyborg station. Giant spotlights fixed on the train as patrols with guard dogs paced up and down the barren platform outside. Flashbacks of train cars from all over Europe converging on the camps overwhelmed me. Crammed into an upper berth in an overheated, four-man compartment with just inches between my face and the ceiling, I felt short of breath and on the verge of bolting out of the car. One of my comrades on the opposite bunk below reached up, grasped my forearm, and told me to calm down, take deep breaths. Our cabin door slammed open, a hand reached in, and a voice bellowed "*dokymenty*"; we handed over our documents and waited several minutes until the arm reappeared with our passports, visas, and customs declarations affixed with all of the proper stamps.

The next morning we arrived at Moscow's Leningradsky Station, were marched to a bus, taken to the Institute, and shown to our living quarters in the wing for "students from the capitalist world." Other wings housed "students from bloc countries" (the eastern European satellites, China, and Cuba) and "students from non-aligned countries" (Finland, India, Vietnam, etc.). Students from Africa and the Middle East were segregated at Patrice Lumumba University, just a ten-minute walk from the Institute along a path through the woods out back. The authorities frowned upon fraternization between the various groups.

Room assignments were based on nationality, and all of the American Jews were assigned to the same room. The spartan accommodations were adequate. A constant barrage of Soviet propaganda emanated from a radio affixed to the wall; we couldn't unplug the radio and were certain that when it was silent it listened to us. All of our classes were conducted in Russian by competent and enthusiastic instructors, specially vetted for their loyalty, we assumed, and so able to withstand the corrupting influence of their American charges. One could go to a special window and pay for a breakfast of cold hot dogs, canned peas, and luke-warm tea, or stand in the cafeteria line for a free bowl of a slimy, fishy gruel that left an unpleasant aftertaste.

As soon as classes ended at 2 PM sharp, I bolted out of the Institute and began exploring Moscow, slowly establishing contact with the network of *refuseniks* to whom I had been assigned. I had brought several expensive editions of the Koran with me to Moscow because they fetched high prices on the black market, and I had passed them along to my contacts; in return, they fed me home-cooked meals. Soon enough, I was shuttling between Moscow's best-stocked *beriozhka* to families scattered throughout the city delivering cases of Similac baby formula.

I spent most of my free time with a couple my age who had applied to emigrate to Israel but had been denied exit visas for several years running; we spoke Hebrew with one another in preparation for their eventual emigration. They lived in a room in his mother's two-room apartment in the Taganskaya neighborhood and introduced me to their circle of friends at frequent gatherings that lasted late into the night.

I spent hours with Zhenya, who was in the midst of a hunger strike to protest the imprisonment of her husband, who had organized Hebrew classes throughout Moscow. I taped a lengthy interview with her, transcribed it, translated it into English, and delivered it to the lead reporter of a major Western weekly magazine. I was directed to Natasha,[3] a former history teacher, who met with me over two months and introduced me to several works of *samizdat*— government-banned literature that had been secretly published and distributed.

Finally, at the end of our semester, we took the overnight train to Leningrad and spent several days sightseeing before continuing along to Helsinki. At that same crossing at Vyborg, several border guards, led by a tall and portly man with bloated cheeks and sporting a fedora, entered our car and headed straight for my compartment. Dismissing my cabin mates, they crowded in and ordered me to undress as they began rummaging through my luggage. The angry man crushed several rolls of film underfoot as he glowered at me; when they found a couple of cassettes, the angry man took them, posted a guard at the door, and left. When he returned, he handed me a form and demanded that I sign. I feigned incomprehension, but he kept insisting; I kept repeating that our ambassador instructed us not to sign any documents without his approval. Eventually, he exited, I got dressed, and we continued along to Helsinki.

Churchill famously described Russia as a "riddle wrapped in a mystery inside an enigma." I discovered that I reveled in the riddle, was intoxicated by mystery, and vowed to return.

*

After a few weeks in Chicago, I repacked my bags and headed out to Arizona to begin a graduate program in international management at Thunderbird.[4] I enrolled in a seminar on East/West trade, won faculty approval for an independent study project in which I created a database containing hundreds of entries on U.S. business interests in the Soviet Union, and wrote a thesis on Soviet industrial espionage. In order to graduate, students were required to pass a proficiency exam in a foreign language but since Thunderbird did not teach Russian or Hebrew, I was required to take another language and so selected Chinese.

Shortly after graduating from Thunderbird, I wound up in Moscow manning a booth at a medical equipment exhibition but when that was over, I was thirty and jobless, dead broke, and in hock to the purveyors of student loans. I fixed on joining the corporate world as the most logical and rewarding cover for more foreign adventures as I continued on my quest to "find something no one else knows."

That was more than twenty years ago. Since then I have traveled all over the world and have lived in Moscow and Nizhny Novgorod (Gorky) during the free-for-all of the Yeltsin era, in Shanghai when the United States bombed the Chinese embassy in Belgrade, in Hong Kong after the handover, in D.C. during 9/11 and Iraq war fever; and most recently, in Tianjin, China. I have worked on a World Bank project with the Russian Employment Service, set up the American Business Center in Nizhny, turned around a Russian IT company on the verge of bankruptcy, served in a senior managerial position with *The Asian Wall Street Journal* and the *Far Eastern Economic Review,* and stepped in at a critical juncture to manage an American company in China under investigation for violations of the Foreign Corrupt Practices Act.

My years of training on the island taught me how to operate below the radar even under close observation, and so the secretive and conspiratorial environments of Russia and China seemed natural milieus for me. At the same time, I came to see the world from a unique perspective, unfettered by the restrictions placed on government officials, unburdened by the rivalries that stifle academia.

Like many others, I have come to believe that, while the United States now stands as the undisputed Great Power, China's reemergence after a 500-year hiatus to its place of preeminence in East Asia will shape the twenty-first century. China is the only nation with the potential to challenge America on the world stage in a process that will unfold over the next several decades. U.S. hegemony and unilateralism will not prevail indefinitely; the world is on the verge of a historic transition from Western to Asian dominance, and such "systemic power transitions have usually been accompanied by war."[5]

I have also come to believe that Russia, even in its post-Cold War diminished capacity, is the "swing player" in a future clash between the United States and China. Russia controls continental gateways to the Chinese heartland, sits astride vast amounts of oil and gas that China desperately needs, and supplies the People's Liberation Army with military hardware and technology worth billions.

My theory then, is that a Sino-Russian alliance against the United States will constitute *The Next Great Clash*. America's current involvement in its Global War on Terror has diverted attention from the implications of these monumental shifts.

\*

I keep a list of all the books I've read, and I've pasted William Safire's wise observation at the top of my list: "Reading is the collecting of intellectual income; writing is the spending of it." However, I always remind myself of a comment made by John King Fairbank, the dean of American Sinologists: "The expansion of our knowledge has expanded the circumference of our ignorance." Thus, I accept full responsibility for any accidental errors in fact, in logic or of omission. The views presented here are mine and mine alone.

# Part One

# EYE OF THE STORM:
# THE THEORETICAL LENS

*Should the United States use all the means at its disposal to delay as long as possible the emergence of China as a major power?*

—Henry Kissinger

When considering global political power at the dawn of the twenty-first century, it is not the mechanical application of a theory or two portending doom and gloom that is so troubling, but it is a profusion of converging patterns and transitions in these uncertain times. Nor is the purpose to critique the validity of a particular model or theory, but to highlight the overwhelming confluence of these disturbing trends.

Global political developments do not flow as smoothly as the transitions between paragraphs, nor do events always fit neatly into the many patterns, cycles, and paradigms presented here. Nevertheless, the breathtaking pace of change accelerates with each passing decade, and so the need to step back and reflect on what may come to pass is even more critical.

The seven theories discussed in this chapter were chosen because they represent a cross section of ideas, each with a different focus, covering different time spans and places. One theory looks at economic innovations as the key to global competition (Modelski and Thompson), another at the pace of economic modernization (Organski and Kugler). Philip Bobbitt analyzes the evolution of the nation-state and the emergence of a new form of constitutional order, the market-state, while John Mearsheimer emphasizes imbalances in the global political order. Samuel Huntington makes the case for an impending "clash of civilizations," while David Abernethy demonstrates how patterns of colonization and decolonization have exacerbated the current wave of political fragmentation. All of these processes are taking place during a transition to a post-petroleum economy, and so Michael Klare believes that the competition for scarce resources will lead to the outbreak of resource wars.

What is most striking about these various theories is that they all lead to or support the conclusion that America is heading toward a major war with China.

**Table 2.1  Summary of Theories**

| Theory/Focus | Theorists | Timeframe | Place | Possible outcome |
|---|---|---|---|---|
| Long cycles Kondratieff waves | Modelski and Thompson | 900s to the present | China and Western Europe | Global war in the 2030s |
| Constitutional order Epochal wars | Bobbitt | 1500s–1991 | Great Powers | Epochal ("cataclysmic") war with Russia and/or China |
| "Offensive realism" System structure Balance of power | Mearsheimer | 1792–1990 | Great Powers | War with China |
| Power transition model Pace and sequence of modernization | Organski and Kugler | 20th century | Global | War with China after "point of intersection"; Chinese-Russian alliance? |
| Clash of civilizations | Huntington | 20th century | Global | Chinese-Islamic alliance: an "arms-for-oil axis" |
| Colonization and decolonization | Abernethy | 1415–1980 | European imperial powers | Political fragmentation; Ethnic cleansing |
| Resource wars/ Peak production | Klare | 21st century | Global | Global oil production peak → post-petroleum economy |

*Sources* (in order of appearance): George Modelski and William R. Thompson, *Leading Sectors and World Powers: The Coevolution of Global Politics and Economics* (Columbia: University of South Carolina Press, 1996); Philip Bobbitt, *The Shield of Achilles: War, Peace and the Course of History* (New York: Knopf, 2002); John J. Mearsheimer, *The Tragedy of Great Power Politics* (New York: W.W. Norton, 2001); A. F. K. Organski and Jacek Kugler, *The War Ledger* (University of Chicago Press, 1980); Samuel P. Huntington, *The Clash of Civilizations and the Remaking of the World Order* (New York: Simon & Schuster, 1996); David B. Abernethy, *The Dynamics of Global Dominance: European Overseas Empires 1415–1980* (New Haven, CT: Yale University Press, 2000); Michael T. Klare, *Resource Wars: The New Landscape of Global Conflict* (New York: Metropolitan Books, 2001).

## LONG CYCLES AND KONDRATIEFF WAVES

In a survey of global political and economic trends extending back to China's Northern Sung era (960–1279), George Modelski and William Thompson, in *Leading Sectors and World Powers,* posit a strong correlation between long cycles (LCs) of global political leadership and the appearance of major economic innovations.

Two chapters in *Leading Sectors* are devoted to China's rise to preeminence during the tenth century and the later transition to the Italian city-states of Genoa and Venice. But Modelski and Thompson's more general focus is on the long cycles beginning with Portugal in the 1400s and extends to the current era of American global predominance.

According to their model, each long cycle of global political dominance—averaging 110 years—consists of four phases: agenda-setting, coalition-building, macrodecision, and execution. Because each macrodecision phase over the past five hundred years has been characterized by a global war, this phase is the "major beat of each long cycle."[1]

At the same time, Kondratieff waves[2] (K-waves), harnessed by the emerging power to propel the advance toward hegemony, represent movement from one leading economic sector to the next. Each K-wave has averaged fifty to sixty years in duration, and so one long cycle corresponds to two K-waves.

The first spurt of economic innovation (odd-numbered K-waves) has historically tended to signal the approach of a major war. Indeed, the peak of the first spurt of innovation "almost always arrived in the decade immediately before the decade in which global war began,"[3] that is, in the 1480s, the 1670s, the 1780s, the 1900s, and by extrapolating, in the 2020s.[4]

Further, according to Modelski and Thompson, major global economic processes are comprised of four K-waves, and there is "no instance of a series of more than four K-waves centered upon one major region."[5]

By using Modelski and Thompson's model, we can see that the current world power, the United States, is at the intersection of a long cycle approaching the macrodecision (global war) phase and an odd-numbered Kondratieff wave; and major wars of the modern era have occurred during odd-numbered K-waves:

We have documented, moreover, the regularity with which global wars have paced the transitions between [odd- and even-numbered] K-waves since the mid-fifteenth century. In the twentieth century the interval between K17 and K18, the period between 1914 and 1945, that included severe global warfare as well as the Great Depression, was particularly memorable.... [In] the current era, the start-up time for K19, is a time of transition and bears the characteristics of transition crisis.... The result is economic slowdown, an air of depression, high structural unemployment, political turmoil, and the surfacing of fundamentalist ideologies.[6]

**Table 2.2   Long Cycles and Kondratieff Waves**

| Global economic process | Long cycles | Duration | K-waves | Leading economic sector | Peak of innovation | Global war |
|---|---|---|---|---|---|---|
| Oceanic trading | LC5 Portugal | 1430–1540 | K9 K10 | Guinea gold Indian spices | 1480s | Italian wars (1494) |
| | LC6 Dutch Republic | 1540–1640 | K11 K12 | Atlantic trade Asian trade | 1580 | Spanish-Dutch wars (1580) |
| Industrial takeoff | LC7 Britain | 1640–1740 | K13 K14 | Amerasian trade Amerasian trade | 1670s | War of Louis XIV (1680) |
| | LC8 Britain | 1740–1850 | K15 K16 | Cotton, iron Steam, railroad | 1780s | Napoleanic wars (1792) |
| Information economy | LC9 U.S. | 1850–1973 | K17 K18 | Steel, chemicals, electrics Autos, aerospace, electronics | 1900s | World War I (1914) World War II (1945) |
| | LC10 ? | 1973– ? | K19 K20 | Information industries | 2020s | ? (2030s) |

*Source:* Adapted from George Modelski and William R. Thompson, *Leading Sectors and World Powers: The Coevolution of Global Politics and Economics* (Columbia: University of South Carolina Press, 1996).

## CONSTITUTIONAL ORDERS AND EPOCHAL WARS

Rather than emphasizing transition phases between economic innovations, Philip Bobbitt, in *The Shield of Achilles: War, Peace, and the Course of History,* melds the history of warfare, international relations, and constitutional law into a theory of epochal wars—"great coalitional conflicts that extend over decades"[7]—ignited by a breakdown in the legitimacy of the existing constitutional order.

According to Bobbitt, the most recent epochal war—the Long War—consisted of a series of conflicts (World War I, World War II, and the Cold War) spanning seventy-six years from 1914 to 1990, in which the major powers fought over competing visions for the new constitutional order of the day—the nation-state. With the fall of the Soviet Union, liberal democracy emerged victorious in the ideological battle against fascism and Communism. The peace settlement that marked the end of the Long War was different from its predecessors in that the United States emerged from the Long War in a seemingly unassailable position of unprecedented power.

Because globalization—increased global integration in all spheres of life, largely driven by international trade and aided by the information revolution —has weakened the foundations of the nation-state, a new form of constitutional order is emerging: The global political system is undergoing a transition to the "market-state." Just as the great powers battled over what form the nation-state would take, so too will they do battle over the three competing varieties of the nascent market-state that Bobbitt identifies: the entrepreneurial (for example, the United States), the managerial (for example, France and Germany), and the mercantile (for example, Korea and Japan). The uncertainty that permeates the international system—the challenge to national sovereignty posed by terrorists, the proliferation of low-intensity conflicts, the assault on civil liberties in response to the war on terrorism, the apparent ineffectiveness of the United Nations—are all symptoms of systemic transitional friction.

Accordingly, "if the pattern of earlier eras is to be repeated, then we await a new, epochal war with state-shattering consequences"[8] heralding the arrival of the market-state. Moreover, "the new era that we are entering makes their use [of nuclear weapons] by a great power more likely than in the last half century"[9] because nothing else will be effective against a nation with such overwhelming military superiority as the United States now possesses. "Because their own constitutional forms are still at issue and because they are both nuclear powers,"[10] Bobbitt concludes that Russia and China pose the most immediate threat to the global political order.

## OFFENSIVE REALISM: SYSTEM STRUCTURE/BALANCE OF POWER

John Mearsheimer's theory of "offensive realism"[11] is based on two key assertions: that great powers, primed to compete and motivated by an innate drive toward hegemony, relentlessly seek more power; and that multipolar systems characterized by a potential hegemon (unbalanced multipolarity) are most prone to war. War between great powers, according to Mearsheimer, is caused primarily by the distribution of power in the international political system rather than by the introduction of economic innovations or ideological struggles to determine the constitutional order of the day.

The theory of offensive realism asserts that great powers exist in an anarchic and uncertain international system but are nevertheless rational actors whose overriding goal is survival. Fear motivates great powers to act aggressively; hegemony, the ultimate guarantor of survival, is the endgame. A direct correlation between fear and power exists: As the global political order approaches hegemony, more fear permeates the system.

As long as nation-states are defined territorially, armies hold the key to power as conquerors and occupiers; therefore, a nation's military power—especially the size of its land forces—is of paramount importance in an assessment of overall strength. However, as "large bodies of water profoundly limit the power-projection capabilities of land forces,"[12] great powers have been limited to regional hegemony due to the "stopping power of water."

Although land power, sea power, strategic air power, and nuclear forces are all elements of military strength, Mearsheimer concludes that naval blockades (sea power) and strategic bombing campaigns (air power), while useful in lengthy wars of attrition, are rarely decisive.[13] Rather, in a review of ten wars between the great powers over the past two centuries, Mearsheimer demonstrates that land power was decisive in all but one instance—the defeat of Japan in World War II.[14] Further, insular great powers—that is, those that enjoy a strategic advantage by being buffered from aggressors, such as the United States—have not been invaded by other great powers, whereas continental great powers, such as France and Russia, have been invaded by other great powers twelve times since 1792.[15] This suggests that in a showdown between China and the United States, China's home advantage as a continental power with the largest army in the world and millions of reserve troops trumps America's massive power projection capability.

Mearsheimer contends that the United States has maintained its dominant position in North America for more than a century because it is sandwiched between two relatively weak countries, insulated by two oceans, has built a large, conventional army supported by naval and air power, and maintains a vast nuclear arsenal. Europe currently displays a bipolar distribution of power with Russia and the United States as the primary rivals for hegemony. In Northeast Asia, a system of "balanced multipolarity" characterized by competition between China, Russia, and the United States prevails.

To prevent the emergence of other regional hegemons that might challenge its primacy, the United States has intervened as an "offshore balancer" in the major twentieth century wars: in World War I against Wilhelmine Germany, in World War II against Nazi Germany and Japan, and in the Cold War against the Soviet Union.

Simply put, "regional hegemons...do not want peers,"[16] but China is emerging as a potential peer competitor. If China succeeds, Mearsheimer believes the power structure in Northeast Asia will shift to "the most war-prone and deadly distribution of power"[17]—that of unbalanced multipolarity.

The European political system was characterized by unbalanced multipolarity during forty-four of the two hundred years examined in *The Tragedy of Great Power Politics*. Warfare involving the great powers occurred during thirty-five of those forty-four years—or almost 80 percent of the time—and accounted for 96 percent of all military deaths across all countries during the entire period.[18]

If the primacy of land power tempered by the "stopping power of water" impedes a great power's aspirations to regional hegemony, then is the proliferation of U.S. forward bases and the global deployment of its carrier battle groups intended to compensate for the limitations imposed on its power projection capabilities? Is the U.S. invocation of projective power a strategy to encircle an emerging peer competitor, China, on the verge of challenging the United States? After all, "the most dangerous states in the international system are continental powers with large armies,"[19] and China is a continental power with the largest army in the world.

## THE POWER TRANSITION MODEL

According to A. F. K. Organski and Jacek Kugler's power transition model[20] internal (domestic) dynamics are the key indicator of impending conflict between nations. While Mearsheimer's balance-of-power model focuses on asymmetries in the international political order that may be redressed by alliance formation, the power transition model suggests that the pace and developmental sequence of a challenger country's modernization effort, catalyzed by "a general dissatisfaction with its position in the system,"[21] increases the probability of war between the challenger and the dominant power, indeed "sets the whole system sliding almost **irretrievably** [emphasis added] toward war."[22] While alliance formation may temper imbalances in the political system, the dynamics unleashed by disequilibrium—according to the power transition model—are less susceptible to manipulation by external forces (international actors) and so the apparently ineluctable drift toward war, especially between the great powers.

In *The War Ledger*, Organski and Kugler devote a chapter to a measurement of those national capabilities—beyond gross national product (GNP)—that account for "political capacity," which they define as the ability of elites to extract resources for the achievement of national goals.[23] The authors focus on four conflicts—the Arab/*Israeli* wars, *North* v. South Vietnam, India v. *China* (1962) and the Korean War—in which standard measurements, such as GNP, proved to be an unreliable indicator of which party would prevail. The authors conclude that the decisive factor in each instance was a superior level of political mobilization. And how to measure what Paul Kennedy calls "that indefinable 'plus factor' of national self-confidence and willpower in a people whose time has come,"[24] such as is seen in China?

Most efforts to predict when China will overtake the United States, however, focus on models that project economic growth. In two of the four conflicts mentioned above, China surprised the United States by emerging victorious (the stalemate in the Korean War is considered a victory by most Chinese);

in the third conflict, Communist North Vietnam routed the American super-power and ultimately prevailed over South Vietnam.

Communism's mastery of techniques of political control coupled with the Confucian tradition of bowing to authority has led to major gains in the Chinese government's ability to mobilize its political resources and may act as a counter-balance to the West's, and especially America's, increased productivity gains. In other words, China may overtake the United States sooner than expected, and "the largest number of conflicts have occurred after the point of intersection of the power trajectories of the competing countries."[25]

Reliance on the nuclear deterrent to prevent war between China and the United States is not supported by Organski and Kugler's review of fourteen conflicts that occurred between 1945 and 1980.[26] Indeed, in four of these instances—the Chinese Civil War, the Korean War, the Sino-Soviet conflict of 1969, and the Sino-Vietnamese-Soviet confrontation of 1979—China risked nuclear confron-tations with either the United States or the Soviet Union. Counterintuitively, "the tendency to go to war increases as the likelihood of great-power involvement increases and as the possibility that nuclear weapons may be used becomes more real."[27] Moreover, in twelve of the fourteen cases presented, "conventional military superiority on the site of the dispute"[28] determined victory rather than an advantage in nuclear missiles and delivery systems.

> One may speculate about the future, in terms of the power-transition model, and foresee a relatively long period in which China will have surpassed the Soviet Union but not the United States, and when an alliance between the Russians and the Chinese could spell an earlier demise of American dominance in the international system than is currently anticipated. A solid alliance between the United States and the Soviet Union, on the other hand, would delay the moment at which China becomes the dominant power.[29]

## THE CLASH OF CIVILIZATIONS

Whereas Bobbitt and Mearsheimer focus on systemic changes in the constitu-tional order and in the balance of power as the catalyst for major wars between the great powers, Samuel Huntington, in *Clash of Civilizations*, uses a larger canvas. He believes that the contemporary global political order is defined by competition between civilizations rather than nation-states. As such, "the dyna-mism of Islam is the ongoing source of many relatively small fault line wars; the rise of China is the potential source of a big intercivilizational war of core states."[30]

A core, or leading, state ultimately emerges within each civilization; for exam-ple, China is the core state in the Sinic civilization, Russia in the Orthodox grouping, the United States in the West. Civilizations in which a core state has not yet emerged—such as the African, Buddhist, Islamic and Latin American civilizations—are comparatively weak. While religion is the most important defining element of each civilization, racial and class overtones are implicit in the civilizational approach. Huntington's "West versus the Rest" describes, after all, the predominantly white, rich, developed, and aging northern countries in temperate zones, while the Rest—the Africans, Arabs, Asians, Indians, and Latinos—make up the majority of the earth's poor and restless youth in the developing southern tropical zones.

Huntington is convinced that Western civilization's dominant position during the past five hundred years has been secured by "its superiority in applying organized violence,"[31] by perfecting the means to commit state-sanctioned mass murder. Globalization, nonproliferation, and "human rights imperialism" are recent additions to the West's arsenal of domination, a variation on the "triple assault" theme developed by David Abernethy.[32]

However, Asian assertiveness—Huntington notes that "the Chinese economy will become the world's largest early in the twenty-first century"[33]—and a Muslim resurgence have emerged as challengers to Western civilization, and Huntington foresees a Chinese-Islamic alliance—an "arms-for-oil axis"—against the West. An alliance between these two most populous civilizations would contain more than half of the world's total population and would create a most lethal combination, as "among the major powers only China's violence propensity exceeded that of the Muslim states; it employed violence in 76.9 percent of its crises."[34]

An alliance between China and Islam would be a grave challenge for the United States but a double bonanza for Russia, whose

> interests lie in the emergence of a major Chinese geopolitical threat in East and South-East Asia, or a genuine Islamic threat to Western interests which would include the overthrow of pro-Western regimes in the centers of the Middle Eastern oil economy. In the face of such a crisis the price of Russian gas and oil would soar, and Russia's indispensability to the West would give her greater leverage in Washington and Brussels.[35]

According to Huntington, the Soviet Union's war with Afghanistan (1979–1989) and the Gulf Wars are examples of fault line wars between civilizations. While the West may have viewed the Soviet defeat in Afghanistan as a major cause of the USSR's demise and thus a victory against its Cold War rival, the Muslim world saw it as their heroic victory against a superpower, similar to North Vietnam's view of its defeat of America.

As Western political leaders who did not consult with the subjects of their manipulations created many Arab nations in the aftermath of World War I, the concept of the nation-state itself was undermined in the Arab world and so was illegitimate at birth. Although the Islamic world presents several contenders for

**Table 2.3 The Clash of Civilizations, or The West against The Rest (14% : 86%)**

| | Western (White) | Latin American | African (Sub-Saharan) | Japanese | Sinic (Confucian) | Islamic | Orthodox | Hindu |
|---|---|---|---|---|---|---|---|---|
| % world territory | 24.2 | 14.9 | 10.8 | 0.3 | 7.5 | 21.1 | 13.7 | 2.4 |
| 2002 population % world total | 882 million 14.0 | 532 million 8.4 | 608 million 9.7 | 127.6 million 2.0 | 1,500 billion 23.8 | 1,134 billion 18.0 | 236 million 3.7 | 915.8 14.9 |
| GDP as % of world total | 64.4 | 5.0 | <1.0 | 11.7 | 7.0 | 4.0 | 4.4 | 1.6 |
| Nuclear capability (possibly) | +U.S. in 1945 +Britain in 1957 +France in 1960 (Germany) | (Brazil and Argentina reportedly abandoned their programs) | (South Africa destroyed its weapons) | Able, but proscribed by constitution; fast-breeder reactor and ABM technology; U.S. security umbrella | +China in 1964 North Korea (Taiwan and South Korea reportedly abandoned their programs) | Pakistan in 1998 (Iran, Libya, Algeria) | +Russia in 1949 (Ukraine) | India in 1974 |
| Core, or leading, states | United States | *(Brazil, Mexico, Argentina, Venezuela) | *(South Africa, Nigeria) | Japan | China | *(Egypt, Indonesia, Iran, Pakistan, Saudi Arabia, Turkey) | Russia | India |

+Permanent member of the United Nations Security Council.

*Undefined, with contenders.

*Notes:* 1) Huntington also includes a civilizational category based upon Buddhism and a catch-all category of Other that includes such countries as Ethiopia, Haiti, and Israel that are not included in this table. 2) Population and GDP figures are based on data in the *CIA World Factbook 2003* and International Institute of Strategic Studies, *The Military Balance 2003/2004*; however, the data were apportioned into civilizational categories, and calculations are presented as approximations only.

*Source:* Table based on Samuel P. Huntington, *The Clash of Civilizations and the Remaking of the World Order* (New York: Simon & Schuster, 1996).

the role of core state, all of the candidate countries—Egypt, Indonesia, Iran, Pakistan, Saudi Arabia, and Turkey—are in the throes of ongoing crises. As such, it is difficult to predict which country, if any, will emerge as Islam's core state, although the non-Arab countries of Iran and Turkey seem to be the frontrunners.

While it may be in the West's best interest to prevent the emergence of a regional hegemon in the Middle East, it is also possible that leadership will emerge from outside the state structure in the form of an unusually charismatic leader, such as Osama bin Laden.

## IMPERIAL EXPANSION AND CONTRACTION

The decolonization process has compounded the proclivity for intercivilizational war and conflict as the number of independent states has more than tripled since 1914, making the management of international relations even more complex.

**Table 2.4  The Number of States**

| Year | 1914 | 1945 | 1960 | 1978 | Late 90s | Current |
|------|------|------|------|------|----------|---------|
| Number of states | 44 | 64 | 107 | 148 | 180 | 191 |

David Abernethy, in *The Dynamics of Global Dominance,* develops a conceptual framework that divides the expansion and contraction of European empires since 1415 into five phases. In doing so, he focuses on how each major power, or metropole, mixed political, economic and religious elements in a "triple assault" to dominate its colonial territories.[36] "They [the Europeans] were ingenious in devising methods to humiliate non-Europeans and unusually skilled at encouraging those they ruled to internalize an inferiority complex."[37]

Abernethy then demonstrates how four great power wars for hegemony not only undermined the metropole's capacity and will to sustain colonial possessions, but also stimulated colonial opposition against the center.[38] From this perspective, the Seven Years' War and World War I are *catalytic wars* that triggered the push for independence in British North America and energized the leadership of the Indian National Congress, respectively. Both wars presaged decolonization phases characterized by *follow-up conflicts*—the Napoleanic Wars and World War II.

During the last decolonization phase (1940–80), eighty-one former colonies achieved independence as the European imperial powers withdrew from overseas possessions in Asia, Africa and the Middle East following World War II.

Extrapolating from Abernethy's analysis, a new and distinct post-1980 phase would include the fall of the seven eastern and central European Communist satellite regimes in 1989,[39] followed by the dissolution of Yugoslavia into five components,[40] and the emergence of fifteen republics from the fallen Soviet Union in

1991, signaling the independence of twenty-seven more countries. Whereas the European empires held sway in overseas possessions, the Soviet republics and adjacent satellites formed a contiguous continental empire. In addition, "in the Soviet case empire's end came unexpectedly, in peacetime, almost overnight and with minimal foreign intervention."[41] In this scenario, the Cold War represents a *catalytic war* between the two superpowers; America's victory in the Cold War is one feature in a new, expansionary phase of economic globalization.

This global shedding of empire leaves "very little additional real estate...to reward the winner of a peaceful great-power confrontation or to compensate the loser."[42] Is war more likely now because the proliferation of so many new states leaves less territory to trade for peace? Does this portend further fragmentation, tribalization, and an upsurge in ethnic cleansing, as suggested by the series of Yugoslav wars throughout the 1990s?

...the postcolonial and post-Communist division of countries into separate states has uprooted millions of people, fomented internecine wars, degraded the citizenship of trapped minorities and perpetuated ancient grievances, closing both minds and frontiers. Give or take a little, this has been true of Pakistan, Kashmir, Ireland,

**Table 2.5    Phases of Imperial Expansion and Contraction**

| Phase | Duration | Direction | Focus | War |
|-------|----------|-----------|-------|-----|
| 1 | 1415–1773 (358 years) | Expansion/ colonization | New World (mainland) | Seven Years' War (1756–1763) |
| 2 | 1775–1824 (49 years) | Contraction/ decolonization (U.S. and 19 Latin American countries gain independence) | New World (mainland) | Napoleonic wars (1789–1815) |
| 3 | 1824–1912 (88 years) | Expansion | Old World (coastal) | |
| 4 | 1914–1939 (25 years) | Unstable equilibrium | Old World | World War I (1914–1918) |
| 5 | 1940–1980 (40 years) | Contraction/ decolonization (81 colonies gain independence) | Old World (≈ 30% islands) | World War II (1939–1945) |
| 6 | 1980–present | Expansion: globalization | Old World | |

*Note:* In column five, "War," the Seven Years' War and World War I are catalytic wars, whereas the Napoleonic wars and World War II are follow-up conflicts.

*Source:* Adapted and expanded based on Table 2.1, "Imperial Phases," in David B. Abernethy, *The Dynamics of Global Dominance: European Overseas Empires 1415–1980* (New Haven, CT: Yale University Press, 2000), 24.

Palestine and Cyprus, as well as, most recently, the former Yugoslavia. That the United States should condone or encourage partition seems especially ironic, since Americans fought a civil war to preserve a federal union that remains a beacon for others.[43]

## RESOURCE WARS AND OIL PRODUCTION PEAKS

A different viewpoint is offered by Michael Klare, who argues that competition for the world's scarce resources—arable land, copper, diamonds, fisheries, gold, timber, water, and especially oil—is the root cause of many contemporary conflicts.[44]

Petroleum, for example, currently accounts for about 40 percent of the annual global energy consumption mix, or almost 30 billion barrels a year.[45] By 2025, annual global consumption of oil is projected to reach *44 billion barrels.*[46] Since world crude production is depleted at an annual rate of 4 to 5 percent, and since global consumption grows at about 2 percent annually, at least 1.8 billion to 2.1 billion new barrels of replacement oil must come online every year, assuming that petroleum's proportion of the energy mix remains stable at 40 percent.[47]

However, since the depletion of the world's oil fields outpaces the discovery and exploitation of replacement sources, some industry experts have predicted a global oil production peak.[48] Although there is disagreement as to when the peak will be reached, "previous energy transitions (wood to coal and coal to oil) were gradual and evolutionary; oil peaking will be abrupt and revolutionary."[49]

According to one analyst,[50] the first phase of this peak began early in 2004 with a spike in the price of oil; the second phase will start around 2009–2010 when non-OPEC producers reach their highest level of output; and the third phase will begin sometime around 2020, when OPEC reaches its maximum production capacity.[51] The interval between the second and third phases will be a period of maximum advantage for OPEC—especially for the most oil-rich members of the cartel, such as Saudi Arabia, Iraq, Kuwait, the United Arab Emirates, and Iran—since oil prices are projected to be in the range of $50–100 per barrel, with an average price of $70.

Once peak production capacity is reached, the long transition to a post-petroleum economy will begin. Regardless of when peaking actually occurs, "the world community will need to invest $3 trillion over the next thirty years to raise global oil production to a level adequate to meet world demand in 2030."[52] Implementation of mitigation strategies to limit the impact of peaking will require more than a decade to yield substantial relief,[53] but the global political leadership required for this monumental task has yet to assert itself. In the meantime, "oil supply disruptions over the past three decades have cost the U.S. economy about $4 trillion, so supply shortfalls associated with the approach of peaking could cost the U.S. as much as all of the supply disruptions since the early 1970s combined."[54] So the global economy will be faced with the double whammy of additional trillions to extract petroleum under peaking conditions and trillions more to prepare for the transition to a post-petroleum world.

The United States currently comprises 5 percent of the world's population but consumes 25 percent of its oil. Oil represents 40 percent of the U.S. energy mix:[55] A full 97 percent of America's transportation system—its trains, planes, cars, buses, and ships—runs on oil. And U.S. consumption of oil is projected to increase by more than 33 percent from 2004 to 2025, as domestic production of crude oil will correspondingly decrease by about 20 percent. Since 1998, the United States has imported more than half of its petroleum and imported oil is projected to reach almost 70 percent of U.S. consumption by 2025.

Saudi Arabia, whose productive capacity is expected to increase 54 percent by 2025, currently provides 12.2 percent of total U.S. oil imports.[56] Almost 65 percent of the world's proven oil reserves are in the Persian Gulf countries, but even under the most optimistic conditions, production capacity in the Gulf countries cannot keep pace with world demand, especially because China and India are growing at a frenetic rate and increases in their projected petroleum needs far outpace America's. The more developed economies of Asia—Hong Kong, Japan, Singapore, South Korea and Taiwan—are almost *totally* dependent on oil imports, 80 percent of which originate in the Middle East.[57]

Because of the massive energy inputs required to sustain its unprecedented economic growth—coupled with the steady depletion of its more mature oil fields at Daqing, Shengli, and Liaohe—China seems especially vulnerable to any disruption in the supply of oil from the Middle East, where chronic instability is the norm rather than the exception. But China faces a double risk: Not only is it dependent on oil from the Middle East, but it also relies on U.S. naval forces to guarantee the safe passage of that oil through the critical sea-lines-of-communication from the Persian Gulf through the Strait of Hormuz across the Indian Ocean to the Strait of Malacca and up through the South and East China Seas.

**Table 2.6   Petroleum Consumption 2005, Projected for 2025**

|  | 2005 | Imported | 2025 | Growth | Imported |
|---|---|---|---|---|---|
| China | 7.0 | 49% | 14.2 | 103% | 77% |
| India | 2.5 | 69% | 4.9 | 96% | 80% |
| United States | 20.7 | 67% | 27.3 | 32% | ≈ 70% |
| World | 82.5 | – | 119.2 | 44% | – |

*Note:* All figures in millions of barrels per day, except percentages.

*Sources:* 2005 figures from *BP Statistical Review of World Energy June 2006*, p. 11. Percentage of imports derived by subtracting each country's annual production from its annual consumption. Annual production figures from the *BP Statistical Review*, p. 8.   2025 figures from U.S. Department of Energy, Energy Information Administration, *International Energy Outlook 2005*, Table A4, "World Oil Consumption by Region, Reference Case."

Faced with this double dependency, and because "China's natural endowments feature large quantities of the environmentally wrong type of resources (massive coal reserves) in the wrong places (the North and West) and the strategically right type of resources (oil) in the wrong places (North and West), while China's largest and fastest-growing energy demand is in the southern and eastern coastal provinces,"[58] China has adopted a national energy strategy that includes greater exploitation of its abundant coal reserves and diversification of petroleum imports via land routes from Kazakhstan, Iran, and the Russian Far East.

The need to secure an ever greater supply of a resource that may be nearing its peak of production has stimulated a global competition that is especially acute in the Asia Pacific region, creating what Kent Calder calls a "deadly triangle of growth, energy shortage, and armament."[59] He goes on to say that the situation "has the explosive potential—given underlying resource rivalries and the dual shadows of Chinese and Korean unification—to generate destructive, wasteful regional arms races, and possibly to stimulate Japanese rearmament,"[60] while enriching the Persian Gulf and Russian petrocracies.

*

As we have seen, Modelski and Thompson have established a correlation between the appearance of major economic innovations and global wars, and many theorists believe we are on the cusp of a transition from the information revolution to a new wave of innovations that will unleash a revolution in nanotechnology, genetic engineering, and space exploration. At the same time, the erosion of the legitimacy of the nation-state, and the emergence of the market-state, may lead to what Bobbitt calls an epochal, or "cataclysmic," war. Regardless, the United States will most likely intervene to prevent China's rise as a potential peer competitor, especially because, as China's economy grows, the likelihood of war with the United States increases. Huntington believes that a Chinese-Islamic alliance against the West may erupt into an intercivilizational war.

All of these dynamics are taking place within a system made even more complex by the proliferation of states, coupled with greater political fragmentation and increased competition for scarce resources due to an impending global oil production peak that will trigger resource wars.

# U.S. FOREIGN POLICY, THE DEBT EXPLOSION, AND DEMOGRAPHIC TRENDS

*What, for our survival, must we seek to prevent no matter how painful the means?*

—Henry Kissinger

*The Persian empires of Achaemenids and the Sassanids each lasted several hundred years, as did each of the five conquering Chinese dynasties, to say nothing of Rome. Byzantium lasted a millennium, as did Venice. Portuguese, Hapsburg, Ottoman, and British dominance must be measured in centuries, not decades. Even the Vandal empire of Genseric dominated the Western world's Mediterranean core for the better part of a hundred years while Rome was collapsing. Because it was a fomenter of dynamic change, a liberal empire like the United States was likely to create the conditions for its own demise, and thus to be particularly short lived.*

—Robert Kaplan

While this gathering storm of global systemic trends points to conflict between the United States and China, recent developments in U.S. foreign policy, combined with historic debt levels and emerging demographic patterns, are sapping America's ability to respond to China's rise. Writing in the mid-1980s, at the height of the Reagan military buildup, Paul Kennedy noted:

> The United States now runs the risk, so familiar to historians of the rise and fall of previous Great Powers, of what might roughly be called "imperial overstretch": that is to say, decision-makers in Washington must face the awkward and enduring fact that the sum total of the United States' global interests and obligations is nowadays far larger than the country's power to defend them all simultaneously.[1]

Two decades later, America's proliferating web of global military commitments and entanglements borders on strategic overextension and far exceeds what Kennedy described. As a result, the long-term strength of the nation may be imperiled at precisely that time when it faces the ultimate challenge, if, as anticipated, there is another cataclysmic showdown between the great powers—this time, China and the United States. Recent trends in the formulation of American foreign policy almost guarantee a massive collision.

## TRENDS IN AMERICAN FOREIGN POLICY

The Bush administration's unilateralism and its disdain for the United Nations have alienated and offended many of America's European allies. As a result, two pillars of post-WWII American foreign policy have been weakened: the primacy of the Atlantic Alliance, and the leading role of the United Nations as a global forum for conflict resolution. "The United States [has] exchanged its long-established reputation as the principal *stabilizer* of the international system for one as its chief *destabilizer*"[2] and has become "the world-transforming society, even revolutionary in its subversive impact on sovereignty-based international politics"[3] under the leadership of Republican foreign policy elites that call themselves the Vulcans.[4]

Several trends that characterize the evolution of the U.S. foreign policy establishment over the past several decades magnify the transformation that has occurred under the Vulcans. First, a generational shift within the foreign policy elite has taken place: from the "Wise Men"[5] who lived through WWI and became the country's premier strategists during the early phase of the Cold War, to the "Best and the Brightest"[6] of the 1960s and Vietnam, to the self-proclaimed "Vulcans"[7] (Donald Rumsfeld, Dick Cheney, Colin Powell, Paul Wolfowitz, Richard Armitage, and Condoleezza Rice) who all cut their teeth in the Pentagon, and whose "pronounced emphasis upon military perspectives to foreign policy problems was the principal distinguishing characteristic."[8]

In addition, in the bureaucratic turf wars between the office of the National Security Advisor, on the one hand, and the State and Defense Department on the other, that have characterized all administrations since President Nixon's, either the National Security Advisor or the Secretary of State emerged victorious.[9] That pattern ended when Donald Rumsfeld returned as Secretary of Defense (he had earlier served in this post during the Ford administration) and won his stealth war against Secretary of State Colin Powell, who resigned early in George W. Bush's second term. As *Washington Post* reporter David Von Drahle colorfully put it, Powell "has returned to private life, having been dropped, flipped and pinned in short order by the king of bureaucratic wrestlers."[10] This shift in power from the State Department to the Department of Defense is consistent with the militarization of American foreign policy; at the same time, a gradual politicization of the Department of Defense has occurred: For example, nine of the past thirteen Defense Secretaries have been appointed based on political considerations rather than expertise.[11]

Thus in a brief period a generational transition characterized by the militarization of American foreign policy and the politicization of the Defense Department has occurred in the upper echelons of a foreign policy establishment that has alienated America's European allies and undermined the usefulness of the United Nations.

Within the Republican Party itself, a factional and generational dispute pitting foreign policy realists against the vanguard of the neoconservative movement[12] emerged during the Ford administration, primarily in response to Henry Kissinger's unprecedented accumulation of power as Nixon's Secretary of State *and* National Security Advisor. As former Israeli Foreign Minister Abba Eban wryly put it, Kissinger was "the only U.S. Secretary of State under whom two presidents served."[13]

President Ford, seeking to place his own imprint on the executive branch after Nixon's resignation and attempting to bolster his chances of winning the 1976 presidential election, made several personnel changes that curtailed Kissinger's power while setting the stage for the eventual domination of the Vulcans. Ford fired James Schlesinger at Defense and replaced him with Rumsfeld, while Dick Cheney replaced Rumsfeld as Ford's chief-of-staff; Brent Scowcroft succeeded Kissinger as National Security Advisor, and George H.W. Bush replaced William Colby at the Central Intelligence Agency (CIA). There is speculation that Rumsfeld engineered these changes to position himself as Ford's running mate in the 1976 election, but no matter—Ford selected Robert Dole instead.[14]

The neocons, and the Vulcans in particular, abhorred Kissinger's policy of détente with the Soviet Union and so sought confrontation rather than accommodation; they favored ballistic missile defense and so objected to Nixon's 1972 *Anti-Ballistic Missile Treaty* (ABM) with the Soviet Union as an impediment to U.S. national security. The Vulcans' purge of Republican realists continued under Ronald Reagan, who introduced the Strategic Defense Initiative (Star Wars) and opted for a decidedly confrontational approach to the Soviet Union. Kissinger was relegated to the political wilderness during the Reagan era, and his protégé, Brent Scowcroft, who returned as George H.W. Bush's National Security Advisor, has lately become a pariah within the Republican Party after he publicly opposed the current war in Iraq.[15] The administration of George W. Bush abrogated the *ABM Treaty* with Russia on December 13, 2001.

The Vulcans' chief ideologist, Paul Wolfowitz, had studied at the University of Chicago under Leo Strauss, regarded by many as the godfather of neoconservatism. A recent study of the Straussians[16] portrays a tight-knit network of predominantly white male disciples who honeycomb the upper echelons of the Republican foreign policy apparatus and are waging a domestic war against

America's perceived moral relativism—hence family values—while advocating militarism abroad—hence Afghanistan and Iraq.

In a sense, they are America's counterrevolutionary shock troops of the Right who have forged an alliance of convenience with born-again Christians to maintain a lock on political power in the United States. Conveniently, "conservative Christians have conferred a presumptive moral palatability on any occasion on which the United States resorts to force. They have fostered among the legions of believing Americans a predisposition to see U.S. military power as inherently good, perhaps even a necessary adjunct to the accomplishment of Christ's saving mission. In doing so, they have nurtured the preconditions that have enabled the American infatuation with military power to flourish."[17] Further, "the followers of Strauss see themselves. . .standing for the defense of the West, for the revival of ancient teachings and lost morality."[18] In a sense, then, they are America's jihadists.

*

A review of American force deployments overseas reveals that the number of U.S. troops stationed abroad has more than doubled from 2002 to 2003—from about 205,000 to 418,500 troops—with almost 75 percent of the additional forces deployed in Afghanistan and Iraq.[19] As of late 2004, at least 458,449 U.S. military personnel[20] were assigned to some 737 American military bases in 38 countries.[21]

If the forces assigned to America's twelve aircraft carriers that ply the world's oceans and seas—escorted by battle groups composed of a bevy of cruisers, frigates, destroyers, submarines and supply vessels—were included, the actual level of troop deployments would be much higher: Approximately 3,200 crew and 2,400 pilots and aircrew man a single aircraft carrier. These vast flotillas function as movable forward staging bases and are deployable globally;[22] the United States has more aircraft carriers than all other countries combined.[23]

Moreover, even before the United States launched Operation Enduring Freedom in Afghanistan on October 2001, "teams of Special Forces were discreetly operating in 125 countries."[24] Finally, the U.S. Department of Defense has outsourced many of its training activities in some forty-two countries to corporations whose proprietary work is shielded from disclosure under the Freedom of Information Act.[25] For all of these reasons, it is difficult to form a complete picture of the scope and nature of U.S. military deployments abroad.

In addition to the increased number of U.S. military personnel abroad, the U.S. government also provides direct military aid to foreign governments.[26] Further, the Pentagon's arms sales bureaucracy, the Defense Security Cooperation Agency, coordinated the delivery of $10.24 billion worth of arms in 2002, almost more than the total deliveries of arms originating from the United Kingdom, Russia, France, and China combined.[27] The Pentagon also helps to fund the purchase of these arms through its Foreign Military Financing program; in

**Table 3.1   U.S. Troops Deployed Abroad**

|  | 2002 | 2003 | 2004 |
|---|---|---|---|
| **EUCOM**—U.S. European Command (HQ: Stuttgart-Vaihingen) | **97,423** | **102,967** | **121,525** |
| Germany | 68,950 | 73,500 | 90,700 |
| Belgium | 1,290 | 1,400 | 1,390 |
| Greece | 290 | 310 | 538 |
| Italy | 10,790 | 11,965 | 15.474 |
| Netherlands | 550 | 800 | 303 |
| Norway | 53 | 73 | 50 |
| Portugal | 50 | 50 | 1,058 |
| Spain | 2,190 | 2,030 | 562 |
| Turkey | 3,860 | 1,742 | 1,650 |
| United Kingdom | 9,400 | 11,097 | 9,800 |
| (Mediterranean 6th Fleet includes one carrier battle group) |  |  | (14,000) |
| **PACOM**—U.S. Pacific Command (HQ: Hawaii) | **80,060** | **89,228** | **83,769** |
| Australia | 110 | 110 | 90 |
| Diego Garcia | 668 | 668 | 1,071 |
| (Guam + Northern Marianas Islands) | 3,460 | 4,490 | 4,400 |
| Japan | 38,450 | 40,680 | 43,550 |
| Singapore | 124 | 151 | 89 |
| South Korea | 37,140 | 43,060 | 34,500 |
| Thailand | 108 | 69 | 69 |
| (Pacific 3rd–San Diego and 7th Fleet: four carrier battle groups) |  |  | (140,400) |
| **CENTCOM**—U.S. Central Command (HQ: MacDill AFB, Tampa, Florida) | **20,958** | **215,550** | **179,260** |
| Afghanistan[+] | – | 8,500 | 18,000 |
| Bahrain | 4,200 | 4,500 | 3,000 |
| Djibouti | – | 800 | 1,000 |
| Iraq[*] | – | 146,400 | 121,600 |
| Kuwait | 8,388 | 38,160 | 25,250 |
| Kyrgyzstan[+] | – | 700 | 700 |
| Nigeria | 12 | – | – |

| | | | |
|---|---|---|---|
| Oman | 260 | 270 | 270 |
| Pakistan[+] | – | 1,300 | 400 |
| Qatar | 3,300 | 3,300 | 6,540 |
| Saudi Arabia | 4,408 | 10,000 | 300 |
| United Arab Emirates | 390 | 570 | 1,300 |
| Uzbekistan[+] | – | 1,050 | 900 |
| (Indian Ocean/Persian Gulf/Red Sea 5th Fleet: one carrier battle group) | | | |
| **NORCOM**—U.S. Northern Command (HQ: Peterson AFB, Colorado Springs) | **6,437** | **6,954** | **6,883** |
| Bermuda | 800 | 800 | 800 |
| Cuba | 2,209 | 2,306 | 2,255 |
| Iceland | 1,478 | 1,658 | 1,758 |
| Portugal | 730 | 970 | 850 |
| United Kingdom | 1,220 | 1,220 | 1,220 |
| (Atlantic 2nd Fleet—Norfolk, Virginia: four to five carrier battle groups) | | | |
| **SOUTHCOM**—U.S. Southern Command (HQ: Miami, Florida) | **371** | **390** | **1,767** |
| Colombia | 15 | – | 890 |
| Ecuador | | | 290 |
| Honduras | 356 | 390 | 587 |
| **Other**—U.S. Peacekeeping Troops Abroad | | **5,060** | **3,649** |
| Bosnia Stabilization Force (SFOR) | | 1,800 | 839 |
| Kosovo Force (KFOR) | | 260 | 260 |
| Serbia/Montenegro KFOR | | 2,250 | 1,800 |
| Egypt Multilateral Forces (MFO) | | 750 | 750 |
| **TOTAL (Countries)** | **205,249 ( 29)** | **420,149 ( 36)** | **396,853 (41)** |

[+]Operation Enduring Freedom.
[*]Operation Iraqi Freedom.
Sources: Based on material in International Institute of Strategic Studies, *The Military Balance 2002/2003, 2003/2004, 2004/2005;* Chalmers Johnson, *The Sorrows of Empire: Militarism, Secrecy, and the End of the Republic* (New York: Metropolitan Books/Henry Holt, 2004); Robert D. Kaplan, *Imperial Grunts: The American Military on the Ground* (New York: Random House, 2005); Dana Priest, *The Mission: Waging War and Keeping Peace with America's Military* (New York: W.W. Norton, 2003); press reports in *The Nation, The New York Times, The Washington Post,* and *Stratfor;* extensive coverage on www.GlobalSecurity.org; and annual U.S. Department of Defense *Defense Base Structure Reports* and *Worldwide Manpower Distribution by Geographical Area.*

2003, it requested $4.1 billion to fund this program.[28] The U.S. Department of Defense is also engaged in ongoing negotiations with other countries to secure overflight and docking rights, access to storage facilities (for ammunition, refueling equipment, and vehicles), and status of force agreements (SOFAs) that grant U.S. troops immunity from prosecution by local authorities (extraterritoriality).[29] Recent examples of U.S. military activity abroad, organized here according to the U.S. command structure, are summarized below:

## U.S. European Command

- *The Military Balance 2003/2004* reports that U.S. military personnel based in Germany may be relocated to Hungary, Poland, Romania, and Bulgaria, all former bulwarks of the defunct Warsaw Pact.[30] In advance of these force redeployments, "in February 2003, the United States also began to build two new military bases at Burgas [a port in Bulgaria]... [and] at the Romanian port of Constanta, the air force is building a similar base complex."[31] With these bases, NATO and U.S. forces will have edged even closer to the Russian frontier and will have an even greater ability to seal off the Black Sea outlet. NATO forces will also have alternative access routes to the Middle East via the land bridge provided by Georgia and Azerbaijan. U.S. and NATO forces in Iraq, Turkey, Afghanistan, and Pakistan—and potentially in the north from Azerbaijan, will thus surround Iran. The missing link is egress across the Caspian Sea through Kazakhstan or Turkmenistan to U.S. bases in Uzbekistan, although the United States is exploring the possibility of establishing a base at Shymkent Airport in Kazakhstan.
- *The Caucasus.* U.S. Secretary of Defense Donald Rumsfeld visited Azerbaijan in December 2003 to discuss closer military ties.[32] In neighboring Georgia, the United States has launched a $64 million program to train troops in counterterrorism in an effort to halt the flow of Chechen guerillas from Russia to Georgia through the Pankisi Gorge.[33] U.S. aid to Georgia was increased to $166 million in 2004.[34] Azerbaijan and Georgia are ripe for further U.S. interventions due to presidential successions in both countries.[35]
- The United States also reportedly seeks to establish forward bases in Morocco, Algeria, and Tunisia and to conclude aircraft refueling agreements with Senegal and Uganda.[36]

## U.S. Central Command

- *Central Asia.* In addition to the U.S. military presence in Kyrgyzstan and Uzbekistan, the United States has also gained access to the Khujand, Kulyab, and Kurgan-Tyube bases in Tajikistan.[37] Recently, however, the government of Uzbekistan expelled the United States from its territory after claiming that the United States was somehow involved in riots that broke out in the city of Andijan on May 13, 2005.
- Ethiopia has granted overfly rights to and shares intelligence with the United States.[38] In addition, the United States is training Ethiopian forces in counterterror tactics and has conducted joint operations with U.S. forces based in Djibouti.[39]
- The United States "has pledged $40 million to help upgrade Kenya's aviation infrastructure and enhance airport security"[40]—and conducts joint military exercises

with Kenya (Edged Mallet), most likely as a precursor to access rights to the air base and naval station at Manda Bay.[41]

- U.S. Special Forces in Nigeria engaged in Operation Focus Relief are training Nigerian battalions. The combined cost of training and of the military equipment that has been supplied is estimated at $55 million annually.[42]

- Pakistan has been granted the status of a "major non-NATO ally."

- The United States is also considering "the possibility of building a signals intelligence base on the Yemeni island of Socotra."[43] In addition, the United States awarded $22 million in military aid to Yemen after it "signed on to the War on Terrorism."[44]

## U.S. Pacific Command

- The Australian government may grant the United States access to a "staging post" in Darwin.[45]

- In August 2002, the United States reportedly resumed military ties with Indonesia and U.S. Special Forces are training an indigenous counterterrorism unit.[46] There are also unconfirmed reports that a naval dock is under construction in Bitung, on the island of Sulawesi, and that the U.S. Navy will be granted docking rights at this facility.[47]

- The United States may seek access rights to an air base built by the Soviets outside the city of Choir in Mongolia. Regardless, "the majority of Mongolia's foreign military training and assistance came from the United States."[48]

- U.S. and Philippine forces are reportedly conducting joint training exercises in counterterrorism tactics. In addition, details of a Mutual Logistics Support Agreement (MLSA) that grants the United States access to supply depots in the Philippines are being finalized.[49]

- The United States has also reportedly accorded the status of "major non-NATO ally" to the Philippines and Thailand. Unconfirmed reports suggest that U.S. and Thai officials are in discussions over U.S. access to the Sattahip naval base and the U-Tapao air base.[50] *The Washington Post* reported that Thailand had granted the United States access to its military bases and had "allowed the CIA to transport high-level al Qaeda prisoners to Thailand for interrogation."[51]

- U.S. aircraft carriers have access to Singapore's Changi naval base.

- The United States and Vietnam are considering terms for U.S. access to Cam Ranh Bay air and naval facilities, vacated by Russia in the summer of 2003.

## U.S. Southern Command

- The United States has reportedly been granted access to "three aerial logistics bases"[52] that are used by the Southern Command for drug-interdiction activities in Latin America: in Manta, Ecuador; in Aruba and Curacao; and at Comalapa International Airport, located outside of San Salvador, El Salvador.[53]

- "Plan Colombia" includes a $1.3 billion aid package to the Colombian government, of which $519 million was allocated for military training and the purchase of Black Hawk helicopters.[54] U.S. Special Forces in Colombia focus on training elite military units and also *junglas,* counternarcotics jungle fighters.[55]

This ongoing campaign to project America's military might abroad, symbolic of the militarization of American foreign policy, threatens to undermine the nation's democratic ideals and has gravely tarnished America's image. The symbolism of the Statue of Liberty is in danger of being displaced by the image of America, the global jackboot, imposing its will abroad with brutal force based on the Bush doctrine of preemption. Mark Danner, pointing to abuses at a U.S.-controlled prison in Iraq, Abu Ghraib, makes the point succinctly: "What better image of Arab ill-treatment and oppression could be devised than that of a naked Arab man lying at the feet of a short-haired American woman in camouflage garb, who stares immodestly at her Arab pet while holding him by the throat with a leash?"[56]

At home, the Bush administration tramples on the civil liberties of U.S. citizens under cover of the disingenuously named Patriot Act and the recently revealed domestic spying program. At the U.S. base in Guantanamo Bay, Cuba, 650 "unlawful combatants" are being held indefinitely pending adjudication by military tribunals whose decisions are not subject to civilian review; and the United States has been engaged in exporting these "illegal enemy combatants" to Egypt, Jordan, and Morocco—where they are presumably tortured—as part of its "extraordinary-rendition" program.[57]

And so, in the words of the historian and Canadian politician Michael Ignatieff, America is in danger of becoming weak "in the elements of power that do not subdue by force of arms but inspire by force of example."[58]

This trend is exemplified by the widening gap between U.S. budgetary allocations to the Departments of Defense and State, where "spending on *national defense* increased from $335.5 billion in FY01 to 400.5 billion in FY04...while, the *foreign affairs* budget has gone from $26.2 billion in FY02 to 28.7 billion requested in FY04."[59] Clearly, force trumps diplomacy.

Recent descriptions of U.S. foreign policy refer to the current administration's unilateralism, its "king-of-the-hill approach," its disdain for allies and alliances, and its brazen disregard for international law.[60] A *Newsweek* cover story, "The Arrogant Empire," portrays a unipolar world in which the American imperium practices diplomatic intimidation and humiliation based on threats and denunciation.[61] President Bush, alternately characterized as haughty, surly, abrasive, and bombastic, has come to embody this approach to foreign relations.

Michael Howard, writing soon after the fall of the Soviet Union in *The Lessons of History,* noted that "once the Soviet banners were seen as being not liberating but oppressive, representing not a universally valid ideology but an alien Empire intent on maintaining and extending its power...they lost all their universalist moral authority."[62] America, now bereft of the Soviet bogeyman, has one-upped the Soviets by transforming itself into an empire that is feared. America's loss of credibility, of its moral authority and political capital, may be far more deleterious to the national wealth than its massive budget and trade deficits because "in becoming an empire it risks losing its soul as a republic."[63]

> [It] is the perceived hegemony that the US already exercises throughout the world that fuels not only terrorism, the classic weapon of the desperate underdog but, worse, sympathy for terrorism and for the hatred that breeds it. Military power may acquire empires, but it is not enough to sustain them. It needs to be complemented by that "soft power" that confers respect, authority, and above all, legitimacy.[64]

## DOMESTIC CONUNDRUMS

It may be tempting to dismiss many of these concerns about U.S. military spending by noting that while U.S. defense spending has started to increase again, it remains comparatively low as a percentage of the gross domestic product (GDP); however, U.S. defense expenditures in 2002, relative to other countries, increased to *40 percent of the global total.*[65] At the same time, the U.S. share of the gross world product has also reached a new high of about 30 percent in 2002. Because of the combined effect of economic growth and a low rate of inflation, the United States has managed to purchase its status as "the world's single superpower on the cheap,"[66] or so it may seem.

But lest we become complacent, U.S. defense expenditures during the Vietnam War—also incurred at a time when its global share of GDP was at a high point— failed to purchase victory against Ho Chi Minh's forces, doomed Lyndon Johnson's Great Society domestic programs, and afforded the Soviets a window of opportunity during which they achieved nuclear parity with the United States. It seems foolhardy to assume that might alone will be more successful in the Middle East—or anywhere else—than it was in Southeast Asia.

The fatal domestic condition this time around may be America's aging population. Baby boomers are on the verge of retiring en masse, and so federal outlays for Social Security and Medicare are projected to mushroom.[67] At the same time, the gloomy prospects for America's financial future are deepened by the Bush administration's debt explosion. Fueled by three tax cuts and by steadily increasing budget requests for the Department of Defense, these deficits far exceed those of the Reagan administration.[68]

In fact, "global aging [in the developed world, here defined as North America, Western Europe, Japan and Australia]...is the most *economically consequential* of all predictions we can now make."[69] The global aging scenario is locked in; those approaching retirement age already exist and have been counted and recounted. The magnitude of the impending crisis will be determined by the manner in which governments act—or fail to act—now.

**Table 3.2  Defense Budgets: China, Russia, and the United States, 1995–2004**

| | (1985) | 1995 | 1996 | 1997 | 1998 | 1999 | 2000 | 2001 | 2002 | 2003 | 2004 | % Change 1995–2004 |
|---|---|---|---|---|---|---|---|---|---|---|---|---|
| **China** | | | | | | | | | | | | |
| Official defense budget | | 7.5 | 8.4 | 9.7 | 11.0 | 12.6 | 14.5 | 17.0 | 20.0 | 22.3 | 25.0 | 233% |
| Actual expenditures* | 21.6 | 31.7 | 36.1 | 36.5 | 37.5 | 39.5 | 42.0 | 47.0 | 51.0 | 55.9 | 84.3 | 166% |
| Defense as % of GDP | 4.9 | 5.9 | 5.7 | 5.7 | 5.3 | 5.4 | 5.3 | 4.0 | 4.1 | 4.7 | 6.1 | |
| Defense as % world total | 1.8 | 3.8 | 4.4 | 4.5 | 4.7 | 5.3 | 5.0 | 5.5 | 5.7 | 3.9 | – | |
| **USSR/ Russia** | | | | | | | | | | | | |
| Official defense budget | 368.3 | 62.8 | 73.9 | 64.0 | 57.1 | 56.8 | 58.8 | 46.1 | 50.8 | 65.2 | 59.6 | -5.1% |
| Defense as % of GDP | 16.1 | 7.4 | 6.4 | 5.8 | 5.3 | 5.1 | 4.3 | 4.5 | 4.8 | 5.0 | 3.5 | |
| Defense as % world total | 31.4 | 10.0 | 8.7 | 8.0 | 7.0 | 7.0 | 7.2 | 7.6 | 5.7 | 4.9 | – | |
| **United States** | | | | | | | | | | | | |
| Official defense budget | 380.9 | 252.6 | 277.3 | 273.0 | 279.0 | 283.0 | 304.1 | 329.1 | 362.1 | 456.0 | 490.0 | 94% |
| Defense as % of GDP | 6.1 | 3.8 | 3.5 | 3.3 | 3.1 | 3.2 | 3.0 | 3.1 | 3.3 | 4.1 | 4.1 | |
| Defense as % world total | 32.5 | 34.0 | 33.0 | 34.0 | 34.0 | 35.0 | 36.0 | 38.6 | 40.0 | 37.0 | – | |

*Based on International Institute of Strategic Studies' estimates of actual Chinese defense expenditures.

*Notes:* All figures in U.S.$ billions, except percentages. Since 2004, "Defense as % world total" figures no longer given.

*Source:* International Institute of Strategic Studies (IISS), *The Military Balance,* 1986 and 1993–2006 editions.

In general, a global demographic revolution is underway and will further erode the West's ability to prevent a shift to Asian dominance in the international political order. The developed world faces a longevity revolution brought about by the unprecedented number of persons who survive into old age—as indeed, "global life expectancies have grown more over the last fifty years than over the previous five thousand."[70] People are living longer *and* retiring at a younger age.

At the same time, Western countries are experiencing a decline in fertility rates—a "birth dearth"—and so the ratio between taxpaying workers and pensioned beneficiaries is steadily falling. Ballooning federal deficits aggravated by tax cuts and coupled with an imminent stampede of retiring baby boomers spells disaster for America's "pay-as-you-go" Social Security retirement system that is saddled with an unfunded liability estimated at $10 trillion. This figure *does not include* health care obligations under Medicare or other federal entitlement programs such as Medicaid and federal civilian and military pensions.[71] A "national cost explosion" in health care and a very low national savings rate make the forecast for the United States even more dismal.

An uptick in fertility rates will not affect these projections because the resulting offspring will not enter the labor market for another twenty years or so. Public policies that encourage immigration will most likely clash with and stimulate a rise in protectionism and would, even if enacted, have a minor impact due to the magnitude of the projected demographic imbalances. Increases in productivity may be limited by the continuing shift in employment from the manufacturing to the service sector, traditionally less susceptible to productivity gains. In addition, as more elderly retire, the ranks of those employed in the service sector will swell to meet an increase in demand. Finally, a basic pillar of future productivity gains has been compromised because U.S. per capita spending on the elderly continues to exceed per capita spending on children by a ratio of eleven to one,[72] highlighting America's propensity to consume now rather than to invest for the long-term.

The tendency to save less during retirement, coupled with massive fiscal deficits and unfunded obligations to future retirees, may trigger a global capital shortage. Currently Japan and China recycle the proceeds of their trade surpluses with the United States back into U.S. treasury securities and so have amassed a great deal of leverage over U.S. financial markets. As of January 2007, China, Japan, and Korea owned more than $1.145 trillion in U.S. treasuries. China's share, at $455 billion,[73] accounted for almost half of that total, and its purchases of U.S. government securities have increased more than fivefold since the beginning of 2002.

"A world economy where one radical imbalance (the American deficit) sustains another (the Asian surplus)"[74] now faces an onslaught of millions of retirees over the next twenty to thirty years that may force this "radical imbalance" over the edge into uncharted territory. Peter Drucker, the management guru, may be correct when he asserts that due to the aging of Japanese society, "Japan . . . [is] drifting toward collective national suicide by the end of the 21st century"[75] and so will gradually lose its ability to finance the U.S. deficit. On the other hand:

> The developed world's role in world affairs could also be constrained by a reversal in the identity of creditors and debtors. If some of today's largest low-income societies —most notably, China—set up fully funded retirement systems to prepare for their own future aging, will they produce ever-larger capital surpluses? More to the point, will today's great powers someday depend on these surpluses to keep themselves financially afloat—and look to the demographically growing developing countries as the world's new economic engine? If so, how can we expect these new suppliers of capital to use their newly acquired leverage? Will they call for wholesale changes in the priorities of global financial institutions? Will they turn the tables in international diplomacy? For example, will the Chinese someday demand that the United States shore up its Medicare system the way it once demanded the Chinese change their human rights policies as a condition of lending?[76]

Will China's National People's Congress convene annually to review America's progress in managing its federal budget deficit before extending most-favored nation status as a prerequisite for the release of credits?

The United States is presented with a window of opportunity to reform its federal entitlement programs before the baby boomers start retiring in 2010 and before Social Security outlays start to exceed revenues sometime between 2013 and 2016.[77] Reform efforts, however, may face stiff resistance by seniors in the voting booth who will comprise a much larger percentage of eligible and actual voters, and by highly effective lobbying groups that advocate on behalf of seniors. The political clout of seniors will be magnified even more in key "retirement states," such as California and Florida.

In summary, "instead of yesterday's 'imperial overstretch' that pushed the military hegemony of so many great powers beyond endurance, what may break today's developed countries will be 'domestic overstretch'—excessive commitments to an entitlements empire, consisting of unsustainable public retirement promises."[78]

What about the combination of imperial and domestic overstretch, tinged with vanity and hubris?

> The weight of global history suggests that China as a rising power will exhibit increasingly assertive behaviors over time, especially during the phase surrounding a systemic power transition, but that the triumph of the United States would be truly evanescent if, in the process of successfully combating such assertiveness, it enervated itself to the point where another rising power assumes global leadership simply because the victorious but now exhausted hegemon has no further capacity to resist.[79]

# PATTERNS IN CHINESE HISTORY

*Every revolution evaporated, leaving behind the slime of bureaucracy.*

—Kafka

Shifting from trends in the United States that may sap its ability to respond to China's rise, this chapter focuses on cycles of Chinese unification and fragmentation, the legacy of China's "century of humiliation," its use of military force, its shifts in primary alliances, and the recent evolution of China's military strategy. My purpose in reviewing these topics is to uncover broad patterns that might serve as guideposts to China's future behavior.

Since China's unification under the Qin in 221 BC, a cyclical pattern of expansion (Yang phases) followed by retreat (Yin phases) has emerged. "Each cycle begins with the launching of a major Chinese dynasty [Han, Tang, Ming, Communist] accompanied by a significant burst of Chinese expansion,"[1] especially toward the northern frontier.

During Yin phases, "barbarians" from the north have exploited China's weakness and so the ensuing fragmentation of the Three Kingdoms era following the fall of the Han Dynasty in 220, the Five Dynasties era following the fall of the Tang in 907, and the dissolution of the Qing Dynasty followed by the Republican era, "warlordism," Japanese occupation, and Civil War. In general, fragmentation begets reunification begets re-division in processes spanning hundreds of years.

The average duration for each of these cycles is 723 years: Yang phases have averaged 345 years, while Yin phases have averaged 378 years. According to this view of Chinese history, China is currently in the early stages of an expansionary Yang phase and "most major external military campaigns carried

**Table 4.1   China Cycles**

|  | Unification/Expansion | Fragmentation/Retreat |
|---|---|---|
|  |  | (Warring states period 475–221BC) |
| **Cycle I:** | **Yang I** | **Yin I** |
| 810 years | 221BC–AD 220<br>Qin unification → Han expansion | 220–589<br>Three Kingdoms era → Jin unified phase (265–317) → Jin southern phase (317–420) → Era of north-south division (420–589) |
| **Cycle II:** | **Yang II** | **Yin II** |
| 779 years | 589–907<br>Sui → Tang expansion | 907–1368<br>Five Dynasties and Ten Kingdoms era (907–960) → Sung unified phase (960–1127) → Sung southern phase (1127–1279) |
| **Cycle III:** | **Yang III** | **Yin III** |
| 581 years | 1368–1644<br>Ming expansion | 1644–1949<br>Qing → Republican era (1911–1949): "warlordism," Japanese occupation, civil war |
| **Cycle IV:** | **Yang IV** |  |
|  | 1949–?<br>Communist Unification |  |

*Notes:* Yin I and II phases are characterized by a north-south division in 317 and 1127, respectively; the Yin III does not share this characteristic.

*Source:* Based on Gari Ledyard, "Yin and Yang in the China-Manchuria-Korea Triangle," in Morris Rossabi, editor, *China among Equals: The Middle Kingdom and Its Neighbors, 10th–14th Centuries* (Berkeley: University of California Press, 1983), 313–353.

out by the unified Chinese state occurred during the first one-third of a regime's existence."[2]

China's reunification in the twentieth century has occurred in three stages thus far: the overthrow of the barbarian Qing (Manchu) Dynasty in 1911, followed by the expulsion of the Western maritime powers in 1949 after the Chinese Communists emerged victorious in the civil war against Nationalist (Kuomintang) forces; the third stage of reunification began with the reacquisition of Hong Kong (1997) and Macau (1999) from the British and Portuguese, respectively. It stands to reason that this stage will not be complete until the Taiwan issue is resolved.

"While the northern peoples are invaded by the Chinese only in the course of the Yang phases, and the Chinese are invaded by the northern peoples only during the Yin phases, the Koreans are invaded in the course of both phases."[3] Thus the Korean War in 1950 and the enduring stalemate (armistice), North Korea's repeated attempts at nuclear brinksmanship, and the precarious situation to the north in the Russian Far East.

China's "controlled apartness,"[4] its attempt to strike a balance between autonomy (self-reliance) and integration (dependence) in response to the West's unrelenting pressure to open and penetrate the fabled China market, mirrors the push and pull of Yin and Yang phases. The tribute system, the Canton system, the unequal treaty system, and now accession to the World Trade Organization represent China's attempt to regulate foreign economic influences. Likewise, the sinicization of Buddhism, Marxism, and capitalism, and the assimilation of foreign conquerors—the Mongols and the Manchus—symbolize China's efforts to master foreign cultural and political intrusions: "The best way to fight the barbarians...was to learn all their tricks first."[5]

*

The historian Michael Hunt points out that these millennia of history have imbued the Chinese with a "high degree of historical consciousness"[6] and a continuity of tradition, distinguished in the modern era by the "century of humiliation" inaugurated by China's loss to the British in the first Opium War of 1839–42. The lingering residue of the British civilizing mission in China was "about 40 million Chinese consumers of opium, of which about 15 million were addicts" by 1900.[7]

Next the Russians exploited the Qing Dynasty's weakness by exacting treaty concessions in 1858 and 1860 "under pressure" and forcing the cession of lands north of the Amur and Ussuri rivers—consistent with a pattern of depredations from the north during a Yin phase. Just more than one hundred years later in March 1963, Chairman Mao alluded to China's displeasure with its northern border in one of the early public salvos of the Sino-Soviet rift.[8]

Under the terms of the *Treaty of Shimonoseki* that concluded the Sino-Japanese War of 1894–95, a war fought over the domination of Korea, Formosa (Taiwan), which had been claimed by China in 1683—some twenty years after Dutch colonists were expelled from the island—was next ceded to the Japanese. The loss of Taiwan represents China's greatest—and still unredeemed—humiliation, and marks the advent of Japanese colonialism in Asia and a breach in the tributary–vassal relationship between China and Korea.

The litany of diplomatic slights and the betrayals visited upon China by the Western powers continued unabated in the twentieth century, when Qing representatives were not invited to participate in negotiations convened by President Theodore Roosevelt as he mediated an end to the Russo-Japanese War of 1905. The ensuing *Treaty of Portsmouth* established a Japanese protectorate over Korea (formally annexed in 1910) and also acknowledged that Manchuria fell within Japan's sphere of influence. Russia's astounding defeat in this war had initially spurred hopes of an Asia free of white rule, but "Japan's contempt for the backwardness of other Asians"[9] was soon revealed.

Even though China had sided with the Allies in World War I and "approximately 100,000 Chinese laborers assisted British, French, and American forces in France, suffering several thousand casualties,"[10] the Allies betrayed the Chinese at Versailles by entering into a secret agreement that transferred Germany's concession in Shandong to the Japanese.

So much for the lofty idealism of President Woodrow Wilson's Fourteen Points that promised "open covenants of peace, openly arrived at, after which there shall be no private international understandings of any kind but diplomacy shall proceed always frankly and in the public view" and "a free, open-minded, and absolutely impartial adjustment of all colonial claims."[11] Colonel House, the president's most trusted aide and confidante, reportedly told Wilson that Japan would likely expand into China since "so much of the white world was closed to the Japanese."[12]

"The decision to transfer Germany's concession in China to Japan not only alienated the Chinese from the United States but set the stage for the next war in Asia [the Sino-Japanese War]."[13] Twenty-five years later at Yalta, in the final months of World War II, President Franklin Roosevelt, in a side deal with Josef Stalin, agreed to seek Chiang Kai-shek's acquiescence to the restoration of tsarist privileges in Manchuria[14] in exchange for the USSR's abrogation of the Soviet-Japanese nonaggression pact. Once again, the Allies had redistributed "political and military power in the Far East without China's presence or participation."[15]

The image of the West (and Japan) reveling in China's slow-motion dismemberment and feasting on its carcass, the resentments engendered by the Great Powers during China's "century of humiliation," go a long way in explaining China's "hyper-sovereignty values."[16]

As Communism's ideological appeal continues to fade, nationalistic impulses are ripe for exploitation by "an irredentist China with a boulder rather than just a chip on its shoulder."[17] This trend is reinforced by the Chinese Communist leadership's evolution from a core cadre of charismatic founding fathers inured by decades of hardship and guerilla warfare—the "Long March" generation of Mao and Deng—to "fourth generation" technocrats trained in the confines of the Party bureaucracy, such as Hu Jintao, China's president, and Wen Jiaobao, the Prime Minister. As a result, the influence that China's preeminent leader exerts in major foreign policy initiatives has been diluted.[18]

If the past is any guide to how China's new generation of leaders might use its growing military power, "across the long sweep of its four-thousand-year history, China rarely has been aggressively expansionist. It has never had a Hitler or a Napoleon."[19] In addition, "China never carried out territorial expansion across water."[20]

John King Fairbank, the founder of modern Chinese studies in the United States, demonstrates that during the period 1644–1840, China's use of military force to impose control occurred almost exclusively in what he calls the Inner

Asian Zone (Mongolia, Tibet, and Central Asia).[21] China has historically focused on threats emanating from its peripheral territories that form a shield around its core; indeed, China has displayed "an almost mesmerizing continental orientation born of constant danger from the nomads of Inner Asia."[22]

As a result, coastal defense and naval power were neglected—even forbidden. Consistent with a continental power that built up its land forces, the Empire was more successful at staving off encroachments from the Inner Asian Zone rather than from the Maritime Zone (Korea, Formosa, Japan). Indeed, "there is no period in Chinese history when a maritime power...posed the greatest threat to Chinese rule"[23] —but that assertion no longer holds. The United States has extended its primacy as the dominant maritime power in East Asia while expanding its land presence in a creeping, pincer-like movement around the People's Republic of China (PRC) with the establishment of U.S. military bases in Afghanistan and Kyrgyzstan.

More recently, according to an analysis of thirteen major foreign policy crises from 1929–1979[24] (ten of which occurred during the first thirty years of the PRC's existence from 1949 to 1979), threats to China's territorial integrity triggered 60 percent of the PRC's crises.

Six states have acted as the triggering entity in these crises,[25] and the United States was "the most visible in this dimension...triggering two crises on its own"[26] but "involved militarily in six of the 10 PRC crises."[27] China responded with high-intensity violence (full-scale war, serious clashes) in "69% of these crises."[28]

In another study of the frequency of leading power Militarized Interstate Disputes (MIDs),[29] the former Soviet Union and China emerged as the most dispute-prone countries during the period from 1918 to 1992. When the time frame encompassed the shorter Cold War era, the United States and China qualified as the most dispute-prone nations.

An analysis of 118 China-specific MIDs from 1949 to 1992 revealed the following patterns:

- China's MIDs were more often triggered by territorial issues (49 percent).
- When China entered into a dispute, it did so more aggressively than other states.
- In disputes with the United States, China "tended to escalate to a higher level"[30] than it did with other countries.

These findings corroborate the characterization of a modern Chinese state imbued with a "realpolitik strategic culture"[31] in which the PRC's military strategy has complemented its shifting alliance pattern. "Since 1949 Beijing had strategically tilted away from the strongest pole in the international order"[32]— thus, China early on entered into an alliance with its Communist neighbor to the north, the Soviet Union.

Just a little bit more than a decade later, the era of the Sino-Soviet rift ushered in a period of "dual adversaries" during which China confronted both the U.S. and the USSR while struggling through its self-imposed isolation during the Cultural Revolution. The menacing Soviet behemoth amassed troops and deployed missiles along its border with China, lending credence to the perception that the USSR was overtaking the Americans, hopelessly mired in Vietnam.

The Sino-Soviet War of 1969—a series of border clashes—followed by Nixon and Kissinger's adroit diplomacy, led first to the opening of relations with China in 1972 and then the establishment of full diplomatic relations between the U.S. and China in 1979.[33] The early 1980s witnessed a thaw in relations between Beijing and Moscow as the United States, under President Reagan, launched its greatest peacetime military buildup; the pace of reconciliation accelerated once Gorbachev assumed command of the Soviet Politburo. Beijing, in the role of "swing player,"[34] now sought to strike a balance in its relations between the two superpowers. After the U.S. emerged as the sole superpower, China and Russia sought to forge a strategic partnership but their progress was briefly tempered by the events of 9/11.

## THE EVOLUTION OF CHINA'S MILITARY STRATEGY

Prior to China's reunification in 1949, Mao and the Communists waged guerilla warfare against the Nationalist opposition and Japanese occupation forces and so based refinements to the theory of revolutionary war on practical experience.[35] In applying theory and practice to the Chinese situation, Mao emphasized political mobilization at the village level as the key to a strategy of peasant-based guerilla warfare: "lure the enemy in deep," wear them down, strike, and retreat.

Maoism's victory inspired other movements against colonial rule in Asia—especially the Vietnamese under Ho Chi Minh.[36] Results counted: The Chinese Communists defeated Nationalist troops who retreated to the island of Taiwan, the Korean War ended in a stalemate, and the Vietnamese routed the French and then the Americans in the Indochina Wars. That the white man's defeat engendered pride throughout Asia is an understatement.

The Soviet Union and the United States confronted China with an overwhelming margin of military superiority when the Chinese Communists took power in 1949. China responded by adopting a strategy of weakness in order to survive—a strategy compared to that of the European neutral states, such as Austria, Finland, Sweden, and Switzerland—nestled between the Soviet colossus and its expanding empire in Eastern Europe and the Western alliance system that evolved into NATO.[37] Likewise, China sat, spent and exposed, between its putative ally to the north, the Soviet Union, and the American Pacific power across the ocean.

The new Communist government exploited China's geographic and demographic advantages by developing a strategy of "people's war" in which a "mass army prepared to trade space for time and men for weapons"[38] in a protracted struggle against potential enemy intruders. Mao initially derided nuclear weapons as a "paper tiger" because China, of all the major powers, was—and remains—the least vulnerable to a nuclear attack on its cities as approximately 70 percent of its population still lives in rural areas. The regime, however, later augmented its strategy of "people's war" when it decided in 1955 to embark on a crash program to develop a nuclear arsenal.[39]

China's "survival-state posture"[40] lasted for almost thirty years until the post-Mao era. The weak-state strategy, coupled with alternating alliances first with the Soviet Union, then with the United States, succeeded in avoiding nuclear war—although the Kennedy and Johnson administrations had considered a preventive strike against China's nuclear research facility at Lop Nor, possibly in a joint operation with the Soviets.[41] Later, the USSR approached the Nixon administration to determine how the U.S. would respond to such a strike.[42] The Soviet Politburo also reportedly discussed the "unrestricted use of the multimegaton bomb [that] would release enormous amounts of radioactive fallout... killing millions of Chinese" shortly after the outbreak of hostilities between China and the USSR in March 1969.[43]

China's rapprochement with the U.S. and Japan in 1972 checked the threat from the Soviet Union—freeing China to pursue widespread economic reform after Deng Xiaoping consolidated power in 1978. Deng implemented the "four modernizations" that included national defense as a priority—albeit the last of the four modernizations.[44] As a result, in 1985 the Party's Central Military Commission revised its military strategy to reflect "people's war under modern conditions" (also referred to as an "active defense strategy in the new era").

From repelling a large-scale invasion from Taiwan with presumed U.S. support in the 1950s, to avoiding a massive surprise attack from the Soviet Union in the 1960s, the focus in the late 1970s now shifted to developing the means to prevail in a limited, local war on the periphery—"meeting the enemy at the gate"—especially along the northern and coastal frontiers. The leadership also called for the depoliticization of the People's Liberation Army (PLA)—a shift in emphasis from "red" to "expert"—but later undermined this objective by deploying PLA troops against it own citizens to quash the Tiananmen uprising in 1989.

Dengist reforms have propelled China on a trajectory of unparalleled economic growth that continues unabated.[45] If China sustains "average growth rates of approximately 8–9 percent per annum over the next 20 years, China's GDP could surpass that of the United States within 10–15 years."[46] Some analysts have suggested that China is using its unprecedented economic growth fueled by an export-led strategy to underwrite a military modernization campaign that "will likely precipitate some significant changes in the regional balance of power by the year 2020"[47] and have dubbed this new approach China's "calculative security strategy."[48]

With the gradual improvement in relations between the Soviet Union and the People's Republic in the 1980s and the eventual fall of the USSR in 1991, China's emphasis on the active defense of its vast northern border has shifted to development of a forward military posture along the eastern maritime zone.[49] This shift has entailed the development of defensive air power to protect China's surface fleet, vulnerable to attack because of the limited range of its air defense systems; the acquisition of air refueling equipment and Airborne Warning and Control Systems (AWACS) aircraft by 2010 are therefore key priorities.[50] In addition, maritime defense will require the expansion of replenishment-at-sea (RAS) capabilities. Troop redeployments, troop reductions, and a greater emphasis on specialized services, such as rapid response forces, a mountain brigade along the Sino-Indian border, and a jungle brigade along the Sino-Vietnamese border have complemented these changes.

The 1991 Gulf War broadcast live on CNN shocked the PLA's elite. Improvements in precision weaponry and technology, the use of electronic warfare to paralyze Iraq's command, control, communications, and intelligence systems $(C^3I)$ at the start of the operation, the employment of stealth and anti-missile technology, and the display of night-fighting capabilities highlighted China's capabilities gap with the West—a gap magnified by the revolution in military affairs (RMA). China responded by increasing its military expenditures, but its lack of transparency clouds perceptions and breeds even more uncertainty about China's ultimate aims—perhaps intentionally.

Partially in response to the West's imposition of an arms embargo after Tiananmen, China turned to Russia for quick infusions of advanced weaponry and technology, ushering in "a transformation in the Asia-Pacific region's balance of power as dramatic as that created by Japan in the years following the Meiji Restoration."[51]

Because "Russia apparently refused to sell the advanced Su-35,"[52] China purchased Su-27 Flanker long-range fighter jets and also signed a joint production transfer agreement stipulating that approximately 200 Su-27s will be assembled in China over a 10-year period.[53] Many of the Su-27s, located at a base in Wuhu approximately 800 kilometers northwest of Taipei, would play a key role, if not the key role, in securing the air corridor over the Taiwan Strait—"the single most dangerous place on the planet,"[54]—if China decides to use military force to resolve the Taiwan issue. China has also purchased several Sovremenny-class destroyers equipped with supersonic Sunburn SS-N-22 missiles designed to penetrate the U.S.' Aegis air defense system, in addition to four Kilo-class submarines —critical to strengthening its sea-based second-strike nuclear capability.[55]

In the 1990s, China accounted for almost 25 percent of Russia's total arms exports although Russian weapons comprised just 1 to 2 percent of China's

**Table 4.2  China's Primary Alliance Patterns and Military Strategy**

| | 1950s | 1960s | 1970s | 1980s | 1990s | 2015–2020 |
|---|---|---|---|---|---|---|
| **Primary threat perception** | Three-front threat: Korea, Taiwan (w/ U.S. assistance), Vietnam (French assistance) | Massive surprise attack from USSR | USSR | Prevailing in a local, limited war (jubu zhanzheng) | Derailment of economic growth 1993: net oil importer | U.S. |
| **Primary alliance pattern** | Sino-Soviet alliance: "leaning to one side" | Sino-Soviet rift: "dual adversaries" | Normalization of relations with U.S.: triangular diplomacy | Thaw with USSR: balancing | End of Cold War: strategic partnership with Russia | Regional hegemon |
| **Military strategy** | "People's War" = protracted struggle; 1955: China decides to develop atomic bomb | 10/16/1964: China's bomb; Mao's "Third Front" strategy with minimal nuclear deterrence and no first-use pledge; "first-strike uncertainty" | Post-Mao transition → (by late 1970s, capability to deliver nuclear weapons) | 1985: "People's War under modern conditions" aka active defense strategy in the new era ("meet the enemy at the gates") | "Calculative security strategy" with "limited nuclear deterrence"; "limited war under high-tech conditions" Green-water fleet | Strong-state strategy<br><br>Blue-water fleet |
| **Internal events** | Great Leap Forward | The "three hard years" Cultural Revolution | Mao → Deng | Four Modernizations Tiananmen | Unprecedented economic growth | Reunification with Taiwan? |
| **External events** | Korean War French in Indonesia Stalin → Khrushchev | Khrushchev → Brezhnev Sino-Indian War (1962) U.S. in Vietnam Sino-Soviet War (1969) | 1974: Indian test Sino-Vietnamese War Soviets into Afghanistan | Brezhnev → Gorbachev; Reagan, Thatcher, Pope John Paul II; Fall of the Berlin Wall | Fall of the USSR Gulf War (1991) NATO to Kosovo (1999) China's embassy in Belgrade bombed (5/7/1999) | Korean unification? Nuclear Japan? More assertive India? |

*Sources:* Avery Goldstein, *Deterrence and Security in the 21st Century: China, Britain, France and the Enduring Legacy of the Nuclear Revolution* (Stanford, CA.: Stanford University Press, 2000); Michael D. Swaine and Ashley J. Tellis, *Interpreting China's Grand Strategy: Past, Present and Future* (Santa Monica, CA: RAND, 2000); You Ji, *The Armed Forces of China* (New York: I.B. Tauris and Co., 1999).

weapons inventory.[56] In the year 2000, however, China's arms purchases from Russia increased to 49.6 percent of Russia's total arms trade (India accounted for another 22.5 percent).[57] While it is acquiring sophisticated military hardware and technology, China is also underwriting an ailing Russian defense establishment and so benefits from the leverage it creates.

A major threat to China's continued pace of economic growth arose in 1993 when it became a net importer of energy resources. China is now dependent on oil transported from the Middle East through strategically vital sea lines of communication (SLOCs), especially along the corridor extending from the Persian Gulf to the Indian Ocean and then on through the Malacca Strait to the South China Sea, and north to the East China Sea.

To guarantee its future economic and national security, China must enhance its power-projection capabilities beyond its coastal waters in order to secure passage through the region's maritime chokepoints[58] but then runs the risk of triggering a regional, and primarily naval, arms race (like Japan a century ago?). China's predicament is exacerbated by increased competition for energy supplies throughout the region that has stimulated the development of alternative sources of energy, especially nuclear energy.[59] This emerging scenario contains the ingredients for a classic arms race subject to the unpredictable dynamics of spirals of tension.

To guarantee the survivability of its second-strike retaliatory nuclear capability, China has also launched an effort to increase the accuracy of its intercontinental ballistic missiles (ICBMs), expand the capabilities of its submarine-launched ballistic missiles (SLBMs), and improve the penetrability of its missile warheads. These measures indicate that China's earlier policy of minimal nuclear deterrence has been upgraded to a policy of limited deterrence, defined as "having enough capabilities to deter conventional, theater, and strategic nuclear war, and to control and suppress escalation during a nuclear war."[60]

However, if the United States were to build and deploy "an effective missile defense system, both strategic and theater...[then] the bulk of China's nuclear arsenal may be rendered impotent."[61] Even the *belief* that an effective national or theater missile defense (NMD/TMD) system is deployable could prompt China to seek reunification with Taiwan—a topic discussed in the next

**Table 4.3  Russia's Weapons Sales to China, 1995–2005**

| 1995 | 1996 | 1997 | 1998 | 1999 | 2000 | 2001 | 2002 | 2003 | 2004 | 2005 | Total |
|------|------|------|------|------|------|------|------|------|------|------|-------|
| 464 | 1066 | 579 | 111 | 1383 | 1700 | 2964 | 2429 | 1997 | 2581 | 2564 | 17,838 |
| 89% | 85% | 82% | 44% | 85% | 92% | 94% | 92% | 95% | 94% | 95% | 91.2% |

*Note:* Figures are in U.S.$ millions at constant (1990) prices based on SIPRI trend-indicator values and as a percentage of total Chinese arms imports.

*Source:* Stockholm International Peace Research Institute (SIPRI) arms transfer database, available at http://www.sipri.org/contents/armstrad/access.html, last accessed April 2007.

chapter—before the approaching transitional vacuum when China's limited nuclear deterrent capability might become obsolete.[62]

Chinese aggression toward Taiwan becomes even more likely because China, now in a hypernationalistic expansionary phase fueled by its resounding economic success, tends to respond aggressively to territorial issues, especially when the U.S. is involved. It has also shifted to a forward military posture along the eastern maritime zone, and so is facing down three key American allies—Korea, Japan, and Taiwan.

# TAIWAN: THE TRIPWIRE

*Most systemic wars, therefore, come about as a result of cataclysmic interventions by the existing hegemon on behalf of some other victims.*

—Swaine and Tellis, *Interpreting China's Grand Strategy*

Nothing is more important to China than avenging the loss of Taiwan. This "sacred national obligation" propels China, like an amputee reaching out to reclaim the last of its severed limbs (Taiwan, Macau, Hong Kong, Tibet).

In a conversation with Henry Kissinger in 1973, Mao acknowledged that it might take another hundred years or so to settle the Taiwan issue, adding, "I do not believe in a peaceful transition."[1] Two years later, Mao reaffirmed, "A hundred years hence we will want it, and we are going to fight for it."[2] But time has passed, and the younger generation might not be willing to wait so long, especially as China's economic juggernaut and the government's manipulation of nationalistic impulses as a substitute for Communist ideology inflame this revanchist fervor.

Although Japan took control of Taiwan (Formosa) in 1895 under the terms of the *Treaty of Shimonoseki,*[3] Japan's defeat in World War II put Taiwan's status in play again even though the major Allied powers had acknowledged, at the Cairo and Potsdam conferences,[4] that Taiwan was Chinese territory. "Washington now wanted to find a way to deny it [Taiwan] to the Communists."[5]

And so from 1945 to 1957, the United States provided Taiwan with more than $6.75 billion in economic and military aid.[6] With the outbreak of the Korean War in 1950, President Truman dispatched the Seventh Fleet to the Taiwan Strait; over time, "Taiwan became the principal [CIA] base for launching clandestine military operations against mainland China."[7] During the Taiwan

Strait Crisis of 1954, "the United States had come dangerously close to using nuclear weapons against the Chinese mainland,"[8] and in 1955, the United States ratified a *Mutual Defense Treaty* with Taiwan. In January 1958, the United States installed "nuclear-armed Matador missiles" on Taiwan,[9] and later that year, during the Second Taiwan Strait Crisis, the United States again deployed its Seventh Fleet to the region and provided state-of-the-art air-to-air Sidewinder missiles to Taiwan, enabling it to achieve a kill-ratio of 1:30 against China's Soviet-supplied MIG-17s.[10]

All of this occurred during the PRC's infancy – at the onset of the Cold War and against the backdrop of the Korean War and the U.S. reconstruction effort in Japan. The French had begun their withdrawal from Indochina, and by the end of the 1950s, U.S. foreign aid to South Vietnam had approached $2 billion.[11] Taiwan was another piece in a U.S. policy of containment and encirclement, buttressing Secretary of States John Foster Dulles' brainchild, the Southeast Asian Treaty Organization (SEATO).

Until President Nixon sent Henry Kissinger on a secret mission to China in 1971, official U.S. contact with the People's Republic had been limited to the Panmunjom, Geneva, and Warsaw talks.[12] The Watergate scandal, followed by Nixon's resignation, interrupted the momentum toward formal diplomatic relations that followed the opening to China in 1972. President Ford's lack of legitimacy—he assumed office following Nixon's resignation on August 9, 1974 —further hindered progress on normalization.[13]

The conservative wing of the Republican Party, personified by Ronald Reagan, exploited growing dissatisfaction with the administration's moves toward China and away from Taiwan to mount an unsuccessful challenge against the incumbent Ford in the 1976 Republican presidential primaries. In addition, many began to view Kissinger and the policy of détente with the Soviet Union—which they equated with appeasement—as a campaign liability for Ford, who went on to lose the general election to Jimmy Carter.

Monumental shifts were also taking place within China's top leadership circle. Kissinger, during his November 1974 trip to Beijing, met with his chief interlocutor, Premier Zhou Enlai, in a hospital suite where Zhou was undergoing treatment for bladder cancer; the relatively unknown Hua Guofeng succeeded Zhou as Premier shortly after Zhou's death in January 1976.

Chairman Mao, going blind and afflicted with Lou Gehrig's disease, suffered a series of heart attacks, while the Gang of Four, a radical faction led by Jiang Qing,[14] Mao's wife, engineered Deng Xiaoping's removal as First Deputy Premier in April 1976. After Mao's death in September 1976, Hua Guofeng also assumed leadership of the Communist Party; less than a month later, the Gang of Four was arrested and Deng Xiaoping, rehabilitated for the third time, gradually wrested control of the Party from Hua over the next several years.

Many Chinese believe that just rulers are blessed by a Mandate of Heaven, and so interpreted the massive Tangshan earthquake in the summer of 1976—during the Year of the Dragon, representative of the Chinese emperors and the most popular zodiac year—as an omen that the leadership's Mandate of Heaven had been withdrawn.

In the United States, President Jimmy Carter juggled the *Panama Canal Treaty* negotiations, *Strategic Arms Limitation Treaty* (SALT II) talks with Moscow, normalization with China, and the Camp David Accords between Egypt and Israel. All the while, his two most visible foreign policy advisers, Zbigniew Brzezinski, the National Security Adviser, and Cyrus Vance, the Secretary of State, jockeyed for power and influence in a most unseemly fashion, apparently unmindful of the gathering storm in Iran that led to the downfall of the Shah and Ayatollah Khomeini's return. The Carter camp, focused on the upcoming 1978 Congressional elections, decided that normalization with China would have to wait until after the elections.

Deng, however, was not constrained by a fickle electorate. But Vietnam's invasion of China's ally, Cambodia, in late 1978—an attempt to overthrow Pol Pot's odious Khmer Rouge regime—complicated Deng's efforts to consolidate power after the extended leadership struggle—especially as the Chinese considered Vietnam a Soviet proxy on their southeastern border.[15] China decided to "teach Vietnam a lesson," but Deng wanted to conclude the normalization agreement with the United States before China launched an attack against Vietnam and so may have been more amenable to compromise.

China and the United States now faced the diplomatic conundrum of reconciling China's three conditions for normalization—an end to U.S. diplomatic ties with Taiwan, abrogation of the *Mutual Defense Treaty*, and withdrawal of American troops from Taiwan—with America's goals of securing a Chinese commitment to resolve the Taiwan issue peacefully, while maintaining America's right to provide arms to Taiwan.

At first, the Carter team tried to renege on Ford's pledge that the United States would shut down its liaison office in Taiwan, but then relented. Both sides tiptoed around the arms issue—Brzezinski, in his memoirs, states, "we did not talk about arms sales directly."[16] Deng wanted the United States to agree that no additional arms would enter the pipeline to Taiwan during the 1-year cancellation period stipulated under Article 10 of the *Mutual Defense Treaty* with Taiwan; the United States agreed, but intended to resume arms sales after the 1-year moratorium. After some hesitation, Deng agreed, but asked for "an assurance that such sales would be made secretly."[17] The United States, however, would not agree to conceal these future arms deals, and so the parties decided to proceed with normalization and return to the arms issue later. The Chinese agreed that the United States could issue a public statement about the peaceful resolution of Taiwan's status, but stipulated that the statement could not be included in the official communiqué on the establishment of diplomatic relations.

Disregarding all that the executive branch had negotiated, the U.S. Congress, just four months later, passed the Taiwan Relations Act by such a wide margin that it was immune to a presidential veto. On the arms issue, the Act stated, "The United States will make available to Taiwan such defense articles and defense services in such quantity as may be necessary to enable Taiwan to maintain a sufficient self-defense capability."[18] The Act also stated, "The United States decision to establish diplomatic relations with the People's Republic of China rests upon the expectation that the future of Taiwan will be determined by peaceful means."[19]

Needless to say, "Deng felt betrayed."[20] The Chinese, henceforth, questioned the reliability of America's interlocutors, who apparently did not have the political capital required to deliver on all that they had promised; indeed, Nixon and Kissinger had originally pledged to complete the normalization process in 1976.[21] The Chinese must have wondered how to build a stable relationship with a country whose agreements were subjected to the vagaries of 4-year election cycles, the excoriations of an uncontrollable press, and an untamable legislature. The Chinese system does not brook such interference.

In 1980, the Carter administration's last year, arms sales to Taiwan reached $835 million.[22]

Long regarded as "one of the two most fervent supporters of Taiwan in American politics"[23] (Barry Goldwater was the other), "Reagan considered himself a true friend of the Nationalist Chinese and a personal friend of the late Chiang Kai-shek."[24] Statements from Ronald Reagan's presidential campaign that attacked Carter's China policy—Reagan even vowed to reestablish diplomatic relations with Taiwan—infuriated the Chinese.

"Within the Reagan camp, there was no stronger supporter of Taiwan's cause than Richard V. Allen,"[25] later appointed Reagan's first National Security Adviser. In one of his opening salvos, Allen invited several Taiwanese officials to Reagan's inauguration, setting the stage for a diplomatic showdown with the People's Republic that was only resolved when two of the invitees cancelled at the last minute; the third, already in the United States, conveniently contracted a severe case of the flu and checked into a hospital.[26]

When candidate Reagan became President Reagan, the unresolved issue of arms to Taiwan moved to the forefront again. All signals in Washington pointed to the sale of Northrop's advanced FX fighter jets to Taiwan, especially as "Tom Jones, Northrop's chairman, was Reagan's friend and political supporter."[27]

To ameliorate the sting, Alexander Haig, Reagan's first Secretary of State, championed arms sales to China, but Huang Hua, China's foreign minister, told Haig that one billion Chinese "can't be bribed."[28] Rejecting this attempt at linkage, the Chinese instead pushed the Reagan administration to set a cutoff date for arms sales to Taiwan, and so negotiations on this issue resumed.

In *A Great Wall: Six Presidents and China,* Patrick Tyler, a former Beijing bureau chief for *The New York Times,* concludes that the Reagan administration's stubborn insistence on proceeding with arms sales to Taiwan "was all about money, all about saving Northrop, all about bailing out the president's friend."[29]

The looming crisis in Poland, however, convinced Reagan to back down on the FX issue. Reagan calculated that alienating the Chinese at a time when the Soviets might use military force to suppress Poland's Solidarity movement was not in the best interests of the United States; better that the Russians were still worried about protecting their backside. The U.S. administration, however, decided to continue co-producing Northrop's F-5E fighter jet in Taiwan.

Finally, after two years of negotiations, the United States and China issued the August 1982 communiqué that defined the limits on arms sales to Taiwan.[30] Later, seeking to take advantage of every imaginable loophole, "the Reagan administration concluded that the August communiqué did nothing to limit the transfer of advanced defense technology and defense services—as opposed to weapons,"[31] and so discreetly arranged for General Dynamics to transfer technology that enabled the Taiwanese to develop the Indigenous Defense Fighter (IDF).[32]

James Lilley, America's most senior, unofficial diplomat in Taiwan during these negotiations,[33] has revealed that before the August 1982 communiqué had been signed, he delivered "six assurances" that contradicted the communiqué to Taiwan's President Chiang Ching-kuo: "We made sure there would be no paper trail. The assurances were delivered in the form of a blind memo. They were committed to paper but without a signature or letterhead so that there would be no evidence of its origin."[34]

Shortly after the agreement was signed, "Reagan moved, secretly and unilaterally, to eviscerate what he had just signed."[35] In a one-page memo, locked away in a safe, Reagan had spelled out his interpretation of the agreement: "The United States would restrict arms sales to Taiwan so long as the balance of military power between China and Taiwan was preserved."[36] The United States appointed itself the arbiter of the balance of military power between China and Taiwan, and "The State Department meanwhile announced that it would sell nearly $800 million in weapons to Taiwan in 1983 and about $760 million worth in 1984."[37]

In response to the Tiananmen Massacre in 1989, the Bush administration had suspended all military cooperation with China, and in particular, the Peace Pearl project, "an F-8 avionics program worth $550 million."[38] As succor to the Taiwanese, the United States had provided "comparable avionics kits for its IDF"[39] and so now Taiwan had a qualitative advantage. The U.S. cancellation of the F-8 avionics program with China "probably contributed to its decision to purchase advanced SU-27 fighters from the Soviet Union in 1991."[40]

In the 10-year period from 1983–1992, U.S. government and commercial arms deliveries to Taiwan reached approximately $5.525 billion. In the next 10-year period, 1993–2002, sales nearly tripled to $15.37 billion,[41] of which $6 billion was for 150 F-16 jet fighter aircraft, a transaction approved by President George H.W. Bush.[42] Brent Scowcroft, Bush's National Security Adviser, explained to Zhu Qizhen, China's ambassador to the United States, "This sale of F-16s is not done for Taiwan or for you. It is being done because the production line is in Texas and Texas is crucial to the President"[43] in the upcoming 1992 presidential race against Bill Clinton and H. Ross Perot.

After twelve years of Republican rule, Bill Clinton usurped the patrician Bush by winning the White House in 1992; "Clinton's group of advisors [was] so disposed against China as to preordain the path to confrontation."[44]

Many in the new administration believed that China had shipped M-11 intermediate-range missiles to Pakistan as a quid pro quo for the sale of F-16s to Taiwan, but the evidence was not conclusive. In any event, the United States imposed trade sanctions on China, worth an estimated $500 million annually.[45]

As a precursor to an event that would have international repercussions, President Lee Teng Hui of Taiwan, in a move calibrated to incite Beijing, had requested permission to refuel in Hawaii while en route to Central America. In an attempt to downplay the event—the first visit to the United States by a president of Taiwan (before President Jiang of China had visited the United States)—Lee's chartered 747 was shunted off to a corner of Hickham Air Force Base in Honolulu and greeted by a low-ranking diplomat who was not affiliated with the U.S. government at the time.

But Lee had established a precedent, and, a bit more than a year later and after much wrangling—the House and the Senate resoundingly passed a nonbinding "sense of the Congress" resolution supporting him—Lee succeeded in obtaining a visa to attend a reunion at Cornell University, where he had earned a Ph.D. in agricultural economics in 1968. Lee had astutely "hired the Washington lobbying firm Cassidy and Associates for a three-year fee of $4.5 million to push for the visa to be approved,"[46]—and his investment paid off. Lee arrived in Los Angeles on his way to Cornell on June 7, 1995.

In the midst of his presidential election campaign,[47] Lee had brilliantly manipulated the United States and China to garner publicity that buttressed his image as the candidate who had forced America's hand *and* stood up to Beijing. President Clinton, too, was gearing up for his 1996 reelection bid, while China was in the midst of another leadership transition. Paramount leader since the late 1970s, Deng Xiaoping's health had been deteriorating for the past several years, and his handpicked successor, Jiang Zemin, could not afford to appear weak—especially to the generals of the People's Liberation Army (PLA)—in the face of Lee's intransigence.

In a transparent bid to influence Taiwan's 1996 presidential election, the PRC launched the Third Taiwan Strait Crisis with a series of military exercises, and later, six missile tests north of Taiwan in the summer of 1995; on August 17, the Chinese conducted an underground nuclear test at the Lop Nor facility in Xinjiang Province.

A barrage of diplomatic communications between Beijing and Washington ensued; Xiong Guangkai, then deputy chief of the PLA general staff, reportedly warned a retired American diplomat, "China was prepared to sacrifice millions of people, even entire cities, in a nuclear exchange to defend its interests in preventing Taiwan's independence."[48]

As Taiwan's election approached, the PLA positioned 150,000 troops along its coast facing Taiwan, and several weeks later, began another round of ballistic missile tests within twenty-five miles of Taiwan's two largest ports at Kaohsiung and Keelung. The United States responded by deploying two carrier battle groups, the USS Independence and the USS Nimitz, to the waters near the Taiwan Strait. President Lee went on to win his reelection bid—Taiwan's first-ever direct election for president—with almost 55 percent of the vote.

Even though China had attempted to intimidate the Taiwanese with this massive show of force, the U.S. "deployment of March 1996 was the first act of American coercion against China since 1958...[and] it deeply humiliated the new Chinese leadership and the People's Liberation Army."[49]

By the mid-1990s,

> The United States allowed President Lee of Taiwan to come to the United States, sold 150 F-16s to Taiwan, designated Tibet an "occupied sovereign territory," denounced China for its human rights abuses, denied Beijing the 2000 Olympics, normalized relations with Vietnam, accused China of exporting chemical weapons components to Iran, imposed trade sanctions on China for sales of missile equipment to Pakistan, and threatened China with additional sanctions over economic issues while at the same time barring China's admission to the World Trade Organization.[50]

Unconfirmed rumors at the time posited, "Taiwan has also been building a secret reprocessing facility and shaping bomb cores."[51]

In 2001, President George W. Bush approved the sale of a $4 billion arms package to Taiwan. In 2003, U.S. government arms deliveries to Taiwan dropped to approximately $540 million,[52] but then skyrocketed in 2004 with an arms sales package valued at $1.776 billion.[53]

Taiwan's declining defense budget—while China's is growing[54]—has led to questions about whether Taiwan is free-riding under the U.S. security umbrella. As a result, the United States has been pressuring Taiwan's Legislative Yuan to approve a $15 billion special budget allocation—separate from its annual defense budget—for procurement of eight diesel submarines valued at $8 to 10 billion, twelve anti-submarine P-3C Orion patrol aircraft valued at $4 billion, and four Kidd-class destroyers.[55]

In April 2002, the U.S. House of Representatives established the Congressional Taiwan Caucus; as of January 2007, it had 143 members, or almost 33 percent of House membership. The Senate formed its Taiwan Caucus in September 2003, and as of January 2007, it had 23 members.[56]

No doubt, the highly organized and efficient Taiwan lobby in Washington is advocating for Taiwan's inclusion in a theater missile defense system (TMD); one of the arms packages approved by Washington in April 2000 included a Pave Paws[57] long-range radar system that "could eventually be linked to a theater missile defense system."[58]

Might Taiwan approve the special budgetary allocation when Washington agrees to include the island in a TMD system? Will Taiwan's inclusion in TMD foster a false sense of security and encourage its pro-independence proclivities? How might Taiwan respond to Beijing's military buildup—especially the placement of more than 700 ballistic missiles positioned along China's eastern coast and targeted at Taiwan—without further provoking China?[59] Does China fear the United States might act with impunity once it has the ability to neutralize China's second-strike retaliatory capability with a defensive shield? Might China act first against Taiwan to preclude this possibility by invoking its own doctrine of preemption? Under what conditions would the United States intervene on behalf of its unofficial ally, Taiwan? And how would the United States intervene?

Would Japan defend Taiwan? After all, Japan had occupied Taiwan for fifty years, its Taiwan lobby is growing in strength, and under the terms of the 1996 *U.S.-Japanese Treaty,* "the two governments will jointly and individually strive to achieve a more peaceful and stable security environment in the Asia-Pacific region."[60] Would the PLA, therefore, launch a preemptive strike against Japan, or against U.S. forces (hostages) based in Japan? Does Japan have a secret nuclear weapon?

According to Jonathan Mirsky, a renowned journalist and China scholar, "some American experts on the Chinese military, who have held senior political and military positions, suggested at a recent seminar at Oxford that if Taiwan seemed to be losing in a military conflict with China, the U.S. would consider 'taking the war to the Mainland.'"[61] This is consistent with the abrupt shift from strategic ambiguity in Taiwan policy enunciated by President George W. Bush when he declared that the United States would do "whatever it took to help Taiwan defend itself."[62] Conversely, "Exactly how much blood and treasure China would be willing to expend over the issue is unclear, but it might be considerably more than the United States would be prepared to shoulder. Indeed, many Chinese believe that, in the final analysis, Taiwan matters far more to China than it does to the United States."[63] The "balance of fervor"[64] makes it clear that the Taiwan issue is a vital interest of China's.

For all of these reasons, Thomas Christensen, a leading scholar on China's foreign relations, asserts that "the most dangerous period in cross-strait relations may be between the years 2005–2010"[65]—that is, during the window of opportunity before the United States deploys NMD or TMD.

It is worth noting that Taiwan's next presidential election in March 2008 occurs just a few months before the start of the Summer Olympics in Beijing. This has led to speculation that Taiwan will ratchet up its pro-independence rhetoric and activities under the assumption that Beijing would not respond in its usual manner out of fear of jeopardizing the Games.

But "without firing a shot... [China] could cause chaos in Taiwan"[66] by manipulating the vast economic leverage that it has gradually accumulated over the past decade. In 2004, exports to China accounted for an astounding 23 percent of Taiwan's GDP;[67] and according to private estimates, Taiwan has approximately $100 billion invested in China.[68] More than 1 million Taiwanese, out of almost 23 million in 2004, live and work on the mainland.

All the while, Taiwan has shed its image as a corrupt, authoritarian regime and has embraced democracy *and* unabashed capitalism and so stands as a viable alternative to the mainland. As Taiwan continues to democratize, calls for independence have become more volatile, especially as Chen Shui-bian's Democratic Progressive Party (DPP) favors independence and has supplanted the Kuomintang (KMT), the once-predominant political party comprised primarily of mainlanders who fled to Taiwan as Mao's Communists took power; the KMT has traditionally advocated reunification with the mainland. Taiwan's New Party, the most ardent supporter of reunification, has seen its share of the popular vote decline from 12.8 percent in 1995 to a miniscule 0.44 percent in 2004.[69]

A December 2004 poll on national identity conducted by Taiwan Thinktank indicates that 61 percent of respondents viewed themselves as "Taiwanese-only," whereas 14 percent chose "Chinese-only" and 16 percent chose "both."[70] In another sign of creeping Taiwanization, the island's Minnanese dialect is increasingly replacing Mandarin, and so "Mandarin-speaking Taiwanese must read subtitles to understand the sit-coms and talk shows with the highest ratings."[71]

As a result, it is likely that over time, Taiwan's Pan Green alliance—composed of the DPP and the Taiwan Solidarity Union, or TSU—will gain control of the Legislative Yuan from the Pan Blue alliance—composed of the KMT and the People's First Party, or PFP—and so will be free to act with less restraint.

The Taiwan Strait, "the most dangerous place on the planet,"[72] has become the new Fulda Gap[73] in an emerging showdown between the United States and China. The diplomats who drafted the communiqués that define the

Sino-American relationship sing their own praises and herald their linguistic adroitness in crafting a policy toward Taiwan based on "strategic ambiguity." But the Shanghai Communiqué, "a masterpiece of diplomatic obfuscation,"[74] is built on a basic "untruth that China is prepared to go to war to defend,"[75] and the United States seems hell-bent on being drawn into, or precipitating, *The Next Great Clash*.

Events, rather than policy, seem to drive the Sino-American relationship; and Taiwan has repeatedly emerged, or has positioned itself, as the main driver in cycles of action and reaction. John Gaddis, in a superlative history of the Cold War, observes, "By sticking their necks out over Quemoy and Matsu [in the first Taiwan Strait Crisis of 1954], the Americans had handed him a noose, which he could relax—or tighten—at will. Mao chose to tighten the noose again in August 1958"[76]—and the United States threatened to use nuclear weapons. Again in the Third Taiwan Strait Crisis of 1995–1996, "U.S.-China relations [were]... hostage to the condition of Taiwan-PRC relations,"[77] but this time China reportedly threatened the use of nuclear weapons.

General MacArthur referred to Taiwan as an "unsinkable aircraft carrier and submarine tender," and America, at least in China's eyes—apparently intends to keep it that way, even though China's legal claim to Taiwan predates the founding of the United States.

The purpose here has not been to disparage U.S. support for Taiwan over the years, but rather to demonstrate how America's actions have consistently been at loggerheads with China over Taiwan. It is no wonder that many Chinese believe America has been obstructing its reunification effort and "busily preparing Taiwan for war"[78] from the get-go. "Beijing considers that the heart of the 'Taiwan problem' is not Taiwan's separation from the mainland but the American role in perpetuating it."[79] Perhaps that is why China has now drawn closer to Russia than at any time in its long history—the subject of Part Two of this book.

# Part Two ───────────────────

# WHEN RUSSIA MET CHINA: FROM THE 1600s TO 1911

*The Russian advance, it bears repeating, possessed its own inner logic and could not stop until it had reached a line of an optimum of conquest linking Vladivostok and Port Arthur around the Korean peninsula. Korea was part of an organic frontier stretching from Kamchatka to the strait separating the Liaotung and Shantung peninsulas, the gateway to Peking, and the Russian advance could no more stop short of Korea than it could have stopped short of Sakhalin. There could be no peace until Russia or Japan had imposed its hegemony in the narrow seas. Japan's hegemony in Korea threatened Russia's hegemony in the Liaotung Peninsula and destroyed the usefulness of Vladivostok, "the dominator of the east." Russia was building a continental railroad to Vladivostok and Port Arthur; Japan was threatening to turn these two terminal bases into dead ends.*[1]

Emphasizing broad patterns of interaction at the elite level, this chapter focuses on relations between China and Russia since their first official contact in the 1600s until the fall of the Qing Dynasty in 1911. As the relative strength of China and Russia ebbed and flowed, borders have contracted and expanded in response to the advancing power, the declining power. Is there any reason to think that this will not happen as China rises again?

## FROM THE 1600s TO THE 1840s: NERCHINSK, KIAKHTA, AND THE UNEQUAL TREATIES

In the earliest phases of state-to-state contact between Russia and China—dating back to the 1600s—Russian emissaries traveled across the Siberian plains to Peking, a round-trip journey that often took four years to complete under dangerous and even deadly conditions. The Russians typically traveled to Peking to present various trade-related requests, while the Chinese repeatedly resisted the barbarians by citing violations of ceremonial form and etiquette, corroborating the observation that "the history of Sino-Russian relations in the seventeenth century was to be basically one of Russian demand and Chinese/Manchu reaction."[2] The Russians kept reappearing at the Emperor's court as supplicants bent on penetrating China's "controlled apartness."[3]

In Russia's quest to fill its royal coffers, it sought to expand its market for Siberian furs and pelts—after all, "the entire Siberian economy was considered the tsar's private property"[4]—but the repeated refusal of its emissaries to kowtow before the Chinese emperor and to make tribute limited the success of its missions to Peking.

In one of the first Russian expeditions in 1618, Ivan Petlin failed to present a tribute gift to the emperor Wan-li and so was refused a meeting at court. The emperor, however, had approved a written message to the tsar to be conveyed by Petlin—"permission [was granted] for the Russians to send envoys and trade with China"[5]—but this message was not read until 1675 because the Russian imperial court had not yet trained any of its functionaries to translate Chinese documents into Russian.

Fyodor Baikov's 1656 mission to Peking to establish trade and diplomatic ties failed because he too refused to kowtow and declined "the emperor's gift of tea boiled with butter and milk."[6] Two years later in 1658, Setkul Ablin and Ivan Perfiliev arrived in Peking but were denied an audience with the emperor because of their lowly status as mere couriers; they returned to Moscow in 1662 with a written message for the tsar that again went untranslated. Nikolai Milescu kowtowed before the Chinese emperor Kangxi in 1675 and so was granted an audience, but his mission was derailed when he "refused to kowtow in a muddy courtyard in the rain when receiving, from subordinate officials, the emperor's presents for the tsar."[7]

Milescu, however, did establish contact with several influential foreign Jesuit priests in Peking who provided valuable information and insights, highlighting another pattern that emerged in the early stages of Sino–Russian relations. Whereas the Russians frequently employed the services of foreigners from different lands as their emissaries to Peking,[8] the Chinese and Manchus relied almost exclusively on one group of foreigners, the Jesuits, as advisers—especially in their relations with other foreign powers. The Russians consistently managed to extract confidential information from the Jesuits, who hoped to expedite their communications with Rome by gaining access to an overland transportation route across Russia in exchange for their insights into the inscrutable ways of the Chinese court.[9]

In 1685, the Manchu general Sabsu, who had been appointed military governor in Heilungkiang and placed in charge of Russian affairs two years earlier, launched an attack on the Russian fortress at Albazin and destroyed its recently built fortifications. At about the same time, the emperor Kangxi sent two letters written in Latin to the tsar, who responded by dispatching Fyodor Alekseevich Golovin to Nerchinsk for negotiations. Golovin met with the chief Manchu envoys Songgotu and T'ung Kuo-kang (Kangxi's uncle) to discuss a settlement. The Jesuits brokered these negotiations and served as interpreters, giving the Chinese an advantage over the Russians, who had to rely on their adversaries' interpreters.[10]

Seventy years after Petlin's expedition to Peking, China and Russia concluded the *Treaty of Nerchinsk* (1689), an attempt to contain Russia's advance into the Amur River basin by defining borders in the region. This treaty, written in Latin and the first between China and Russia, has been described as "essentially a Chinese success...which governed Sino-Russian relations in peace for the next 170 or so years, a period that was to see the gradual reversal of Chinese predominance over Russia in East Asia."[11] While the Russians were motivated by a desire to expand their market for furs, the Chinese Emperor Kangxi sought to prevent a Russian-Jungar alliance (the Jungars were a Mongolian tribe) by acceding to Russia's trade imperatives.

In 1720, Lev Vasilevich Izmailov, appointed by Peter the Great, embarked on the arduous journey to Peking with instructions to increase trade between Russia and China and to secure land in Peking for the construction of an Orthodox Church and a consular office. His mission was generally successful, and he also "at last solved the vexed problem of ceremonial. It was agreed that Russian envoys should perform the kowtow to the Manchu emperor at Peking, and China's envoys when sent to St. Petersburg should repay this compliment in kind."[12] The Middle Kingdom had finally acknowledged an implied equality in relations with the northern barbarians.

The *Treaty of Kiakhta,* signed in 1728, formalized agreement on many of the issues raised during Izmailov's mission of 1720. Kiakhta was designated the center of Sino-Russian frontier trade (officially limited to barter until 1854) and a border was delimited that specified the point at which Mongols—many of whom had fled into Siberia to escape the Manchu tribute tax—were subject to extradition. The treaty also institutionalized Russia's China trade by regulating the frequency of caravans, by allowing Russian Orthodox missions to Peking for periods of ten years each, and by establishing a Chinese language school for Russians in Peking.

The Russian team spent six months in Peking negotiating the *Treaty of Kiakhta;* "relations between the negotiators became so strained at times that the Russian embassy was denied food and for more than a month was given only brackish water, which caused over half the staff to fall ill."[13] Even though the Russians seem to have accomplished all of their goals, the *Kiakhta Treaty* has been characterized as the "Mongolization of Sino-Russian relations,"[14] because Russia had submitted to the wishes of the Chinese, as had the

Mongols. The barbarians were fenced in and allowed to trade from their frontier post at Kiakhta.[15]

Just a year later, the Manchus appointed To-shih, the vice-president of the Li-fan Yuan (the Office of Barbarian Control),[16] to head a mission to St. Petersburg, the first time an official Chinese envoy was sent to the tsar's court. China's first diplomatic mission to Western Europe occurred more than a century later during the reign of Tongzhi.

After the *Treaty of Kiakhta,* relative calm between Russia and China prevailed throughout the rest of the eighteenth century, although trade was suspended from 1764 to 1768 and from 1785 to 1792. On both occasions, successful negotiations—enshrined in the *Supplemental Treaty of Kiakhta* and the *Accord of 1792,* respectively—allowed for the resumption of trade. However, Mongol pressure on the nomadic Kazakh hordes had led the Kazakhs closer to the Russians, whereas the Manchus, under Qianlong, the emperor from 1735 to 1796, violently suppressed the Mongols and moved Chinese forces into Mongol territory.

There is an unusual parallelism in that each country's most effective and most capable leaders reigned—or at least died—at about the same time: Kangxi (1662–1723) and Peter the Great (1689–1725), Qianlong (1735–1796) and Catherine the Great (1762–1796).[17] Even though Catherine the Great and the Emperor Qianlong both ended their reign by the close of the 1700s, a shift in relative power had occurred as Russia had expanded under Catherine and its reform campaign had gathered momentum.

The old patterns reemerged when Count Yuri Golovkin journeyed to China in 1805 seeking to expand Russian trade into Canton and Nanking. His mission failed because he too "refused to perform the kowtow before a silk screen concealing a tablet representing the emperor."[18] Just a few years later, in discussions with Nikolai Treskin, the military governor of Irkutsk, the Manchus expressed an interest in the establishment of a permanent Russian embassy in Peking but refused to reciprocate by opening an embassy in St. Petersburg.

If the "ceremonial was the outward expression of the Confucian world order... the Russians simply didn't know the drill"[19] after almost 200 years of contact with their neighbor. It is just as likely, though, that Russia's mastery of form and etiquette would have been met by new and unexpected hurdles concocted by the Chinese to frustrate their interlocutors' progress.

The early 1800s also witnessed changes in the Russian Orthodox Church missions to Peking. The Russians began to display a marked interest in Chinese affairs by acquiring books and manuscripts and developing a specialized Asia collection; the Russian monk Iakinf, who served in Peking for fourteen years (1807–21), has since become known as the "father of Russian Sinology."[20] During the same period, the Kazan and St. Petersburg universities introduced Chinese-language studies, and in 1819, the Russian Ministry of Foreign Affairs established its Asiatic Department.

The Kiakhta frontier trade and the growing influence of the Russian Orthodox mission in Peking were the primary outlets for the expression of Russia's interests in China, but the First Opium War of 1839–42 and the ensuing Anglo-Chinese *Treaty of Nanking* (1842), inaugurating the unequal treaty system and the treaty ports, struck a "mortal blow to the Kiakhta trade."[21]

The sea powers—Britain, France and the United States—had gained a competitive advantage over Russia as the cost of transporting goods from European Russia across Siberia and down into China exceeded the cost of shipping goods to the treaty ports. The *Treaty of Nanking* marked the beginning of China's "century of humiliation" by foreign powers bent on exploiting China's weakness, and Russia stepped in to lay claim to its share of the spoils.

> In the history of Russo-Chinese relations, a triumphant Manchu China played the role of containing power from the last quarter of the seventeenth century to the 1840s, when the arrival of "western barbarians" from the European Coastland destabilized the area and facilitated a Russian advance into the Chinese Empire.[22]

## RUSSIAN EXPANSION

Russia's thrust into Central Asia and the Caucasus triggered British fears of Russian designs on India—the beginning of the "Great Game"—and paralleled the sea powers' intrusions into China. In addition, the Manchu dynasty faced domestic upheaval in the form of the Taiping Rebellion while a weak emperor, Xianfeng, sat at the helm. The British, French, and Americans "were all involved in some way or another with the final suppression of the Taiping revolutionaries on behalf of the Manchu rule, [but] the land power Russia was not."[23] This telling detail points to another tactic that the Russians had now applied to the Asian arena:

> It had always been the Russian government's assumption, in Sweden, in Poland, in Persia, and even in Turkey, that Russia's interest was to encourage the rotting process in the surrounding core areas in the name of legitimism, in order to obtain maximum advantages from weak rulers, governments, and dynasties willing to "cling to a serpent" to save their power. Subversion in the name of conservatism was always the hallmark of Russian foreign policy.[24]

As if on cue, the Russians, who had appointed the very talented and capable General Nikolai Muraviev as governor of Eastern Siberia in 1847, advanced unimpeded along the Amur River and established several towns, in violation of the *Treaty of Nerchinsk*. Apparently recognizing the threat now posed by the Russians in the north, the Chinese transferred Prince I-shan, military governor of Ili since 1850, to Heilungkiang.

During I-shan's tenure in Ili, he and Major E.P. Kovalevskii had negotiated the *Treaty of Kuldja* (1851), which expanded frontier trade between Russia and China to the Central Asian cities of Ili and Tarbagatai. Prince I-shan and Muraviev then went on to negotiate the *Treaty of Aigun* of 1858, in which Russia acquired a vast swath of territory along the northern bank of the Amur River from the Argun. In the same year, the *Treaty of Tientsin* granted Russia the same privileges as those exacted by Britain, France and the United States under the *Treaty of Nanking:* complete equality in the conduct of relations, extraterritoriality, all benefits that accrued under a most-favored-nation clause, and access to the treaty ports. Just two years later, in 1860, the *Treaty of Peking* sanctified Sino-Russian trade in Kashgar and thus "opened the entire northern frontier of the Ch'ing empire, from Manchuria to Sinkiang, to Russia's political and commercial influence."[25]

Now Russian ships offered the most advantageous trade route from Canton and Shanghai to the port of Odessa in the Black Sea. Although Russia had succeeded in expanding territorially and in securing a more competitive trade route, "Aigun has been described by the Chinese as the first of the Russo-Chinese 'unequal treaties'...Tientsin was more truly unequal than Aigun, for it gave nothing in return for what it took."[26]

Russia's territorial acquisitions by treaty during the span of a few years exceeded 665,000 square miles, and are "the only remaining territorial legacy of the age of imperialism in China."[27] Furthermore, "in Chinese eyes, this represented a gross dereliction of filial duty to retain all of the lands so carefully accumulated by previous generations and still considered to be part of China's rightful patrimony."[28] Emperor Xianfeng, whose Mandate of Heaven had apparently been withdrawn, fled Peking in 1860, never returned to the capital, and died a year later.

While "Han Chinese colonization...might have saved the lands east of the Ussuri"[29] from Russian encroachment at this early stage, the Manchus had decided against this option only to reverse themselves later as more and more Russians migrated east. Siberia's population had almost doubled between 1815 and 1854, from 1.5 million to 2.9 million.[30] After the abolition of serfdom in Russia in 1861, followed by Dmitri Miliutin's military reforms of 1874 in which active service had been reduced from twenty-five years to ten years, resettlement to Siberia accelerated, and by the end of the nineteenth century its population had reached 7.8 million.[31]

Increased contact between Russians and Chinese in the border regions exacerbated the xenophobic tendencies of both countries. Nikolai Mikhailovich Przhevalsky, a Polish Russophile who became one of Russia's most adulated explorers of Asia, enthralled intellectual circles in Moscow and St. Petersburg with tales of his expeditions. Przhevalsky, however, "stood apart in his contempt for Asian peoples,"[32] whom he described as "unimaginable filth, people squatting and relieving themselves right and left in the street...the Chinaman here is a Jew plus a Muscovite pickpocket, both squared."[33] This harbinger of the racism that characterizes Russian stereotypes of the Chinese neighbor remains a constant theme in Sino-Russian relations.

After its defeat in the Crimean War of 1854–56, Russia had shifted its focus to conquering all of modern-day Central Asia and accomplished this goal by the mid-1880s. Russia's need to find a replacement source for cotton imports after the precipitous drop in production in the American South during the U.S. Civil War prompted its initial expansionary thrust into Central Asia, but a series of Muslim rebellions in Chinese Turkestan (today's Xinjiang) erupted in the 1860s—exacerbated by Britain's apparent support for the local leader, Yakub Beg.

By 1866, China had lost control of this territory to Beg's forces, and Russia, sensing an opportunity and having already advanced far into adjacent territory in Central Asia, moved its forces into the Ili Valley, promising to withdraw once order had been reestablished. Several years later, Chinese forces under General Tso Tsungtang set out to reconquer this territory and succeeded in their mission after Yakub Beg died in 1877.

To formalize Russia's promised return of these contested lands, the Manchu Throne deployed its emissary Chung Ho—the military governor of Mukden (Shenyang)—to St. Petersburg, the first such mission by a Chinese official since To-Shih's visit in 1729. Chung Ho and his Russian counterparts negotiated the *Treaty of Livadia* (1879), in which Russia gained control over parts of Chinese Turkestan and exacted further trade concessions from China. China also agreed to pay an indemnity of five million rubles for the costs incurred by the Russians during their occupation of Ili.

After his return to Peking, the Manchu court condemned Chung Ho to death for his inept diplomacy but the sentence was later commuted after his family made a substantial contribution to the state's budget. Zeng Jizi, China's minister to England, was sent to St. Petersburg to reopen these negotiations; the ensuing *Treaty of St. Petersburg* (1881) allowed the Manchus to reestablish their preeminence in Chinese Turkestan, and by 1884, Eastern Turkestan and the Jungarian Basin were consolidated into Sinkiang Province.

Although this was "the first time that China had been able to force a European power into retreat,"[34] "there was a net territorial gain to Russia in the western sector of the Ili region, the 'indemnity'...was substantial, and the Russians had won additional trade facilities. In the end, the Russian empire was still the winner."[35]

## THE RISE OF JAPAN: THE SINO-JAPANESE WAR AND THE RUSSO-JAPANESE WAR

While Russia had been expanding into the Amur valley region and Central Asia and as China reestablished its dominance in Sinkiang, Japan had been forced to rescind its foreign exclusion policy by America's Commodore Perry in 1854; Japan's Meiji Restoration followed in 1868. Russia, "faithful to their diplomatic tradition, preferred to encourage the rotting process"[36] in Japan and so had dissociated itself from the maritime powers' infringement on Japan's isolation. In summary, then:

> The history of the Russian advance into the Pacific frontier after 1848 is thus the history of a struggle for the redistribution of space among a dynamic Russia, a China determined to resist despite its growing weakness, and a vigorous Japan bent on building an empire to the detriment of both.[37]

In 1891, the Russian government authorized the construction of the Trans-Siberian railway. Besides the obvious trade motive, Russia sought to construct "a ring fence around the valley of the Amur and the Maritime Province"[38] and to provide a means for the expeditious deployment of military troops to this faraway region.

Increasing tensions between China and Japan over the status of Korea precipitated the transmission of an unusual diplomatic message from the Chinese to the Russians. The governor general of the Chihli region, Li Hungchang, "who wielded major influence in foreign affairs, informed Count Cassini, the Russian minister, that China... would appreciate Russian mediation"[39] on its behalf with the Japanese. Diplomatic niceties and Russian mediation, however, did not prevent the outbreak of the Sino-Japanese War of 1894, because

> Japanese officials felt directly threatened as Russia moved into what they regarded as their country's sphere of influence. The response was to intervene directly on the Asian mainland, somewhat as the British had done in India. Japan's defeat of China (1895) gave it treaty-port rights there and enabled it to assert growing influence in Korea.[40]

Under the pretext of attending Nicholas II's coronation, Li Hungchang traveled to St. Petersburg in the spring of 1896. After lengthy negotiations, Russia agreed to finance China's indemnity to Japan after China's defeat in the 1894 war. Russia and China also concluded a secret military alliance, the *Li-Lobanov Treaty*, that would be triggered by Japanese aggression against Russia, China, or Korea. The Russians also pressed Li for further railway concessions by reportedly promising him "three million rubles for expediting the matter of the railway concession"[41] but this accusation of bribery "has not been conclusively proved."[42] In any event, Li Hungchang's death in November 1901 was "a crippling blow to Russia's influence in Peking."[43]

China's glaring weakness after its defeat in the Sino-Japanese war prompted a "Battle for Concessions" amongst the great powers who used the opportunity to extend their spheres of influence in China. The Russians benefited by claiming the ice-free port of Lü-shun (later renamed Port Arthur) at the southern tip of the Liaotung peninsula and extracted permission from the Chinese to build the South Manchurian Railway line from Harbin to Dalien, a 650-mile spur.

In 1900, the Boxer Rebellion erupted in China, an expression of both antiforeign and antidynastic sentiment. When the rebels attacked and destroyed parts of the Russian railway system, "a large Russian expeditionary force of about 100,000 men invaded Manchuria from six directions."[44] The Russians assured the Chinese that they would withdraw their troops as soon as order was restored —a tactic they had used in the Ili Valley in the 1870s. The British, bogged down in the Boer War, were not in a position to resist Russia's advance into China.

After the Boxer Rebellion was quelled, an influential group of Russian foreign policy advisers advocating further expansion into Korea and Manchuria—the "Bezobrazov clique"[45]—emerged in St. Petersburg. Although Russia had reached agreement with Peking on a phased withdrawal from Manchuria to take place over eighteen months, it later reneged on this agreement.

The Japanese attack on Port Arthur in December 1904, signaled the start of the Russo-Japanese War "to determine the extent of the Heartland power's [Russia's] ability to consolidate its position in the Monsoon Coastland."[46]

> The high point of Meiji militarism was the brutal war against Russia, which began with a Pearl Harbor-type raid on the Russian fleet in 1904. The Japanese were still feeling bruised because Western powers forced them to hand over some of their victory spoils in 1895. This included the southern tip of Liaotung peninsula in Manchuria, which was then leased to the Russians. Western powers were feasting on Chinese territory just then: Germans in Shandong, the French in Canton, the British in various treaty ports along the coast. The Americans were expanding their Asian empire in the Pacific. The Russians acquired railway concessions in Manchuria and were moving into north Korea, which Japan saw as its turf. So the Japanese had ample reason to feel left out of the party.[47]

After the Russo-Japanese War, the government in Peking began to encourage Chinese colonization into Heilungkiang, whose population had reached approximately 2.5 million in 1907, five times the population of the Russian Far East.[48] Russia had shifted its focus to Mongolia, traditionally aligned with the Manchu dynasty.

During the fall of the Qing empire and the abdication of the child emperor Puyi in 1912, Russia and Japan had entered into a series of secret agreements that carved up the region: Henceforth, Northern Manchuria and Outer Mongolia became Russian spheres of influence, whereas Southern Manchuria and parts of Inner Mongolia now fell within Japan's purview. But two world wars—and the Bolshevik Revolution in Russia heralding the rise of Communism—changed all of that.

# CAVIAR AND CHOPSTICKS:[1]
# THE REPUBLICAN ERA IN CHINA (1911–1949)

*Were the Chinese, for instance, organized by the Japanese, to overthrow the Russian Empire and conquer its territory, they might constitute the yellow peril to the world's freedom just because they would add an oceanic frontage to the resources of the great continent, an advantage as yet denied to the Russian tenant of the pivot region.*

—H.J. Mackinder

*In joining in the World War on the side of the Allied Powers, Japan failed to utilize the golden opportunity of making Asia exclusive for the Asiatics. Such an Asia would have opposed the Whites, especially the Anglo-Saxons…As Japan has shown herself incapable of seizing this opportunity, it will be China that will be called upon to make Asia a place for the Asiatics in the future.*

—Sun Yat-sen

After the decades-long disintegration of the foreign Manchu dynasty in China, political authority fragmented even further into a myriad of competing blocs and alliances, cliques and factions, a maze of "polycentric chaos"[2] assaulted from every direction by foreign powers vying for and buying influence.

Sun Yat-sen, inspired by Japan's stunning victory against the Russians in 1905, had traveled to Tokyo with thousands of other Chinese students—"one of the modern world's first large-scale student migrations"[3]—to learn and apply the lessons of the Meiji Reformation to China. Later, Sun founded the Kuomintang (KMT) and emerged as the provisional president of the Chinese Republic at Nanjing that succeeded the Qing dynasty in 1912. Displaced by Yuan Shih-kai just a few months later, Sun retreated to his base in Canton, in southern China, as the country disintegrated into the era of warlordism.

World War I and then the outbreak of the Bolshevik Revolution of 1917 had diverted Russia's attention from developments on its vast frontier with China. During the Russian civil war that followed the Bolshevik seizure of power, Japanese, British, French and American troops intervened in Russia, with only token Chinese participation. Indeed, "by the end of 1918, there were over 180,000 foreign troops on Russian soil and several White Russian armies receiving Allied money and Allied guns."[4]

Although China had sided with the Allies during World War I, one of the decisions imposed by Versailles—granting control of China's Shandong province to Japan—triggered the May Fourth Movement[5] of 1919, student protests in China fueled by anti-Japanese sentiment and perceived betrayal by the United States. However, it was not widely known at the time that "as the price of a new Japanese loan, [China's] Premier Duan Qirui had made a secret agreement...signing away Shandong to Japanese control."[6]

Still smarting from laws that prohibited their ownership of land in California and from limitations placed on their entry into British colonies, the Japanese had sponsored a "racial equality clause" to be included in the League of Nations' Covenant under discussion at Versailles. However, "along the West Coast of the United States, political leaders warned of the serious consequences to the white race if the clause passed."[7] The Japanese traded the Council's failure to pass the racial equality clause for the Shandong concessions in China.

Moscow exploited the May Fourth demonstrations and the hypocrisy of Versailles to score a major propaganda coup by issuing the *Karakhan Manifesto* in which it "declared its willingness to give up all privileges extorted from other nations by Tsarist Russia under unequal treaties...a standard which went far beyond that of Woodrow Wilson."[8]

Later, while defining which concessions to disavow, a series of disagreements erupted over what constituted an unequal treaty and over the disposition of the Chinese Eastern Railway (CER), which was to be returned to China "without any kind of compensation"; subsequent versions of the Manifesto, however, omitted this reference. As before, a parade of high-level dignitaries anointed by the Kremlin—including Adolf Joffe, Leo Karakhan, Aleksandr Paikes, and M.I. Yurin—journeyed to Peking to negotiate the terms of a new treaty.

In general, China's emerging political groupings came to be identified with their geographical location: for example, the KMT in Canton, the Chinese Communist Party (CCP) in Shanghai, warlords in the center (especially in Peking), Japanese collaborators in the Three Eastern Provinces (Manchuria), Russian anti-Bolshevik forces (Whites) in Harbin, and the Soviets in Outer Mongolia. Other foreign powers held sway in the treaty ports along the eastern seaboard, and all parties competed for the fickle loyalty of this or that warlord.

Initially, the Soviets were aligned with the CCP that later formed several united fronts with the KMT, while the Japanese focused on influencing pliable warlords and White Russians. Amongst the Chinese, further gradations along the political spectrum were defined by a pro- or anti-Manchu orientation, and by whether one identified with Duan Qirui's Anfu clique, or with the Chihli clique that overthrew the Anfu regime in Peking in 1920.[9] Within the KMT, the left-KMT (associated with Wang Jingwei and based in Wuhan) vied with the right-KMT (Chiang Kai-shek's faction based in Jiangxi) for power, while the CCP's "28 Bolsheviks" faction, educated in Moscow, competed against Mao and his allies—and this is a simplified version.

As revealed in Jung Chang and Jon Halliday's recent biography of Mao that draws on previously undisclosed archival materials, Moscow's tentacles soon enveloped Mao. For example, in 1918, at the age of twenty-five, Mao began taking Russian lessons "from a Russian émigré (and agent), Sergei Polevoy,"[10] but stymied, eventually abandoned his studies.

Undeterred, in 1921 Russian agents reportedly gave Mao 200 yuan—a sizable sum at the time and Mao's "first known cash payment from Moscow" [11]—to travel to Shanghai to participate in the organization of the first Party Congress. By the end of the CCP's first year, almost 95 percent of its funding had come from the Soviets; Mao also began to receive a monthly stipend.[12] In 1924, Mao was removed from the Party's Central Committee at Moscow's behest; he then embarked on what is portrayed as his opportunistic involvement with the Nationalists during the first KMT/CCP alliance, but was restored to the Central Committee in April 1927.[13]

Moscow, however, had been hedging its bets by persuading Sun Yat-sen to "learn from the Soviets," and deployed Mikhail Borodin, a Comintern agent, as its adviser to the KMT. At about the same time, the Soviet Politburo approved—and Stalin signed-off on—a payment of "roughly 2 million gold rubles" to Sun, who sought Russian assistance so that his forces could take control of all of China. In return, Sun acquiesced to Soviet control over Outer Mongolia and Xinjiang.[14] Sun sent Chiang Kai-shek, his trusted lieutenant, to Russia for military training; when Chiang returned to China, he took charge of the Whampoa Military Academy—funded by Moscow—where Zhou Enlai served as his second-in-command.

To accelerate its goal of influencing developments in China by indoctrinating China's emerging leadership cadre, the USSR opened the Moscow-based Communist University for Toilers of the East in 1921. The Sun Yat-sen University for Toilers of China, established in honor of the 1924 *Treaty of Friendship* with the USSR, opened its doors in Moscow in 1925.

By the time of Sun's death in 1925, "with about 1,000 agents in the Nationalist base, Moscow was now the master of Canton."[15] By 1926, Soviet intelligence agents had established fourteen bases throughout China.[16] Moscow had succeeded in its "bloc within" strategy, its "Trojan horse,"[17] and thus was forged the first KMT/CCP alliance.

"While negotiating a treaty of recognition in the North, Soviet Russia officially strengthened a rival regime in the South."[18] Unofficially, though, the Soviets were apparently trying to influence the outcome of a power struggle within the KMT by plotting to kidnap Chiang Kai-shek in 1926 so that his rival, Wang Jingwei, would emerge as Sun's successor in 1927.[19]

In April 1927, Chiang Kai-shek launched the Shanghai Massacre, slaughtering thousands of Communists; he also purged leftists within the KMT, and expelled his Soviet advisers. The first KMT/CCP alliance had ended, but Moscow's network of sleeper agents remained riddled throughout the Nationalist system.

In mid-1929, Zhang Xueliang, the Manchurian warlord who inherited his post after the assassination of his father in 1928,[20] attacked the Soviet consulate in Harbin and briefly seized the Chinese Eastern Railway, which had been under Soviet control. Chiang Kai-shek had sanctioned Zhang's actions because the Soviets used the area "as a major base for Russian funding and sponsorship of Chinese Communists,"[21] but a decisive Soviet response that included air attacks easily repelled Zhang's ill-fated adventure.

By late 1930, Chiang had consolidated his power within the KMT and launched an extermination campaign against the Communists. The Communists' survival during this period has been attributed to Russia's myriad covert activities:

> What really tipped the scale was Russian assistance—though this remains virtually unknown. Moscow set up a top-level Military Advisory Group in the Soviet Union to plan strategy, and a military committee in Shanghai, staffed by Russian and other (especially German) advisers. The critical help came from Soviet military intelligence, the GRU, which had a network of more than 100 agents in China, mostly Chinese operating in Nationalist offices near the Red Army, whose main job was to provide information to the Chinese Communists. In early 1930, Moscow had dispatched a star officer, the half-German, half-Russian Richard Sorge, to Shanghai to run this operation. Sorge's main coup was to infiltrate the German military advisers' group at Chiang's forward intelligence HQ, where he worked on the disgruntled wife of one of the advisers, Stölzner, to steal the Nationalist codes, including those used for communications between the General Staff and units in the field. This information from Russian spies gave Mao an incalculable advantage. The CCP also had its own agents working in the heart of Nationalist intelligence. One, Qian Zhuangfei, became the confidential secretary of the Nationalist intelligence chief U.T. Hsü, and played a big role in Mao's success.[22]

Early in 1932, the Japanese army entered Harbin and by March had established the colony of Manchukuo, while the KMT and the CCP continued to battle one another. Mao's forces, facing unremitting pressure, set out on the Long March, but—as recently revealed—Chiang let the Communists escape in "a carefully crafted swap: the survival of the CCP for [his son] Ching-kuo,"[23] who had been kidnapped and "taken to Moscow by a little-known but pivotal figure called Shao Li-tzu, who was a key Red mole inside the Nationalist Party."[24]

Zhang Xueliang, the Manchurian warlord who favored the formation of another United Front against the Japanese, opposed Chiang Kai-shek's decision to launch a new suppression campaign against the Communists and so kidnapped Chiang during the KMT leader's visit to Xian. During what has come to be known as the Xian Incident, the Russians pressured the captive Chiang to meet with the CCP's Zhou Enlai by intimating that Chiang's son, Ching-kuo, would be permitted to return to China.[25] After Chiang and Zhou hammered out the details of a second United Front, the Soviet Politburo approved the release of Chiang Ching-kuo.[26] Stalin's direct intervention, "in such a casual, chauvinistic manner, so contemptuous of Chinese communist interests...left [Mao] speechless with rage."[27]

Since the formation of the CCP in 1921, Stalin had focused on strengthening the Soviet faction within the CCP by replacing Chen Duxiu, the first secretary of the CCP, with the Russian-educated Qu Qiubai.[28] In short order, Besso Lominadze, a Comintern agent deployed to China on Stalin's direct order, spearheaded Mao's temporary dismissal from the Politburo.[29] Moscow later engineered Li Lisan's removal as the Party leader in late 1930 by issuing a letter of denunciation and then forcing Li to make a public confession.[30] Li was replaced by Wang Ming, one of the Russian-educated "28 Bolsheviks" and Stalin's "most loyal Chinese acolyte"[31] who "was smuggled to Yenan from Moscow with orders to assume leadership in place of Mao;"[32] Wang represented Stalin's line in support of a United Front to smash the Japanese.

> One of the oddities of Mao's position in the late 1920s and early '30s was that, while his relations with the Chinese leaders whom Moscow promoted to head the CCP were often extremely poor, the Russians themselves took an increasingly positive view of his role. From the Sixth Congress in 1928 onwards, Mao was the only major Chinese leader who was consistently in agreement with Stalin on all three of the key issues in the Chinese revolution: the primary role of the peasantry, of the Red Army and of the rural base areas. In the Kremlin, this did not go unnoticed.[33]

As such, Stalin arranged to bring Anying and Anching, Mao's two sons from his second marriage to Yang Kaihui, to Russia to study.[34] KMT forces had beheaded Kaihui in 1930, but by then Mao had already taken a third wife, Guiyuan, who, in need of medical treatment for lingering shrapnel wounds, followed the boys to Moscow. While in Russia, Guiyuan gave birth to a boy, Lyova, who died six months later from pneumonia. Guiyuan's 4-year-old daughter Chiao-chiao, who had remained in China, was reunited with her mother in Russia;[35] later, Guiyuan "spent two years in a provincial psychiatric hospital"[36] in Russia. None of this mattered much to Mao, who had already moved onto his fourth wife, Jiang Qing.

Throughout the years, the Soviets had also been funneling substantial amounts of military aid to Feng Yuxiang, a warlord in northern China,[37] and intervened "in Sinkiang in support of the Chinese warlord Sheng Shih-ts'ai against his enemies, the Dungans."[38] During Sheng's 1938 trip to the Soviet Union, he met with Stalin and even joined the Communist Party of the Soviet Union.

The Soviets extended significant support to China during its war of resistance against Japan in the form of loans, credits—"Stalin advanced Chiang U.S. $250 million for arms purchases from Russia"[39]—and war materiel: "some 200 or more Soviet pilots flew on active service against the Japanese. No other country gave China any assistance against Japan at this time."[40] But the United States and Britain continued to rake in profits from their brisk trade with Japan. By 1940, Stalin had also personally approved "massive clandestine sponsorship [of the CCP]...set at U.S. $300,000 per month...(worth perhaps U.S. $45–50 million a year today)."[41]

However, the Soviet Union's primary aim was "to keep Japan bogged down in a war of attrition with China"[42] so that, weakened, Japan would be unable to attack Russia from the east. Chang and Halliday claim that Zhang Zhizhong, a general in the Nationalist Army and a Soviet sleeper agent, provoked the Japanese attack on Shanghai in August 1937, triggering an all-out war with Japan. "This was probably one of Stalin's greatest coups. With just one sleeper he warded off the Japanese threat to Soviet Russia."[43]

Ever since Wang Ming—the most prominent of the "28 Bolsheviks"— returned to China in 1937, he and Mao had continuously clashed over party policy, especially toward the United Front. In early 1942, Mao instigated a Rectification Campaign to enforce obeisance to the CCP line and to extirpate "dogmatism"—that is, subservience to the Soviet line. Wang Ming, Mao's main target, obediently made a public confession, but Mao, unsatisfied, arranged for Wang Ming to be poisoned.[44] Numerous unsuccessful attempts severely weakened Wang, Stalin's "most loyal acolyte," and so the Soviets, who held Mao's eldest son, discreetly suggested a trade: Wang Ming for Anying.[45] This minuet with Moscow continued for several years, until Anying was returned to China in 1946; Mao had last seen him in 1927, when he was four (Anying was later killed in the Korean War during an American air raid). Mao kept Wang Ming dangling in a number of insignificant posts until finally, in 1956, he was permitted to travel to Moscow for medical treatment; he remained in Russia, where he died in exile in 1974.

While China continued to wage its war of resistance against Japan, Roosevelt, Churchill, and Stalin met in Yalta in February 1945 and agreed upon the terms of the Soviet Union's entry into the Allied war against Japan. Harry Truman's sudden ascendancy after President Roosevelt's death in April 1945, and then the decision to drop the atomic bomb on Japan in order to hasten the end of the Pacific war, obviated the need for Soviet assistance. However:

The Soviet Union, which declared war only days before Japan surrendered, insisted on retaining the *quid pro quo* Roosevelt had promised Stalin at the Yalta conference: port and railroad rights in Manchuria, together with the southern half of Sakhalin and all of the Kurile Islands. Soviet and American forces each occupied half of Korea.[46]

A million and a half Soviet troops swept into Manchuria the day after the USSR declared war against Japan. In one swift strike, Stalin had restored Russia's pre-1905 sphere of influence in China; the Russians now held sway over more territory in China than in occupied Eastern Europe. With the Japanese out and the Soviets now secure in Manchuria, the situation was ripe for the expansion of Communist power. Before withdrawing almost a year later, the Soviets had stripped Manchuria of its industrial equipment—"worth an estimated U.S. $858 million"—and hauled it back to the USSR as war booty—along with scores of Japanese war prisoners.[47]

U.S. General George Marshall's pressure on Chiang to enter into a cease-fire with Mao in late 1946 was "probably the single most important decision affecting the outcome of the civil war."[48] Mao's spent forces in Manchuria, granted a brief respite, reinforced their lifeline to Russia, through which massive Russian military assistance flowed. The tide had turned; over the next several years, Mao and his forces seized the Mandate of Heaven—the right to rule China.

The Soviet Union's all-pervasive duplicity and its mind-boggling efforts to honeycomb China's nascent political movements and to dominate the personal lives of China's leaders highlighted the ruthless means that the Stalinist regime employed. The Soviets excelled at developing agents of influence and seeding them throughout China's emerging political elite to hasten "the rotting process" in China. Stalin, the omnipotent puppeteer, had masterfully applied Sun Tzu's teachings on the usefulness of the five kinds of spies to weave an imperceptible web in the Chinese theater of operations.[49]

Stalin placed pragmatism above ideology and so supported Mao and the Chinese Communists: He did not want the American-supported KMT[50] as a neighbor and viewed an alliance with the CCP as a means of neutralizing China. With the Chinese Communists in power, China became a vast buffer zone protecting the Soviet Union from an attack by the maritime powers launched from China's eastern seaboard, akin to the protective ring of satellites that the Soviets were erecting in Eastern Europe to ward off encroachments from the continent.[51] Yet throughout all of these years of intrigue and betrayal, Stalin and Mao had never met.

# MAOTAI AND VODKA:[1]
# THE COMMUNIST DYNASTY

*To my mind all the imperialist countries are in a position which is like the position of the sun at 6 PM, but ours is like the position of the sun at 6 AM. Thus the tide has turned. And this means that the Western countries have been left behind, that we have outdistanced them considerably. Undoubtedly, it is not the Western wind that prevails over the Eastern wind, for the wind from the West is so weak. Undoubtedly, the Eastern wind prevails over the Western wind, for we are strong.*

—Mao Zedong, during his 1957 visit to the Soviet Union[2]

*Nixon believed that eventually there would "be a race war between the whites of the world and the people of color, with the Soviet Union breaking down into its European and Asian halves."[3]*

## MAO AND STALIN

According to Chairman Mao's private doctor, "Mao despised Stalin...[and] had a deep-seated personal antagonism toward Stalin that traced back to the days of the Jiangxi soviet, in the early 1930s."[4] In Mao's view, "during the civil war between the nationalists and the communists, Stalin offered no help, refusing to give the communist forces a single gun or bullet, not even a fart."[5]

Even so, just sixty-seven days after the establishment of the People's Republic of China (PRC) on October 1, 1949, Chairman Mao left Beijing's Central Railway Station in an armored train car that used to transport Chiang Kai-shek. Some Party members criticized Mao's sojourn to Moscow—his first foreign trip—because "the Chinese emperor never traveled to meet the barbarians."[6]

For the first time in the more than three hundred years of Sino-Russian relations, emperor and tsar were set to meet face-to-face.

Before Mao's train arrived at Moscow's Yaroslavl Station at about noon on December 16, 1949, after ten days en route from Beijing, "the war of nerves between the two overweening egos had begun";[7] Stalin had earlier rebuffed Mao's request to meet, and then postponed meetings that had been scheduled[8]—compounding the loss of face. Now Mao had accepted an invitation to attend Stalin's seventieth birthday jubilee. Mao's "entourage was devoid of specialists who would have made up a negotiating delegation," but did include Chen Boda, his secretary, and Shi Zhe, his interpreter.[9]

Whisked "off to his bugged residence, Stalin's No. 2 dacha, 27 kilometres outside Moscow,"[10] Mao returned to St. Catherine's Hall in the Kremlin at 6:00 PM for a 2-hour audience with Stalin. The titans wrangled over the existing *Sino-Soviet Treaty* of 1945—based on the Yalta Agreement and negotiated with China's former Nationalist regime—and discussed the disposition of Soviet troops in Lü-shun (Port Arthur) and the Chinese Changchun Railway. Stalin announced that he and "his inner circle have decided not to modify any of the points" in the existing treaty since this might rile the other Yalta signatories, the United Kingdom and the United States—a convenient pretext for maintaining Russia's advantages in China. Mao, temporarily acceding to this view, declared that "the question merits further consideration," and asked to send for Zhou Enlai, who had remained in China. On other matters, Stalin summarily agreed to extend a $300 million line of credit; air transportation routes and trade issues were also discussed. Concerning Taiwan, Stalin emphasized, "what is most important here is not to give Americans a pretext to intervene."[11] Mao was then conveyed back to his isolated dacha nestled in a snow-blanketed birch forest.

Mao and Stalin met again on December 21, Stalin's seventieth birthday, at the Bolshoi Theater, for an evening extravaganza estimated to have cost 5.6 million rubles.[12] Mao sat to Stalin's right in the seat of honor, a prop amongst the Communist ingathering come to pay tribute to Stalin. Mao was also accorded the privilege of rising to praise Stalin ahead of other foreigners in the audience.

The theater troupe performed *Krasny Mak* (Red Poppy), trumpeting the imaginary heroic role of Soviet sailors who came to the aid of the besieged Communists in Shanghai during Chiang Kaishek's 1927 massacre. This distorted interpretation of events incensed many of the Chinese guests; what's more, "to present the poppy as the symbol of the Revolution"—a reminder of Britain's humiliating opium trade in China—"was like a prostitute presiding over a mass."[13]

After the performance, the celebrants decamped to the Kremlin's Georgievsky Hall for an elegant dinner banquet.

Deposited back into Stalin's secluded guesthouse, Mao began to feel cooped up, antsy, and impatient for his next meeting with Stalin; Mao groused, "Am I here just to eat, shit and sleep?"

Of this trio of bodily functions, none was problem-free. On the food front, Mao vented his discontent on the fact that his hosts were delivering frozen fish, which he hated. "I will only eat live fish," he told his staff. "Throw these back at them!" Shitting was a major problem, as Mao not only suffered from constipation, but could not adapt to the pedestal toilet, preferring to squat. And he did not like the soft Russian mattress, or the pillows: "How can you sleep on this?" he said, poking at the down-filled pillows. "Your head will disappear!" He had them swapped for his own, filled with buckwheat husks, and the mattress replaced by wooden planks.[14]

Mao and Stalin met three more times before the end of the year, but these meetings were brief and dealt with trivial matters—except for the meeting on December 24, in which Stalin tried to ascertain "Mao's appetite for turf" in the international Communist movement.[15]

Mao's fifty-sixth birthday on December 26 passed unobserved by his hosts.

Several of Stalin's underlings visited Mao at the guesthouse, but they came as messengers, not negotiators. Because Mao was absent from public view during so much of his visit, the foreign media began to speculate that he might have been detained by his Soviet hosts.[16] To dispel these rumors and to counteract foreign attempts to influence the discussions, Mao held an interview with a TASS correspondent "that proved to be a turning point in the visit."[17] Later that day, on January 2, Anastas Mikoyan and Vyacheslav Molotov, two Politburo members, visited with Mao to discuss his views on a new Sino-Soviet treaty and agreed that Mao should now summon Zhou Enlai to Moscow for the negotiations.[18] By assigning the role of chief negotiator to Zhou, Mao avoided direct culpability for the final agreement.

President Truman announced his hands-off policy toward Taiwan on January 5; on January 6, Britain announced its intention to recognize the PRC. At this point, "Stalin now changed course and encouraged the PRC's plan to seize Taiwan...[and] Hong Kong,"[19]—hoping to incite China to take actions that would drive a wedge between the United States and China, and forestall U.S. recognition of the PRC.

While waiting for Zhou to arrive, Mao busied himself with a visit to a model cooperative farm in Krasnogorsk to witness advances in animal husbandry, followed by the obligatory pilgrimage to Lenin's tomb in Red Square. He departed for Leningrad on the overnight express train on January 14, and put up at the Smolny Institute, Lenin's headquarters during the October Revolution of 1917. After perfunctory visits to the island of Kronstadt, the Winter Palace, the Hermitage, and Peterhof Palace, Mao, unimpressed, left Leningrad on the evening of January 17.

On January 21, the day after Zhou Enlai arrived, Stalin, irate that Mao's rebuttal to a provocative January 12 speech made by U.S. Secretary of State Acheson appeared under the name of a low-ranking official, "hauled Mao into the Kremlin for a mighty dressing-down...[and] made a point of staging the tongue-lashing in front of Chou En-lai."[20] Reportedly, "Mao was so enraged that he became visibly sullen and made no response."[21]

Afterwards, a motorcade of black armored Zils transported the contingent—Stalin and Mao rode in the same vehicle—to Stalin's dacha in Kuntsovo. Stalin, gearing up for one of his notorious nocturnal bacchanalias, turned on his gramophone and invited Mao to join in a jig, but Mao demurred.[22]

And all of this as a prelude to the treaty negotiations that finally commenced.

The resulting treaty's[23] most important section—a mutual security obligation—would be triggered "in the event of one of the Contracting Parties being attacked by Japan or *any state allied with her*," i.e., the United States. "Mao pressed for a cast-iron Soviet commitment to come to China's aid in the event of a U.S. attack, only for Stalin to finagle by adding the condition that a state of war must have been declared."[24]

In the treaty's second section, the Soviets agreed to convey their rights and property in the Chinese Changchun Railroad to China by no later than the end of 1952, although the composition of the railroad's management would periodically alternate. The Soviets also agreed to withdraw their troops from the Lü-shun naval base by no later than the end of 1952 (they actually withdrew in 1955, after the Korean War). The administration and property of Dalian (Dairen) reverted to the Chinese, although the final status of the harbor would be determined "on the conclusion of a peace treaty with Japan."

In the treaty's third section, the Soviet Union agreed to extend a $300 million credit to be disbursed over five years with an interest rate of 1 percent.

Several sources refer to a secret protocol in which China designated Manchuria and Xinjiang as Soviet spheres of influence[25]—thereby enhancing the USSR's territorial security by providing additional buffer zones. In addition, Soviet technicians and advisers working in the PRC were exempted from Chinese jurisdiction—a throwback to the extraterritoriality of the unequal treaty era.

While inaugurating a new era in Sino-Soviet relations—and a marked improvement over the treaty of 1945—the new treaty contained the seeds of its own destruction: In April 1956, "Mao told Mikoyan the secret deals on Xinjiang and Manchuria were 'two bitter pills' that Stalin forced him to swallow."[26]

To celebrate the new treaty, the Chinese hosted a dinner at Moscow's Metropol Hotel on February 14; Stalin, the hermit of the Kremlin, unexpectedly deigned to attend. Two days later, Stalin bid his guests adieu at a Kremlin banquet (Ho Chi Minh also attended), but never reciprocated with a visit to China.

The two Communist behemoths, now straddling the vast Eurasian landmass and enmeshed in a mutual security treaty, consecrated their alliance by unleashing a war on the Korean Peninsula.

## THE KOREAN WAR[27]

North Korea's Kim Il Sung had received extensive military training in Khabarovsk over a 5-year period, and Soviet military commanders had groomed him as a future leader. With encouragement from Stalin, Kim's forces engaged in provocative border clashes and guerilla warfare in an effort to destabilize and ultimately overthrow Syngman Rhee's government in South Korea. Kim mistakenly believed that the United States would not intervene militarily, just as the United States had refrained from direct intervention in the Chinese civil war; he assumed that the new Sino-Soviet alliance acted as a forceful deterrent against American intervention. According to most accounts, "China was a bit player in the drama being played out in the Korean Peninsula until a few months before the war began."[28]

The Korean War erupted on Sunday, June 25, 1950, signaling the expansion of the Cold War to the Asian arena. The United States responded by deploying its Seventh Fleet to the Taiwan Strait. Rather than directly declaring war against Korea, the United States arranged for the United Nations to approve a command for Korea under U.S. control, a diplomatic nicety that avoided triggering the recently concluded treaty between the Soviet Union and China which was intended to prevent renewed aggression by Japan *or any state allied with her,* such as the United States. The Soviets had absented themselves from the U.N. to protest the continued recognition of Taiwan rather than the PRC, but the ploy backfired because the Soviets were not present to exercise their veto when the U.N. Security Council voted on whether to intervene in Korea.

As the situation in North Korea deteriorated, Mao began to consider military intervention: "Historically speaking, the Chinese emperor regarded Korea as his exclusive domain and attached great importance to his influence there."[29] In an effort to tip the scales, Stalin weighed in with a promise to "provide air cover for PLA troops"[30] as Kim harangued his benefactor in the Kremlin for more support. Stalin later broke his promise to provide air cover and substituted it with "substantial military aid."[31] "For Mao, this decision to renege on military commitments made only weeks earlier was the bitterest of all Stalin's betrayals."[32] Stalin had concluded that if U.S. troops conquered the Korean Peninsula, then "Mao [would become] more dependent on Moscow and [this would] lead to the long-term stationing of Soviet troops in China's Northeast."[33]

After more than a year and five major battles, cease-fire talks began; two years later, at Panmunjom, the hostile parties signed an armistice. Mao has been accused of using the issue of POW repatriation[34] to prolong the war "so that he could extract more from Stalin."[35] Chinese casualties in the Korean War are estimated at close to 1 million, but "for decades the Chinese and the Soviets argued bitterly over the $2 billion bill the Soviets presented Beijing for the aid they gave to China's military."[36]

The nuclear era was ushered in by three milestones: The United States had dropped the first atomic bombs on Hiroshima and Nagasaki in 1945; the Soviet Union tested its first atomic device in 1949; and the United States had refrained from using the bomb during the Korean War in spite of General MacArthur's plan to unleash a storm of nuclear missiles on major Chinese cities.

The Korean War, the first proxy war between the two nuclear powers, set the stage for the expansion and the ultimate denouement of the Sino-Soviet alliance by catalyzing the massive arms buildup in the United States and the Soviet Union that convinced the People's Republic that it, too, had to acquire nuclear weapons. The Soviet Union had agreed to provide technical support and know-how to China in its quest for the atom bomb, but Nikita Khrushchev later reneged on this promise.

Besides their collaboration as leaders of the two largest Communist blocs, Stalin and Mao experienced devastating personal tragedies. Stalin's beloved second wife, Nadezhda Alliluyeva, shot herself in the head with a Mauser pistol and was found on her bedroom floor in the Kremlin; Stalin's eldest son, Yakov, taken prisoner by the Germans during the Battle of Stalingrad, was reportedly shot and killed as he attempted to escape from the Nazi camp at Sachsenhausen.[37] The Germans had offered to exchange Yakov for Field Marshal Friedrich Paulus, but Stalin refused to countenance a swap.

In November 1930, the KMT beheaded Mao's second wife, Yang Kaihui;[38] in 1935, they also killed Mao's youngest brother, Zetan. The warlord Sheng Shicai executed Mao's other brother, Zemin, in 1942.[39] And, as mentioned earlier, Mao's eldest son, Mao Anying, serving as a Russian interpreter on the Korean front, was killed during an American air raid on November 25, 1950.

Stalin died in March 1953; Mao did not travel to Moscow again until 1957. Instead, Khrushchev visited Beijing in October 1954, August 1958, and September 1959. Liu Shaoqi, Deng Xiaoping, and Zhou Enlai reciprocated by visiting Moscow. As the reigning leader of the Communist movement's most populous nation, Mao now expected others to pay homage by making the pilgrimage to Beijing.

## KHRUSHCHEV, THE SINO-SOVIET RIFT, THE SINO-SOVIET WAR OF 1969, AND NIXON'S OPENING

Mao considered Khrushchev's Secret Speech denouncing Stalin and the Stalinist "cult of personality" disloyal and destructive to the unity of the international Communist movement and an affront to his own leadership: "For Mao to agree to the attack against Stalin was to admit that attacks against him were permissible as well."[40] Never mind that it came "just as Mao was entering into his Stalinist phase,"[41] tightening his grip on China with the anti-rightist campaign and gearing up for the Great Leap Forward: "One country shut the doors of concentration camps and the other opened them."[42]

Mao also felt slighted because Khrushchev had not conferred with him before delivering the Speech. Even so, Mao supported Khrushchev against Molotov, Malenkov, and Kaganovich—the Soviet "Anti-Party Group"—in a brief leadership struggle that ensued in the summer of 1957.[43] In exchange for his support, Mao sought a "sample nuclear bomb"[44] from the Soviet Union.

Mao also lent succor to Khrushchev during the Hungarian Uprising of 1956. "Khrushchev agonized over what to do, but in the end, under pressure from Mao Zedong, he ordered Soviet troops to re-enter Hungary and crush the rebellion."[45]

Mao's second—and last—foray abroad in November 1957 took him back to Moscow aboard a Tupolev TU-104 to attend the Soviet Union's fortieth anniversary celebration. Mao returned "to Moscow triumphant, the most senior foreign leader of the communist camp, head of a huge delegation, rival and challenger of Khrushchev."[46] This time, he and his entourage put up in an opulent palace that used to belong to the empress Yekaterina, where Mao "insisted on using his own chamber pot in lieu of the flush-style sit toilet in the adjoining bathroom."[47] Mao was preoccupied with ceremonial and social functions and this visit, unlike his first, passed mostly without incident.

But Khrushchev's proposal to build long wave radio stations in China and his request for nuclear-powered submarine basing rights enraged Mao, who called in Soviet Ambassador Pavel Yudin and imperiously ordered him to summons Khrushchev: "I have invited him to come here immediately,"[48] he bellowed.

During Khrushchev's second visit to Beijing from July 31 to August 4, 1958, "Mao smoked throughout, despite Khrushchev's aversion to cigarettes."[49] Chairman Mao's private doctor, Li Zhisui, captures Mao's antipathy toward Khrushchev in his memoirs:

> Mao returned the extravagant hospitality given him in the Soviet Union with a slap in Khrushchev's face. He received the Soviet leader by the side of his swimming pool, clad only in his swimming trunks.... The Chairman was deliberately playing the role of emperor, treating Khrushchev like the barbarian come to pay tribute. It was a way, Mao told me on the way back to Beidaihe, of "sticking a needle up his ass."[50]

Just nineteen days after Khrushchev left China, Mao launched the second Taiwan Strait Crisis as a challenge to "Khrushchev's appeasement policy" and to "sabotage the emerging détente"[51] between the United States and the Soviet

Union; Mao equated Khrushchev's "peaceful coexistence" with appeasement of the imperialists.

In general, "Mao treated Khrushchev as a superficial upstart, neglecting no opportunity to confound him with petty humiliations, cryptic pronouncements, and veiled provocations."[52] Now he had crossed a crucial divide: During the Korean War, Stalin had reigned as the supreme arbiter, but during the second Crisis, Mao seized the initiative and acted independently, impetuously, and in defiance of Khrushchev. What's more, China's unilateral and reckless actions, an extraordinary affront to party discipline, triggered a nuclear threat from the United States. "Later Mao explicitly said that the shells in the Strait were a response to Khrushchev's détente with the United States."[53] The Kremlin responded by scrapping its nuclear deal with China.

Mao's heightened sense of paranoia toward his colleagues mirrored the steady decline in Sino-Soviet relations. At the July 1959 party conference at Lushan, Defense Minister Peng Dehuai boldly questioned the efficacy of the Great Leap Forward and was attacked by Mao, who suspected that Peng's critique was part of a rightist plot hatched in collusion with Moscow[54] during Peng's April trip to Eastern Europe. As a result, Mao engineered a purge: Lin Biao replaced Peng, who "for the next six years lived a hermetic existence under virtual house arrest."[55] Later, during the Cultural Revolution, Peng, the heroic leader of China's volunteer forces during the Korean War, "was dragged to scores of denunciation meetings...at which he was kicked by Rebels wearing heavy leather boots and beaten ferociously with staves. His ribs were broken and he passed out repeatedly...Peng was interrogated some 260 times, as Mao genuinely feared he might have had some connection with Khrushchev."[56]

In August 1959, Sino-Indian border clashes erupted at Lonju, in October, at the Konga Pass; India claimed that a 1,200-kilometer military road built by the Chinese and connecting Xinjiang and Lhasa through the Aksai Chin desert traversed its territory. China, of course, was hypersensitive about its border with India, especially after India had granted political asylum to the Dalai Lama earlier in the year. "Khrushchev expressed his views by extending generous credits to the Indian government, refusing to endorse China's territorial claims."[57]

In September 1959, Khrushchev spent thirteen whirlwind days in the United States, his first visit to the bastion of capitalism and his first face-to-face with President Eisenhower. Khrushchev's appearance at a private dinner party in New York City hosted by Averell Harrimann prompted one guest to describe the Soviet leader as a "very shapeless man in a rather shapeless suit with a very large pink head and very short legs sitting beneath the large Picasso that hung over the fireplace."[58]

From New York, Khrushchev and his entourage flew to Los Angeles, where a bevy of celebrities feted him—including Marilyn Monroe and Elizabeth Taylor. From Los Angeles, the delegation boarded a train that wended its way north along the scenic coast to San Francisco, where the city's high society turned out to welcome Khrushchev, the peasant from Kalinovka. On their way back east, Khrushchev visited Roswell Garst's farm in Coon Rapids, Iowa; Garst had traveled to the Soviet Union in 1955 and had spent a day with Khrushchev discussing hybrid corn seeds and methods of improving agricultural productivity. The First Secretary's American journey ended with a visit to the Camp David presidential retreat in the Catoctin Mountains, along with a side trip to Ike's farm in Gettysburg, Pennsylvania.

Khrushchev returned to the Soviet Union in a state of hypereuphoria, convinced that his unique skills at personal diplomacy would work their magic on Mao, whom he would see several days later in Beijing during the PRC's tenth anniversary celebrations.

But Mao, who had no doubt been monitoring Khrushchev's progress in the United States, branded Khrushchev's trip to the United States "collusion with the enemy." Moreover, "the Chinese leadership were deeply insulted by Khrushchev's decision to come to Beijing"[59] after the visit to Washington; they felt Khrushchev should have scheduled the Washington trip after the festivities in Beijing. During Khrushchev's third and last visit to China, "the real focus of the talks was...the growing tension between the PRC and India."[60]

Khrushchev finally let loose at the Third Plenum of the Romanian Communist party in June 1960, where he unleashed some of his harshest anti-Mao rhetoric, referring to the Chinese leader as "a Buddha who gets his theory out of his nose," and calling Mao a "*galosh*," or scumbag.[61] The next day, he recalled all Soviet advisers in China and halted further assistance on most ongoing projects.

As the rivalry between Mao and Khrushchev, between the People's Republic and the Soviet Union, intensified, both countries began to use a variety of tools that doomed the unraveling alliance: by engaging proxies, by covertly agitating in buffer zones, by heightened competition in the Third World, and by eventually drawing closer to the United States.

Khrushchev's memoirs, written during his forced retirement, include a chapter on the Sino-Soviet rift, in which he explains: "Politics is a game, and Mao Tse-tung has played politics with Asiatic cunning, following his own rules of cajolery, treachery, savage vengeance, and deceit."[62] Khrushchev goes on to reminisce about his visit to Peking in 1954, and surmised:

Conflict with China is inevitable. I came to this conclusion on the basis of various remarks Mao had made. During my visit to Peking, the atmosphere was typically Oriental. Everyone was unbelievably courteous and ingratiating, but I saw through their hypocrisy. After I had arrived, Mao and I embraced each other warmly and kissed each other on both cheeks. We used to lie around a swimming pool in Peking, chatting like the best of friends about all kinds of things. But it was all sickeningly sweet. The atmosphere was nauseating.[63]

Khrushchev's assessment of China's military capabilities was scathing: "The Soviet Army crushed the crack forces of the German Army, while Mao Tse-tung's men have spent between twenty and twenty-five years poking each other in the backsides with knives and bayonets."[64] Khrushchev reportedly said, "When I look at Mao I see Stalin, a perfect copy."[65]

But that did not stop the two titans from agreeing that Russia would acquiesce to China's strike against India (a full-fledged Sino-Indian War erupted in September 1962) in exchange for China's pledge not to interfere during the Cuban Missile Crisis of October 1962.[66]

When the Sino-Soviet rift openly emerged in 1963, competition between the two countries accelerated—especially in the Third World, where pro-Soviet and Maoist factions competed within the indigenous Communist parties. The Sino-Soviet rift has been interpreted as "the final end of the long period, beginning with the Treaties of Peking of 1860, in which China's foreign policy had been subservient to one or another of the powers in the Oikoumene."[67]

This period also witnessed a transfer of power in the Soviet Union, when the Politburo removed Khrushchev from office and retired him to a new dacha in Petrovo-Dalneye. It is ironic that the Politburo ousted Khrushchev less than a year after debating "the China problem [and] a consensus apparently emerged that Mao must if possible be overthrown."[68] Khrushchev's advocacy of military action against China was cited as one of the reasons for his ouster.[69]

> Responding to Mao's hostile comments on Soviet border rights in the Far East, Khrushchev warned that the Soviets would use all "means at their disposal" to protect the borders, including "up-to-date weapons of annihilation." The Soviets had made their first nuclear threat against China.[70]

Just two days after Khrushchev's ouster, China conducted its first nuclear test.[71] Less than a month later, Soviet Defense Minister Rodion Malinovsky reportedly approached Zhou Enlai at a Kremlin meeting to determine if he was willing to assist in ousting Mao from power, but Zhou did not take the bait.[72]

Mao, justifiably paranoid about Soviet plots to overthrow him, curtailed high-level contact between China and the USSR, and then turned his sights against party members with links to Russia, such as Peng Zhen, the mayor of Shanghai, "who may have thought of seeking Russian help to avert Mao's Purge."[73] Russian-speaking Yang Shangkun, director of the Central Secretaries' Office, was interrogated in prison about contacts with Moscow,[74] "and Shi Zhe, who had interpreted for Liu [Shaoqi] with Stalin...was pressed to say that Liu was a Russian spy."[75] Even Zhou Enlai's adopted daughter, Sun Weishi, was "imprisoned because she had been a top-flight Russian interpreter, and met many Russian leaders, including Stalin; so Mao suspected her."[76]

Jockeying began for the top leadership position after Khrushchev's dismissal, and a hard-line "China containment clique," including Yuri Andropov, Andrei Gromyko, Mikhail Suslov, and Dmitri Ustinov,[77] formed around Leonid Brezhnev; Alexei Kosygin took a more moderate stance. Containment of China emerged as a key policy of the new Soviet regime.

1965 was a particularly turbulent year when viewed through the prism of Sino-Soviet competition. Another Indo-Pakistani War erupted (an example of war by proxy as India was traditionally viewed as a Soviet ally and Pakistan as a Chinese ally); Sukarno's forces massacred an estimated 100,000 Communists of Chinese descent in Indonesia; and U.S. ground forces in Vietnam increased tenfold over the previous year, from approximately 17,000 to more than 185,000.

Beginning in the mid-1960s, the number of Soviet troops deployed along the border with China had steadily increased from thirteen to twenty-one divisions.[78] After concluding a 20-year treaty in 1966, the USSR also began to station troops and missiles armed with nuclear warheads in Mongolia—just 500 kilometers from Beijing across flat and open plains.

After the violent Soviet suppression of Czechoslovakia's reform movement in 1968, the Chinese began to suspect that the Soviet military buildup might be the prelude to a crackdown to reverse China's deviance from Soviet orthodoxy —China was in the throes of Mao's Cultural Revolution—under the pretext of the Brezhnev Doctrine.

A series of clashes, most likely initiated by the Chinese, erupted on March 2, 1969, along the Sino-Soviet border at Zhenbao/Damansky Island in the Ussuri River, and quickly lead to the outbreak of armed conflict; "more than thirty Soviet soldiers lay dead."[79] On March 15, the Soviets responded with an armed attack that lasted for about nine hours. The following month, the conflict spread to China's border with Kazakhstan, and in August, the Soviets launched an armored attack near the border with Xinjiang.

The Soviet Union's minister of defense, Marshal Andrei Grechko, "reportedly advocated a massive attack with weapons that would produce a high level of radioactive fallout and kill millions of Chinese;"[80] alternately, the Soviet Politburo considered a preemptive strike on China's nuclear facilities at Lop Nor in Xinjiang.[81] Kissinger reports, "Later the USSR approached the Nixon administration to determine how the U.S. would respond to such a strike,"[82] and "Nixon took perhaps the most daring step of his presidency by warning the Soviet Union that the United States would not remain indifferent if it were to attack China."[83]

As Soviet Premier Alexei Kosygin was returning to Moscow from Ho Chi Minh's funeral in Hanoi,[84] his plane was abruptly diverted to Beijing's airport, where Zhou Enlai and Kosygin met for four hours and agreed to take steps that contained the escalating crisis. But Mao, in a final display of derring-do, ordered two nuclear tests at the end of September.

With a million Soviet troops at near hair-trigger readiness along the Sino-Soviet border, Mao started setting off hydrogen bombs in his western desert, including a three-megaton "city killer" dropped from a four-engine Chinese bomber so that it would burst in the air over the desert. This display of Chinese power lit up the heavens and made the earth thunder. Radioactive fallout drifted into Kazakhstan and Mongolia, where the Soviet armed forces were poised. Two tests were conducted within six days of each other. China had never conducted two nuclear tests in such rapid succession, and Mao's act carried an unmistakable political message for the Soviet divisions massed across the border: Mao was willing to use his ultimate weapon against any attacker. He was practicing the art of war.[85]

Even so, the tests underscored China's continued vulnerability: It still had no second-strike capability of its own and so could not retaliate against a Soviet first strike.

Some suggest that Lin Biao's campaign to succeed Mao had led to the Sino-Soviet War, inasmuch as Lin "acquired much prominence as a result of the Chinese military response."[86] In September 1971, Lin, who opposed a thaw in relations with the United States, "possibly with Soviet support...attempted a military coup against Mao."[87] When the coup failed, Lin fled with his wife and sons in a Trident airplane headed in the direction of the Soviet Union; the plane ran out of fuel and crashed in Outer Mongolia, killing all on board.

As a prelude to President Nixon's opening to China, during the Indo-Pakistani War of 1971, the United States tilted toward China's ally, Pakistan, against the Soviet Union's client, India, and deployed the nuclear-powered Enterprise task force to the Bay of Bengal.[88] The United States also tried to "induce China to consider an attack on India's frontier"[89] by sharing intelligence on the disposition of forces, but the USSR's military buildup on its border with China, and a treaty of alliance signed earlier in the year with India, may have restrained China. America's "atomic gunboat diplomacy,"[90] however, played a major role in India's decision to develop its own nuclear capability.

Nixon is credited with "playing the China card," with exploiting the Sino-Soviet schism, to end U.S. involvement in Vietnam and to transform the bipolar world order into a strategic triangle. But what if Mao had gamed this out, what if the Chinese were using the American barbarians to control the Soviet barbarians, and Nixon had responded as anticipated? To counter the USSR's alleged achievement of nuclear parity with the United States, "China's whole strategy against Moscow was based on using the West and Japan to bottle up Soviet might."[91]

Regardless, the thaw in relations between the United States and China forced the Soviets to increase military spending dramatically since two adversaries armed with nuclear weapons now confronted them on two fronts. But while China's rapprochement with the United States may have implied extended deterrence under the U.S. nuclear umbrella, the Chinese considered the U.S. policy of détente with the Soviet Union as appeasement that freed up scarce Soviet resources on the European front for deployment against China.

China finally took a seat on the United Nations' Security Council in 1972—after Taiwan's expulsion—while the Soviets racked up more successes in the Third World, especially in Africa, a key battleground for influence with aid, trade and arms shipments. In Angola, a Portuguese colony until 1974, Cuban expeditionary forces joined with Soviet advisers in support of the Marxist-Leninist Popular Movement for the Liberation of Angola, while China and the United States unsuccessfully backed rival factions in a struggle for political control in the newly independent country.

All the while, the number of Soviet troops along China's northern perimeter increased from forty-two divisions in 1972 to forty-six divisions in 1978. To compensate for its lack of strategic depth, in 1974 the Soviets began construction of the Baikal-Amur railway (BAM) 200 miles north of the Trans-Siberian, a project that cost billions "while leaving the Russian Far East underdeveloped—resulting in greater vulnerability."[92] During the 1960s and 1970s, "the Soviet Union had spent no less than 60 billion rubles on strengthening its border with China."[93] By the late 1970s, China had reciprocated by deploying "one and a half million men facing the Soviet Union in seventy-five divisions (a 3:1 numerical advantage)."[94]

During Brezhnev's June 1973 U.S. summit with Nixon, he "pressed Washington for a free hand against China";[95] a year later at the height of the Watergate crisis, when Nixon visited Brezhnev in the Crimea, the Soviet leader again tried to bait the United States into an alliance against China by offering concessions in the SALT negotiations.

Zhou Enlai, Zhu De and Mao died in 1976, the year of the dragon. The Soviet KGB's Service A reportedly fabricated a will in which Zhou Enlai denounced Mao's Cultural Revolution;[96] the Zhou forgery "was intended to disrupt negotiations for a Sino-Japanese peace treaty."[97] The KGB also fabricated Mao's final testament to his wife, Jiang Qing, in which Mao asked her "to continue the work I started."[98]

## DIVERGING PATHS TO REFORM: DENG'S GAIGE KAIFANG, GORBACHEV'S PERESTROIKA

At the Chinese Communist Party's December 1978 Third Plenum, Deng Xiaoping and his allies had won approval for *Gaige Kaifang* (Reform and Opening), and targeted industry, agriculture, science and technology, and national defense—the Four Modernizations. To achieve these goals, the Party developed a package of economic reforms, including a new emphasis on initiative and worker responsibility and a shift away from the agricultural collective; a household incentive system, one of the key innovations, gradually replaced the commune system. "Side occupations" and small enterprises were encouraged; the government also established four special economic zones for exports in Zhuhai, Shenzhen, Shantou, and Xiamen.

After the bland uniformity of the Maoist era, the Party now embraced materialism by promoting the acquisition of the "Eight Bigs": a color television, refrigerator, stereo, camera, motorcycle, furniture set, washing machine, and electric fan. Deng's reforms unleashed a Chinese economic juggernaut that has lifted hundreds of millions out of poverty: China's per capita income doubled in a decade, a feat that took the United States almost fifty years.[99] This path to reform rejected the Stalinist troika of a command economy based on heavy industry and agricultural collectivization in favor of "socialism with Chinese characteristics," but the Soviets lambasted China's divergence as rank revisionism.

Conflagrations on China's borders, however, still had the potential to disrupt Deng's plans for domestic reform. In late 1978, the Vietnamese—spurred on by their Soviet patrons—invaded Cambodia, and overthrew Pol Pot's pro-Beijing Khmer Rouge. The "Vietnamese invasion of Cambodia compelled Chinese leaders to prepare for a retaliatory invasion into Vietnam and the risk of a Soviet strike on Chinese territory"[100] on the eve of Deng Xiaoping's first visit to the United States to celebrate the normalization of relations. "Deng's own top priority for the Washington talks was winning American support for China against Vietnam."[101] During private discussions with President Carter, Deng revealed China's plan to "teach Vietnam a lesson"; Carter simply "urge[d] restraint."[102]

China deployed a quarter-million troops and suffered approximately 20,000 casualties during the brief Sino-Vietnamese War of 1979, "arguably...China's most important foreign policy failure since 1949,"[103] since the Chinese retreated without removing the pro-Vietnamese regime in Cambodia. However, in the newfound spirit of Sino-American cooperation, the U.S. National Security Advisor, Zbigniew "Brzezinski met with Chinese Ambassador Chai Zemin virtually every night throughout the military conflict to turn over American intelligence on Soviet deployments,"[104] just in case the USSR began to mass troops on its border with China.

Later that year, the United States "lost its two vital intelligence collection stations at Tacksman in northern Iran"[105] and thus the ability to monitor Soviet missile tests in Kazakhstan when its ally, the Shah, fled Iran. China, however, agreed to let the United States build listening posts in the Tian Shan Mountains northwest of Xinjiang province's capital, Urumqi, within range of the Soviet Union's primary nuclear testing site in northeastern Kazakhstan, near Semipalatinsk.

The Soviet invasion of Afghanistan in December 1979 aroused fears that the USSR would now leapfrog into Iran—destabilized after the Shah's downfall and the Ayatollah's triumphant return from France—and seize control of the

Persian Gulf. To prevent this, and to rollback Soviet forces, the United States, Pakistan, Saudi Arabia, and China formed an unlikely covert alliance to support the rebel Afghan mujahideen. The United States[106] and China funneled weapons and supplies to the Afghan resistance via Pakistan while the Saudis provided funding and jihadists; from these seeds, the Taliban and al-Qaeda were born.

The increasingly hard line adopted by the United States toward the Soviet Union worked "to distance the Chinese from the United States. Reassured by Reagan's anti-Soviet stance, China can be less vigilant against Soviet 'hegemonism.'"[107] At the same time, the Soviets seized on the Reagan administration's FX jet debacle with Taiwan and used Brezhnev's conciliatory March 1982 Tashkent Speech to signal a willingness to reappraise Sino-Soviet relations. But China's "three obstacles" blocked progress: the massive number of Soviet troops on China's border,[108] the USSR's invasion of Afghanistan,[109] and Moscow's continued support of Vietnam against China's ally, Cambodia. Although the Chinese were receptive to Brezhnev's overture, three successive leadership crises in the Soviet Union over a 28-month period—Brezhnev died in November 1982, Yuri Andropov died in February 1984, and Konstantin Chernenko died in March 1985—stalled progress until Mikhail Gorbachev assumed power after Chernenko's death.

Gorbachev, 54, advocated "new thinking" in Soviet foreign policy. Noninterference in the affairs of other socialist states—a renunciation of the Brezhnev Doctrine in favor of "freedom of choice"—stood as a basic tenet of this radical reorientation, designed to ease international tensions and so free up scarce economic resources for domestic restructuring, or *perestroika*.

To accomplish this, Gorbachev initiated sweeping personnel changes in the foreign policy apparatus—most notably, Eduard Shevardnadze replaced Andrei Gromyko ("Mr. Nyet"), the USSR's Minister of Foreign Affairs for twenty-eight years; Shevarnadze's inexperience strengthened Gorbachev's hand in the formulation and implementation of foreign policy. In addition, Gorbachev, determined to seek rapprochement with China, purged the Central Committee and the Ministry of Foreign Affairs of its "anti-China mafia." Igor Rogachev replaced Mikhail Kapitsa as deputy foreign minister of China policy; Rogachev, who had lived in China for fifteen years and spoke fluent Chinese,[110] later became the USSR's Ambassador to China.[111]

As part of the Soviet Union's more conciliatory approach to China, first enunciated in the Vladivostok Speech of July 1986, Gorbachev announced his intention to reduce the number of troops deployed along the Sino-Soviet border and in Afghanistan; he also supported the normalization of Sino-Vietnamese relations.

Only after the Soviet Union had satisfactorily addressed the "three obstacles" did paramount leader Deng Xiaoping agree to grant Gorbachev an audience in Beijing, inauspiciously scheduled for mid-May 1989. Thirty years had passed since the leaders of China and the Soviet Union last met; now the younger potentate presented himself to the elderly emperor in Beijing. Gorbachev, a hero abroad championing *glasnost* and *perestroika* and savoring the adulation engendered by Gorbymania, arrived in Beijing just days after thousands of students in Tiananmen Square went on a hunger strike.

The students masterfully exploited the presence of the international media on hand for the Deng-Gorbachev summit to broadcast their message worldwide; the summit itself became a sideshow and an unimaginable loss of face for Gorbachev's hosts. These events also "reinforced the party elders' view that the student movement was being fomented by foreigners in order to bring down the government."[112] China's leadership ultimately decided to "clear the Square" (*qingchang*) with brutal force; most Chinese, however, euphemistically refer to the Tiananmen Massacre as the June Fourth Incident (*liu si shijian*).

All at once, international Communism was under siege from within; the authority of the Soviet Union's staunchest East European ally, the German Democratic Republic (East Germany), started to wither away several months after Tiananmen; then the Berlin Wall came tumbling down. The division of Germany had been a central tenet of post-WWII Soviet foreign policy, as a reunified Germany might once again rise up to dominate Europe; remember, 28 million Soviets had perished during the war, more than ninety times the American losses of 300,000.

After it became apparent that reunification was inevitable, the USSR tried to keep the new, reunified Germany out of NATO, but in this the Soviets also failed. "United Germany's adhesion to NATO suggested to many influential Russians that the Soviet Union had not only lost the Cold War, but the Second World War as well";[113] and nary a shot had been fired.

The administration of George H.W. Bush had purchased Gorbachev's acquiescence to German reunification by promising that NATO would not extend its jurisdiction east of the new, unified Germany, "a commitment later repudiated by Bill Clinton's administration, but only after the Soviet Union had ceased to exist."[114]

Gorbachev's initial focus on political perestroika had posed a direct threat to the Communist Party's entrenched apparatchiki, to the Party's central role. Without any economic successes to trumpet, perestroika's only benefit was "the right to speak out about how bad things are."[115] Now the USSR's humiliating loss of its satellite empire—decolonization without bloodshed—was mirrored by a dramatic decline in living standards, widespread impoverishment, and the eventual dissolution of the Soviet Union itself. The magnitude of these serial defeats on the national psyche is unfathomable.

The issue of NATO enlargement—to many Russians as odious as the reparations issue was to the Germans after World War I—became a rallying point for Russia's gradual disillusionment with the United States, and is cited as a key motivation of the August 1991 coup plotters who failed in their attempt to topple Gorbachev during his summer vacation in the Crimea.

The Soviet Union's loss of the Eastern European satellites and the reconstitution of Germany radically altered the political landscape of the past twenty years; equidistance between China, the United States, and the USSR now characterized the strategic triangle. The United States no longer needed China as a counter to the Soviets, and "Beijing's leaders seemingly supported the hard-line coup attempt against Gorbachev"[116] in August 1991 that presaged the dissolution of the Soviet Union and Boris Yeltsin's ascent to the presidency of the Russian Federation.

Shortly after the attempted coup, the Chinese leaked a report criticizing the CPSU for elevating Gorbachev in 1985;[117] the Chinese also castigated Gorbachev for his fatal failure of nerves, for losing the Eastern European satellites by not ordering a Tiananmen-like crackdown. Only Romania had followed the Chinese example, and its leader, Ceausescu, and his wife Elena, were executed on Christmas day. But "the great 1989 revolution was the first one ever in which almost no blood was shed....In both its ends *and* its means, then, this revolution became a triumph of hope. It did so chiefly because Mikhail Gorbachev chose not to act, but rather to be acted upon."[118]

While Tiananmen has tarnished Deng's legacy, Gorbachev is ridiculed and blamed for surrendering to the West; he "dithered in contradictions without resolving them. The largest was this: he wanted to save socialism, but he would not use force to do so"[119]—like the Chinese.

# AFTER THE FALL

*Brezhnev calls President Nixon on the hot line and says, "I've heard you have a new super-computer that can predict events in the year 2000."*
*"Yes, Mr. General Secretary," Nixon replies proudly, "we have such a computer."*
*"Well, Mr. President, could you tell me what the names of the Politburo members will be then?"*
*A long silence.*
*"Aha!" Brezhnev exclaims, "You're computer isn't so sophisticated after all."*
*"No, Mr. General Secretary," Nixon replies, "it answered your question. But I can't read it. It's in Chinese."*

—Arkady Shevchenko, *Breaking with Moscow*

*It was always better for us to be closer to either Moscow or Peking than either was to the other.*

—Henry Kissinger

Soviet Communism's vast experiment in human engineering collapsed, and on December 25, 1991, the Soviet flag—that hammer and sickle emblazoned on red—was lowered from the Kremlin's watchtowers and replaced by the Russian tricolor. President Boris Yeltsin of the Russian Federation had Mikhail Gorbachev unceremoniously hustled out of the Kremlin.

Under Yeltsin, Russia early on introduced economic "shock therapy," —associated with Prime Minister Yegor Gaidar's "kamikaze government,"—consisting of the sudden removal of government subsidies on most staples (except energy), and the rapid privatization of state-owned enterprises that spawned a new breed of kleptogarchs. According to one estimate, inflation soared by 750 per cent annually during the first two years of Russia's attempted conversion to a market economy;[1] a ruble devaluation by stealth wiped out the savings of millions over-night. The humiliating loss of empire was now compounded by the loss of livelihood and dignity for many reduced to penury—especially the elderly.

"The overriding factor which encouraged Gaidar to climb into the kamikaze pilot's seat was the intense atmosphere of political, propagandistic and intellec-tual pressure from Western governments and much of the Western media, who were anxious to see the Communist system destroyed root and branch,"[2] a form of "the 'Dracula Syndrome,' the lurid belief that unless a stake was driven through the heart of the corpse, it might revive."[3] "Others believed the West's aim was to 'de-industrialize' Russia and reduce it to the level of a Third World raw materials exporter,"[4] to declaw it.

Still others assert that, regardless, Yeltsin's "Russia was a malignancy in remis-sion; the Yeltsin era was at best a fleeting opportunity to be seized before Russia relapsed into authoritarianism at home and expansionism abroad."[5] Irrespective of creeping NATO enlargement and parsimonious Western aid to the faltering Russian economy, the United States was doomed to lose Russia, according to this interpretation.

In Strobe Talbott's *The Russia Hand* (Talbott was a U.S. Deputy Secretary of State and special envoy to Russia in the Clinton administration) Boris Yeltsin comes off as a hapless stooge, serially snookered by Clinton, whose diplomatic victories were achieved by taking advantage of Russia's frequently inebriated president, at once boisterous and bullying in public but acquiescent in private. The Clinton-Yeltsin infatuation, like the Reagan-Gorbachev coupling, was a pecu-liarly fateful historical pairing; the younger Clinton's velvety smooth charm and his apprenticeship with a reportedly alcoholic stepfather enabled him to best Yeltsin at every turn. Talbott boasts, "On every major point of contention he [Clinton] had been able to bring Yeltsin around to a position more consonant with U.S. interests than what the Russian political and military establishment favored."[6]

In international relations, the Yeltsin team, initially under the influence of Foreign Minister Andrei Kozyrev, had tacked toward the United States; however, a core group of "Russian proponents of the Chinese model of reform became the strongest supporters of close ties to China."[7]

A struggle between Kozyrev's "Atlanticists" and the "Eurasianists" emerged as a major theme in Russian foreign policy during the 1990s, and the "Eurasianists" ultimately prevailed. The Sino-Russian relationship has emerged as "arguably Russia's most substantive foreign policy success story in its first decade,"[8] and has "paralleled the development of NATO expansion,"[9] just as forty years earlier, the *Sino-Soviet Treaty of Friendship* of 1950 followed NATO's formation in 1949.

In China, although the Tiananmen uprising had been brutally suppressed, ethnic activism in Tibet, Xinjiang and Inner Mongolia was on the rise. Taiwan was becoming more assertive after Lee Teng-hui succeeded Chiang Ching-kuo as president in 1988, while the U.S.-led victory in the Gulf War highlighted

China's military and technological backwardness. In September 1992, China's Foreign Minister, Qian Qichen, commented:

> The USA's hegemonic stance and its attempts to interfere in the internal affairs of other states pose the greatest danger to socialist China. To weaken pressure from Washington, China must broaden relations with Japan, Russia, South Korea and other neighboring countries.[10]

An unprecedented series of eight presidential summits between Jiang Zemin and Boris Yeltsin was held during Yeltsin's tenure. Early on, great strides had been made in the resolution of outstanding border issues: Of the 2,444 islands that fall along the labyrinthine riverine network dotting almost 84 percent of the Sino-Russian border, 1,281 were now allocated to China. "This shift in the longtime status quo indicated a sizable alteration of the balance of power—or more precisely, the imbalance of power—in the border areas to the disadvantage of Russia."[11]

During their second summit in Moscow in September 1994—the first visit by a Chinese leader since Mao's 1957 confab with Khrushchev—Yeltsin proposed a "constructive partnership" with China, considered "unusual as initiatives in the Russian-Chinese relationship were more likely to originate with China than Russia."[12]

In the meantime, in the run up to the first round of Russia's 1996 presidential election, Yeltsin, moving to outflank his critics, ousted Kozyrev as Foreign Minister and replaced him with Yevgeny Primakov, Russia's Kissinger and the Eurasianists' doyen. According to William Safire, a former Nixon speechwriter and New York Times columnist, the appointment of Primakov, an "amiable snake...should send a chill throughout the West...[and] is a harbinger of a new Russo-Chinese entente."[13]

"The same qualities in Primakov that aroused suspicion and distrust in the West were welcomed by China's leaders,"[14] as Primakov's views converged with those of his Chinese counterpart, Qian Qichen. "Primakov has promoted Russia, China, and India as a 'strategic triangle' to counterbalance the United States, and the 'Primakov doctrine' reportedly enjoys substantial support across the entire Russian political spectrum."[15]

Primakov's frequent discussions with U.S. Secretary of State Warren Christopher "left no doubt that our [Russia's] opinion would be ignored during the expansion of NATO."[16] This incensed Primakov, because "the leaders of all the Western countries that belonged to NATO assured Soviet leaders they did not intend to expand NATO."[17] Based upon these assurances, the Soviet Union had agreed to withdraw its military forces from East Germany. Primakov suspected that Christopher was prolonging the discussions over NATO expansion because "the United States seemed to be gambling on Yeltsin's losing the election."[18]

After the string of broken promises regarding reunified Germany's inclusion in NATO and then NATO enlargement, Moscow began to accept—did it have a choice?—the apparent inevitability of NATO sweeping eastward, but sought assurances that countries of the former Soviet Union—especially the Baltic countries of Latvia, Lithuania, and Estonia—would not be included in NATO's embrace. Ultimately, however, that question too was also settled "on our [U.S.] terms,"[19] as Talbott notes.

Following the March 1996 Taiwan Strait crisis and the U.S.-Japan Joint Declaration on Security, Jiang and Yeltsin held their fourth summit in Beijing in April 1996, just weeks before the first round of Russia's presidential election. "According to high-ranking Chinese scholars...many in the leadership secretly hoped that Yeltsin would win...even when the choice was between Yeltsin and Communist Party General Secretary Zyuganov."[20] The summit provided a welcome boost to Yeltsin's flagging campaign.

In view of Russia's gradual disillusionment with the United States, and to assuage Russia's nationalist and Eurasianist factions on the eve of the election, the concept of a "strategic partnership" between Russia and China had moved to the forefront of the summit agenda.

In the meantime, the implementation of confidence-building measures and the establishment of troop and weapons ceilings within a 100-kilometer range on both sides of the Sino-Russian border lead to the gradual demilitarization of the border zones.

Under the stewardship of Primakov and Qian, the "strategic partnership" between Russia and China has flourished, but this time around—unlike during the Sino-Soviet alliance of the 1950s—Russia was at its nadir "in terms of power, economic performance, [and] international influence,"[21] and China needed arms, oil, and gas—not atom bombs, railroads, Marx, or Lenin.[22] A potential alliance against the West fueled by humiliation and redemption and expressing itself in strident nationalism was forming; "Russia, a declining great power, aims to recover its lost status, while China, a rising power, resists efforts to constrain its emerging global role."[23]

A beleaguered Yeltsin beseeched Primakov to take control of the Russian government after the August 17, 1998, collapse of the Russian ruble and the moratorium on Russian government obligations; in short, Russia had defaulted on its debts.

Primakov, who begrudgingly acquiesced to his appointment as Prime Minister on September 12, 1998,[24] was immediately confronted by three crises: the domestic economic catastrophe and the concomitant negotiations for a multi-billion dollar bridge loan from the International Monetary Fund (IMF); a joint U.S.-British strike against Iraq in the winter of 1998; and NATO air strikes against Slobodan Milosevic's Serbia, Russia's Orthodox kin, in the spring of 1999.

IMF representatives responded to Primakov's entreaties for financial relief with "moralizing overtones,"[25] and IMF director Michel Camdessus, "smiling maliciously,"[26] procrastinated in approving the bridge loan. Primakov concluded,

> the United States facilitated the IMF's wait-and-see attitude, which in the opinion of many people in Washington was to serve several purposes. One of its goals was to force a weakened Russia, under threat of bankruptcy if IMF debts were not paid, at least not to resist America's foreign policy....[27]

Strobe Talbott reinforced these perceptions when he presented Primakov with a memo on "Economic Issues" that contained "direct threats" and called the Russian-American talks on the IMF bailout "a dialogue of the deaf."[28]

This must have been especially infuriating to the Russians, many of whom believed that the IMF and the World Bank—America's surrogates, in their opinion—had intentionally engineered the Asian economic crisis and the collapse of the ruble.

During the Iraqi crisis in the winter of 1998, the other permanent members of the U.N. Security Council—China, France, and Russia—opposed U.S. and British plans for a military strike against Iraqi radars and anti-aircraft batteries. According to Talbott, "the Russians were apoplectic,"[29] but this did not prevent the 4-day air strike, dubbed Operation Desert Fox.

At the same time, America's escalating demands in its negotiations with Slobodan Milsosevic, Primakov surmises, were designed to keep Russia out of the Balkans. The U.S.-led coalition that organized NATO air strikes against Serbia once again demonstrated that if international institutions did not serve Western interests, they would be ignored or circumvented.

The Kosovo War in the spring of 1999, "the most severe, dangerous, and consequential crisis in U.S.-Russian relations of the post-cold war period,"[30] challenged a basic premise of the international order that prohibited outside interference in another state's domestic affairs. If the West justified a military strike against Serbia over Kosovo, then why not against Russia over Chechnya, against China over Inner Mongolia, Taiwan, Tibet and Xinjiang?

It is ironic that NATO, under U.S. leadership, took "military action for the first time only after the threat it was created to offset had dissipated."[31] At the same time, "Kosovo was something new, virtual war from fifteen thousand feet or above...an antiseptic war waged by remote control."[32]

Although the United States claims that the bombing of the Chinese embassy in Belgrade that killed three Chinese reporters was accidental, during seventy-eight days, from March 24 to June 10, 1999, of the "nine hundred sites targeted by NATO's bombing campaign, only one had been researched and selected solely by the CIA: the Chinese embassy."[33]

"The bombing of China's embassy in Belgrade was a watershed event for many Chinese, similar in emotional content, if not scale, to the effect of June 4, 1989, [Tiananmen] on many Americans."[34] It transformed the Sino-Russian relationship by compelling China to upgrade its strategic partnership with Russia to a formal treaty arrangement.[35]

**Military.** Most immediately, however, it accelerated negotiations for China's purchase of more advanced weaponry from Russia, including fifty Sukhoi-30MKK jet fighters worth approximately $2 billion.[36] In short order, Russia broke ground on a $3.2 billion nuclear power project in Tianwan, located in China's Jiangsu province.[37] Later that year, "the Russian President [Vladimir Putin] was quoted as instructing the Russian military that, in case the U.S. military involved itself in the Taiwan Strait situation, Russia would dispatch its Pacific Fleet to cut off the route of the U.S. fleet in order to keep the latter far away from the Taiwan Strait."[38] China also began negotiations for the purchase of Russia's early-warning A-50 aircraft that would allow it to "see" Taiwan, after Israel, succumbing to U.S. pressure, cancelled China's outstanding order for its Phalcon radar systems.[39] By mid-2002, Russia had signed a $1.5 billion contract to supply the Chinese navy with eight super-quiet Kilo-class Project 636 diesel submarines armed with long-range Klab missile systems,[40] supplementing a fleet of four Kilo-class subs that had already been delivered.

In 2004, Russian arms sales to China increased by 32 percent, from $4.3 billion to $5.7 billion, the "best" year yet. The first-ever Sino-Russian joint military exercise, Peace Mission 2005, was held in China's Shandong Province from August 18–25, with approximately 2,000 Russian and 8,000 Chinese troops. "While some PRC commentators went as far as to suggest that the terrain of the exercise areas was similar to Taiwan's coast, the Russian media toyed with the idea of a joint occupation of North Korea, if necessary."[41]

**Energy.** The proliferation of energy deals between China and Russia, however, dwarfs their military cooperation and arms sales, while challenging the U.S. strategic goal of containing a nascent energy monopoly by encouraging pipeline routes that bypass Russia and Iran. In the meantime, the United States and its allies in the region—Japan, South Korea, and Taiwan—are competing against one another and against China to reduce their dependence on energy imports from the volatile Middle East, while Russia and China draw closer to Iran—consistent with the basic tenets of the Primakov Doctrine.

The proposed Trans-Siberian pipeline dominates all other energy projects under consideration, and is analogous to Russia's eastward expansion at the end of the nineteenth century when it launched the magnificent Trans-Siberian railway (and China, Japan, and Russia on a path to war).

At issue is whether Russia will opt for a pipeline from Angarsk/Taishet, near Lake Baikal, to Skovorodino (about 40 miles from the Sino-Russian border) and south to Daqing, in China's northeastern province of Manchuria (the China option); or whether the pipeline will continue eastward from Skovorodino to Nakhodka and onto Perevoznaya Bay, 10 miles from Vladivostok and 275 miles from Japan's seaports (the Japan option)?

The "China option" will run 1,400 miles, cost an estimated $2.8 billion, take seven years to build, and will yield approximately 600,000 barrels of oil per day (bpd). The "Japan option" (also referred to as the Eastern Siberia Pacific Ocean Pipeline, or ESPO) will run 2,500 miles, cost between $11.5 and $18 billion, take ten years to build, and will produce somewhere between 1 million and 1.6 million bpd.[42]

Moscow's continued indecision, however, has tested the strategic partnership between Russia and China, while extracting the most favorable concessions from China's archrival, Japan. It also laid low Mikhail Khodorkovsky, the Yukos oil magnate, oligarch extraordinaire, and reported presidential aspirant who now languishes in solitary confinement in Prison Camp IZ-75/1, one of Russia's infamous penal colonies in Krasnokamensk, a 15-hour train ride from the provincial capital of Chita and close to the border with China.

Khodorkovsky, serving a 9-year sentence for tax evasion and fraud,[43] had championed closer ties with the United States and supported political diversity by funding Russian opposition parties, such as the Union of Rightist Forces and Yabloko; many speculated that he intended to run for president in 2008, when Vladimir Putin is supposed to step down from office.

Before his imprisonment, Khodorkovsky had been engineering a merger between Yukos and Sibneft, and reportedly offered a stake in the merged entity to the American oil company ExxonMobil—a move certain to have rankled the Kremlin's disciples of state capitalism. Most importantly, Yukos was the "lone champion for the China pipeline route,"[44] once again encroaching on the Kremlin's bailiwick.

Until its dismemberment, Yukos had been "the sole Russian oil exporter to China... [constituting] almost 30 percent of the whole of Russian exports" in the first half of 2004.[45] The China National Petroleum Corporation (CNPC) had to sue after the interruption and shortfall in deliveries that were finally restored toward the end of 2004. Only after Khodorkovsky and Yukos had been disposed of—and Japan had offered billions in enticements[46]—did Russia officially announce its decision to proceed with the "Japan option."

Russia has assuaged China's supply concerns by ramping up oil deliveries by railway. According to the U.S. Energy Information Administration (EIA), Russia "exported roughly 116,000 bbl/d to China during 2004, expects to export 160,000 bbl/d during 2005, and projects exports of 300,000 bbl/d in 2006."[47]

China still hopes that Russia will build a pipeline spur to Daqing, and may have been trying to influence this process when CNPC leant $6 billion to Russia's Rosneft for the purchase of Yuganskneftegaz, Yukos' main production unit, in exchange for future crude deliveries;[48] CNPC also bought a $500 million stake in Rosneft during its initial public offering in 2006.[49] Comments made by Putin during his March 2006 trip to Beijing, however, have lead one analyst to conclude, "until Russia obtains the contract to construct more nuclear power generators in China, the Russian oil pipeline [spur to Daqing] will remain on paper."[50]

While Russia has masterfully extracted a number of valuable concessions from China and Japan, and has positioned itself as the linchpin in Asia's future energy strategies, there is concern that by 2020 oil resources in the region will not be sufficient for full utilization of the pipeline's projected capacity. However, with the "Japan option," Moscow will maintain territorial control over the pipeline, and will have access to multiple markets—China, Japan, Korea, Taiwan, and the United States.

Other Sino-Russian energy and energy-related projects that are under discussion, or have recently been concluded, include:

- An 870-mile rail connection from Pogranichnyy—a 75-acre free-trade zone on the Sino-Russian border (a modern-day Kiakhta?)—to Daqing, the site of China's largest oil-producing field.[51]
- A Gazprom/CNPC deal to build two pipelines, estimated to cost $10 billion, that will carry 60 to 80 billion cubic meters of gas per year from the Kovytka fields, 350 kilometers north of Irkutsk, to China.[52]
- United Energy Systems' (UES) plan "to spend $8.2 billion to build four giant hydropower complexes on the Aldan, Uchur, and Timpton rivers in eastern Siberia to help meet China's annual demand for 40 billion kilowatt-hours of power."[53]
- Russia's transshipment of oil through Kazakhstan's 620-mile Atasu-Alashankou pipeline to China.[54]
- Sinopec's acquisition of a 97 percent stake in Russia's Udmurtneft for $3.5 billion.[55]

**Trade.** Arms sales, military technology transfers, and the proliferation of energy deals have contributed to the explosive growth in bilateral trade between Russia and China, highlighting the economic synergies between the two countries, while at the same time exacerbating tensions that have characterized Sino-Russian relations throughout history.

Nowhere else do China and Russia confront each other on a day-to-day basis more directly than in Northeast China (NEC)—the three provinces of Heilongjiang, Jilin, and Liaoning—and in the Russian Far East (RFE), where China's Heilongjiang province abuts Russia's Primorskii Krai, Khabarovskii Krai and Amurskaya Oblast. "The RFE has a population of about 8 million spread over 6.2 million square kilometers. The neighboring Chinese provinces have a population of 110 million crammed into 1.9 million square kilometers."[56]

A decrease in the birth rate, an increase in the death rate, and an acceleration of outward migration has lead to a decline in the population of the Russian Far East; demographic projections indicate that the population in the RFE "could fall by as much as an additional 25 percent by 2020."[57] At the same time, many of the large, state-owned enterprises (SOEs) in Heilongjiang Province—originally built with Soviet aid almost fifty years ago—face insolvency and massive layoffs, and so the RFE has become a safety valve for skilled, and comparatively cheaper, migrant laborers from China.

The dissolution of the USSR in 1991 and the inability of the new Russian state to project and enforce its authority, coupled with the precipitous decline in Russia's standard of living, prompted an increase in unregulated trade throughout the former Soviet Union, especially in the Russian Far East. "Suitcase peddlers" and smuggling from China proliferated. China and Russia responded by increasing the number of border checkpoints; more customs agents and border guards presented more opportunities for bribery and corruption, so everyone benefited.

Conflict between Russians and Chinese increased as the volume of trade increased. The Russian press published inflammatory articles decrying the poor quality of Chinese goods and warning of the dangers of an influx of Chinese; the Russians launched "Operation Foreigner" in 1994 to root out illegal migrants in the region. The lack of enforceable arbitration mechanisms in contractual disputes was a boon to Russian and Chinese criminal groups, eager to fill the enforcement gap for a fee. "The result has been orchestrated waves of anti-Chinese sentiment, playing on the fears of the local population. One such anti-Chinese campaign in 1996 saw the publication of *The Yellow Peril*."[58]

The following excerpt resembles a previously cited quote attributed to the Russian explorer Przhevalsky[59] more than a century ago and highlights the continuity of Russian anti-Chinese sentiment:

> Believing that they [the Russians] represented European civilization, they found the Chinese with whom they came into contact to be uncouth standard-bearers of a threatening way of life. In particular, the intelligentsia of Vladivostok and Khabarovsk conceived of themselves as cosmopolitans. While acknowledging the hardworking character of the Chinese, they accused them of deception and criminality and of threatening the moral climate of an area already degenerating from within.... Battles over turf between Russian and Chinese criminal groups, and increasingly among the Chinese themselves, aggravated the impression that uncontrolled migration was bringing a "yellow peril" into the RFE cities.[60]

Local politicians—especially Yuri Nazdratenko, appointed governor of Primorskii Krai by President Yeltsin in 1994[61]—exploited and manipulated these sentiments in a quest for more regional autonomy and less centralized control. At the same time, these regional issues complicated bilateral relations between Russia and China. "Conspiracy theories about China's intentions in the RFE"[62] abounded, suggesting that "Chinese migration to the region...[is] an invasion and...[a] sinister Beijing-sponsored plot to breach Russia's territorial integrity,"[63] annexation by stealth via illegal immigration, contract labor, border trade and investment.

Nevertheless, Sino-Russian trade has more than quadrupled from its low-point after the ruble's collapse in 1998, and the leadership has vowed to triple bilateral trade to $60 billion by 2010.

*

Several other issues have tested the burgeoning Sino-Russian alliance, such as the Russian Duma's vote in December 2002 to prevent CNPC's acquisition of Slavneft, one of Russia's major oil companies.[64] And Russia's arms sales to India are a sore point with China—especially as the weapons sold to India are superior to those sold to China. However, in June 2003, India's Prime Minister Vajpayee visited China for a weeklong state visit, the first by an Indian Prime Minister in ten years. Since then, there has been speculation that "Russia will team up with India and China for the R&D for the fifth generation of [jet] fighters";[65] and in June 2005, a tripartite conference between the foreign ministers of Russia, China and India convened in Vladivostok—all further evidence of the Primakov Doctrine gone operational.

**Table 9.1  China's Trade with Russia, 1991–2005**

| Year | Exports | Imports | Total | +/- % |
|---|---|---|---|---|
| 1991* | 1823 | 2081 | 3904 | |
| 1992 | 2337 | 3512 | 5849 | +50 |
| 1993 | 2692 | 4986 | 7678 | +31 |
| 1994 | 1578 | 3466 | 5044 | -34 |
| 1995 | 1674 | 3799 | 5473 | +9 |
| 1996 | 1693 | 5156 | 6849 | +25 |
| 1997 | 2035 | 4084 | 6119 | -11 |
| 1998 | 1833 | 3627 | 5460 | -11 |
| 1999 | 1497 | 4223 | 5720 | +5 |
| 2000 | 2233 | 5769 | 8002 | +40 |
| 2001 | 2715 | 7959 | 10674 | +33 |
| 2002 | 3522 | 8405 | 11927 | +12 |
| 2003 | 6035 | 9726 | 15761 | +32 |
| 2004 | 9102 | 12129 | 21231 | +35 |
| 2005 | 13211 | 15886 | 29097 | +37 |

*Trade with the former Soviet Union.
*Notes:* Figures are in U.S.$ millions. All percentages are rounded up.
*Source:* International Monetary Fund, *Direction of Trade Statistics Yearbooks.*

The Russian physicist Dr. Valentin Danilov's arrest and acquittal, followed by his retrial and conviction, for passing declassified documents on aerospace technology to a Chinese company,[66] is puzzling, as was Moscow's decision to issue a visa to the Dalai Lama for a visit to Russia's predominantly Buddhist Republic of Kalmykia late in 2004—in spite of China's objections.

Overshadowing these issues was the potentially disastrous explosion at a chemical plant in China's Jilin Province in November 2005 that released more than one hundred tons of benzene into the Songhua River and threatened several major cities in Russia, including Khabarovsk; China and Russia worked together, however, to contain the damage.

"The chumminess of the Russian and Chinese authoritarian leaders...is part of a growing global ideological conflict consolidating democracies and dictatorships,"[67] so these are but minor irritants in an otherwise burgeoning alliance that sees the leadership in Moscow and Beijing drawing closer together in almost all spheres of bilateral cooperation, and coordinating policy on a number of multilateral issues and in international fora—often in response to and at odds with U.S. initiatives and interests.

Polling data reveal that before 9/11,

> More than half (51%) of the Russian political, intellectual, and opinion elite polled in December [2000] by an independent opinion survey center, a Russian subsidiary of the American Gallup organization, saw China as first among Russia's "strategically important allies," surpassing Belarus (49.6%), Germany (39.4%), India (23.5%), the United States (20%) and Britain (15.6%).[68]

A more recent poll conducted by the Russian radio station, Ekho Moskvy, found that "74 percent of listeners thought Russia should join in an alliance with China against the United States,"[69] and according to the Horizon Group in Beijing, "the U.S. was also rated as the world's most unfriendly country toward China."[70]

At a 2006 gathering for foreign Russia experts at his official residence at Novo Ogarevo, President Putin emphasized that the Sino-Russian relationship was the "best ever" and had reached a "historic level." He added, "political forces and trends in the world will dictate the best relations with China."[71] To highlight his personal commitment, Putin, a martial arts buff, went out of his way during a trip to China to visit a Shinto shrine in Xi'an, where he observed a performance by China's master martial artists. One of Putin's daughters is studying Chinese; the other is also a martial arts aficionado.

In "The Sporting Spirit," George Orwell said, "sport[s] mimic warfare."[72] As a platform for national glorification, nothing rivals the Olympics, and in 2008, Beijing will be hosting this most enduring of all sports spectacles. Add in China's obsession with control—its mastery of pageantry, pomp, and protocol—and it's likely the world will be witness to the most spectacular coming-out party in history.

But the likelihood of political hanky-panky of the highest order is also great; the last time the international media descended on Beijing—to witness Gorbachev's historic arrival in May 1989—China's university students rebelled, and Tiananmen erupted. With billions of eyes focused on Beijing, the situation will be ripe for exploitation by human rights activists, members of Falun Gong, Taiwan, and myriad others. China will be completely mobilized for victory, its crack troops deployed, its senior cadre on high alert, its security agents out in force. And all the world will be watching.

As if to consecrate their partnership, though, China and Russia have vowed "to cooperate to best America in Beijing"[73] at the Summer Olympics by winning more medals than the Americans at Athens in 2004. But it is not only in the sports arena where China and Russia are cooperating to best America—the subject of the next chapter.

# IN CONCERT WITH THE AXIS

*Sitting on the sidelines and sneering at America's ineptitude are Russia and China: Russia, because it is delighted to see Muslim hostility diverted from itself towards the US, despite its own crimes in Afghanistan and Chechnya, and is eager to entice America into an anti-Islamic alliance; China, because it patiently follows the advice of its ancient strategic guru, Sun Tzu, who taught that the best way to win is to let your rival defeat himself.*

—Zbigniew Brzezinski

In addition to their flourishing bilateral relationship, China and Russia have joined together to undermine America in the United Nations over Iran and Iraq, while their North Korean ally taunts the United States, Japan, South Korea, and Taiwan with unpredictable missile and nuclear tests and other forms of nuclear brinksmanship. China and Russia have been backing the U.S.-designated "axis of evil"—Iran, Iraq, and North Korea—with arms and investments worth billions for years. They have lured the United States in deep on several fronts, catalyzing the "rotting process" in the United States.[1] They have orchestrated a near perfect storm with a blend of Sun Tzu's subtlety and Stalin's cunning; Mao must be chuckling, Stalin licking his chops.

**SCO.** While the United States prefers to go it alone and has destroyed much of its Cold War alliance structure, China and Russia have been nurturing a regional bloc formed in 1996—the Shanghai Cooperation Organization (SCO)—that encompasses almost half of the world's population. Originally called the Shanghai Five, the organization changed its name in 2001 when Uzbekistan joined. The SCO now consists of six members—China, Kazakhstan, Kyrgyzstan, Russia, Tajikistan, and Uzbekistan—and four countries with observer status—India, Iran, Mongolia, and Pakistan.

Although the SCO is not yet a militarized alliance like NATO, it has conducted small-scale joint antiterrorist exercises on the Sino-Kyrgyz border in October 2002—"the first peacetime joint military exercise China is known to have conducted"[2]—followed by more robust exercises on the Sino-Kazakh border during "Interaction-2003, from August 6–12.

There has been some speculation that the SCO may form a gas cartel, a "gas OPEC" (Russia and Iran control about 45 percent of the world's natural gas reserves), and that it is trying to lure Turkey—frustrated over its decades-long bid to join the European Union—into the SCO.[3]

**ABM/NMD/TMD.** The Bush administration's abrogation of the *Anti-Ballistic Missile (ABM) Treaty* with Russia in July 2001 freed the United States to pursue, test, and deploy a nuclear missile defense (NMD) system that shields the United States from attack, and so "could immediately render China's minimalist nuclear retaliatory force obsolete."[4]

Deployment of a U.S. theater missile defense (TMD) system in the Asia Pacific region, "whose key components (Aegis and Patriot systems) are already operational, would considerably neutralize the PLA's only viable means against Taiwan's move toward independence."[5]

At the same time, America's fourth generation nuclear weapons—for example, the B61-11 earth penetrating warhead (also known as the bunker-buster bomb)—fill a gap between conventional and nuclear weapons and so present the capability to respond flexibly, thus lowering the nuclear threshold.

To China and Russia, these developments exemplify America's unilateralism in the era of preemption. To drive home that point, the United States issued its 2002 *Nuclear Posture Review* and singled out Russia, China, North Korea, Iran, Iraq, Syria, and Libya in a nuclear targeting list.[6]

North Korea and Iran, in asserting their right to possess nuclear weapons and to defend against America, claim that the U.S. approach to nuclear nonproliferation—its accommodative stance toward India, Israel, and Pakistan, its hard-line stance against them—is hypocritical, self-serving, and unprincipled.

**Korea.** China, by virtue of its centuries-long tributary relationship with Korea, is the key to a peaceful resolution of the nuclear dispute with North Korea. "Since the cutoff of U.S. heavy oil in December 2002," China has been underwriting Kim Jong-il's regime by carrying large arrears with North Korea, and has been providing nearly all of Pyongyang's fuel imports.[7] North Korea has also allegedly provided Iran and Syria with Nodong 1 and Scud C missiles in exchange for oil.[8] Of paramount concern is the possibility that North Korea might sell fissile material to Iran, or to a terrorist group, such as al-Qaeda.

China and Russia have repeatedly watered-down, obstructed, and vetoed sanctions that the U.N. sought to impose against North Korea and Iran for their proliferation activities, although some reports suggest China may cooperate, in the North Korean case, if the European Union agrees to lift its Tiananmen-era ban on weapons sales to China. Although China and Russia voted—along with the other members of the U.N. Security Council—to impose meaningless sanctions on North Korea after its nuclear test in October 2006, "somehow or other, it is the Bush administration that is being blamed around the world for the latest explosion, not the Chinese regime that props up the North Korean regime. Somehow or other, it's beginning to seem like another illustration of American impotence."[9]

President Putin has also aggressively reasserted Russia's interest in the Koreas, and has paid special attention to nurturing his personal relationship with North Korea's Kim Jong-il. Putin has staked out a middle ground between the Bush administration's hard-line approach and China's traditional role as Korea's patron.

In the Six-Party talks on North Korea—stalled since November 2005 but resumed in December 2006—Russia is in the enviable position of seeming to have the least to lose. The United States and China, who both have vital interests in the region (the U.S. supports 37,000 troops and spends $20–30 billion annually to maintain its commitment in South Korea),[10] advocate opposing outcomes: The United States favors regime change in North Korea, while China seeks to prevent regime collapse by gradually introducing economic reforms.[11]

China and South Korea have been drawing closer together since the establishment of diplomatic relations in 1992[12]—indeed, "China's Korea policy has gradually moved from a pro-North position to one of balance between the two Koreas, tilting toward South Korea,"[13]—and all three revile Japan, the former colonial occupier and America's closest ally in the region. Just as another wave of anti-Americanism swept through South Korea, "China fever" arrived: Chinese language schools are proliferating, and a record number of Chinese tourists have been visiting the South.[14]

Might China be positioning itself for a future "grand bargain, such as the withdrawal of U.S. security guarantees for Taiwan—in other words, Chinese unification—for some sort of Korean unification scheme?" [15]

**Iran.** A decade after the fall of the Soviet Union, the United States embarked on a crusade to transplant democracy by force of arms in faraway and inhospitable places—presumably in response to its all-encompassing Global War on Terror. Even though Russia and Iran had cooperated with the United States after 9/11—Russia had acquiesced to U.S. military bases in Central Asia, Iran had permitted emergency landing rights for U.S. aircraft—the United States and its allied NATO forces have encircled Iran (excluding Turkmenistan and Armenia), and relations with Russia are at a post-Cold War low.

If U.S. strategic interests in the Persian Gulf consist of keeping Russia out and balancing Iran and Iraq so that neither dominates the region, then the United States has failed—catastrophically. U.S. actions have strengthened Shiite

Iran—American forces routed the (Sunni) Taliban from power in Afghanistan and Iraq's Shiite majority, under U.S. protection, has been installed in power. Hezbollah, Iran's proxy, is ascendant in Lebanon, where the Cedar Revolution of 2005, launched with U.S. encouragement, forced Syria out, thereby strengthening Hezbollah by removing the only power strong enough to hold the country's fractious religious groups together.

An anti-U.S. axis has formed—Iran, Syria, Hezbollah in Lebanon, Hamas and Islamic Jihad in the Palestinian territories, the Muslim Brotherhood in Egypt, and Sudan—all energized by the Iraqi insurgency against the American occupation forces.

For the first time since Nasser ruled Egypt, several young, dynamic, and charismatic leaders have arisen to inflame the passions of and unite many in the Islamic world against the West: the former Revolutionary Guard and current president, Mahmoud Ahmadinejad in Iran, Hezbollah's Sheikh Nasrallah in Lebanon, and Osama bin Laden, still at large.

A countervailing, predominately Sunni coalition, associated with the United States and consisting of Hosni Mubarak's quarter century of martial rule in Egypt, authoritarian and hereditary monarchies in Jordan and Saudi Arabia, and Pakistan's precarious military dictatorship under General Musharraf, seems to be on the defensive.

Pundits have speculated about "a historic shift in the position of the long-subordinated Shiite minority relative to the power and prestige of the Sunni majority," about a "Shiite crescent."[16]

In 2006, as the U.S. position in Iraq and Afghanistan continued to deteriorate, President Putin invited Hamas' Damascus-based leader-in-exile, Khaled Mashaal, to the Kremlin, and Iran has goaded its Lebanese proxy Hezbollah to provoke a war with Israel. Russia has banked on all of the chaos in the Middle East—oil prices are at record levels—and, as of March 2007, had amassed the world's third largest pool of foreign reserves estimated at $322 billion.

Because Israel did not crush Hezbollah in the 34-day summer war of 2006, a "deterrence deficit" has developed which could lead to grave miscalculations by all of these disparate elements. And the USA's gross abuse of its intelligence agencies and its failure to find weapons of mass destruction in Iraq has created a "credibility deficit." After the 2006 mid-term elections in the United States, President Bush, a lame duck, has been unleashed from day-to-day political calculations tempered by the prospect of future elections and so may be even more inclined to take preemptive action—this time against Iran.

All the while, Russia and China have aggressively pursued the Primakov-Qian vision of mulitipolarity by reasserting their interests in the Middle East—especially in Iran. While "anti-Americanism may be the glue which binds the Russia-China-Iran trinity together,"[17] China is driven by its urgent need to diversify its energy mix and suppliers, and so has recently concluded several major deals in Iran:

- China's state-owned Zhuhai Zhenrong Corporation "agreed to import 110 million tons of Iranian liquid natural gas (LNG) over 25 years, a deal worth approximately $20 billion,"[18] in March 2004.

- In October 2004, Sinopec signed a 25-year, $100 billion contract "to import more than 270 million tons of natural gas over the next 30 years from Iran's South Pars field"; the deal also included exploration and purchase rights in the Yadavaran oil field.[19]

- CNPC bought the subsidiary of Canada's Sheer Energy that had been working on Iran's Masjed-I-Suleyman oil field[20] in June 2005.

- A "Sinopec-led consortium" completed a $330 million project to expand storage at Neka, Iran's Caspian Sea port; the China National Offshore Oil Corporation (CNOOC) has expressed an interest in developing Iranian sections of the Caspian Sea.[21]

Because Iran supplies China with approximately 13 percent of its oil imports, by the end of 2005 China had become Iran's main trading partner.

Russia, on the other hand, has focused on resuming its multi-billion dollar arms trade with Iran[22] as a means of shoring up its ailing defense sector, and on completing the nuclear reactor at Bushehr (scheduled to go critical in November 2007), in hopes of winning lucrative contracts to build more reactors worth an estimated $10 billion.[23]

In February 2005, *The Moscow Times* reported that approximately 20 Russian-made Kh-55 Granat strategic missiles capable of carrying nuclear warheads were smuggled to Iran and China.[24] That same year, in another arms deal worth $1 billion, Russia sold Tor M1 surface-to-air missiles that could be used to protect Iran's nuclear installations from attack; the package also included upgrades to Iran's stock of Sukhoi and MIG fighter jets.[25] Finally, there are reports of ongoing discussions regarding the sale of submarine-launched missiles that "would greatly complicate the activities of the U.S. fleet in the Persian Gulf."[26]

What this means is that Russia is helping Iran build a nuclear reactor at Bushehr that will enable it to produce nuclear weapons, is supplying Iran with missiles to deliver its nuclear weapons, and is providing Iran with defensive weapons to protect against a preemptive strike, while collaborating with China to shield Iran from U.N. sanctions. At the same time, Russia has attempted to garner diplomatic kudos by offering to relocate Iran's fissionable nuclear material to Russian soil, a cynical example of diplomatic arbitrage of a situation that it has fostered.

In 2002, the Central Intelligence Agency estimated that Iran would go nuclear in seven years; more recently, Meir Dagan, the head of Israel's foreign intelligence agency, the Mossad, stated, "Iran is one or two years away, at the latest, from having enriched uranium."[27]

A nuclear Iran radically alters the Middle East's strategic landscape by posing an existential threat to Israel and by compelling Egypt, Saudi Arabia and Turkey to go nuclear.

**Iraq.** Some have interpreted the decades-long confrontation-by-proxy in the Middle East between the United States and the Soviet Union as part of an "Eastern Question/Great Game/Cold War continuum" that began with the Crimean War of 1856 and has focused on control over the world's most strategic shipping lanes—the Dardanelles, the Suez Canal, and the Persian Gulf.[28]

Until Deng Xiaoping launched China's economic reform program in 1978, Great Power competition in the Middle East had primarily been limited first to Anglo-Russian, and then to U.S.-Soviet rivalry. With the outbreak of the Iran-Iraq War in 1980, China realized that it could quickly generate "billions of dollars in sales of small arms, artillery, and tanks to both sides,"[29] especially as the Soviet Union had temporarily halted arms sales to the warring parties and U.S. diplomatic relations with Iran and Iraq were at a standstill. The Middle East quickly became China's largest arms market, Iraq its largest customer. China wrapped its arms sales in the ideological patina of a desire "to demonstrate the superiority of 'the Chinese way' to the Middle East states, and to 'supplant' that of the superpowers."[30]

When Iran—then firmly ruled by Ayatollah Khomeini—banned the Communist Tudeh Party in 1982, "the Soviet Union became the major supplier of sophisticated arms to Iraq...[and] the United States began clandestine direct and indirect negotiations with Iranian officials that resulted in several arms shipments to Iran,"[31] and the Iran-contra affair.

After Donald Rumsfeld—deployed as President Reagan's special envoy—met with Saddam Hussein in December 1983, the United States transferred billions worth of weapons to Iraq. Many have questioned whether the major powers armed Iran and Iraq in order to goad both regimes along the path to self-destruction.

Because of the imposition of U.N. sanctions against Iraq in the run up to the 1991 Gulf War, China offset its steep decline in arms transfers to Iraq by increasing its shipments to Iran. Largely due to U.S. pressure over the sale of Silkworm missiles, however, China scaled back its weapons trade with Iran, paving the way for the USSR/Russia to replace China as Iran's main arms supplier by the early 1990s. Yitzhak Shichor, a leading scholar on China's relations with the Middle East, comments:

> While the Western drive against China's arms transfers may reflect a genuine concern about the causes of violence and a genuine aspiration for disarmament and the promotion of peace, it also uncovers a sense of superiority, if not racism, against China's intrusion into domains preserved for "whites alone." It betrays a crude

attempt to shield the economic interests of the Western defense industries and also reflects an insensitivity to China's greatness of the past and to its efforts to restore this glory in the future.[32]

The highest estimate of Iraq's outstanding debt to the former Soviet Union/ Russia is $64 billion,[33] and consists of at least $7 billion for arms provided by the Soviets.[34] In addition, Russian companies had entered into numerous energy deals with Saddam's Iraq, such as Lukoil's 52.5 percent stake in the development of Iraq's 11–15 billion-barrel West Qurna oil field, where "Russia now stands to lose more than $20 billion in oil development contracts."[35] In 2001, Slavneft signed a contract to develop the Lutais oil field, and Zarubezhneft entered Iraq seeking development rights in the Bin Umar field.[36] One study concludes that Russia's decision to join in the Moscow-Berlin-Paris axis against the March 2003 U.S. war in Iraq—was "motivated mostly by financial considerations (the enormous profits that Russian companies and elites had been reaping from the oil-for-food program.)."[37]

Three days after the outbreak of the second Iraq War, *The Washington Post* reported that Russian companies had sold electronic jamming equipment, Kornet antitank missiles, and night-vision goggles to Iraq; one of the companies also sent personnel to Iraq to provide training.[38] Later, it was alleged that Vladimir Titorenko, Russia's ambassador to Iraq, had passed intelligence on U.S. troop movements to Saddam Hussein in the run-up to the 2003 war.[39]

China's interests in Iraq, prior to Operation Iraqi Freedom, were minor in comparison to Russia. In 1997, China had signed a 22-year pact with Iraq valued at $1.2 billion to develop and operate the al-Ahdab oil field.[40] China had also entered into a partnership to develop Iraq's Rafidain field.[41]

China contributed to Iraqi preparations for the second Iraq War by reportedly installing a "nationwide fiber-optic communication system" linking Iraq's air defense sites;[42] in addition, China allegedly transshipped a Kolchuga radar system provided by Ukraine to Iraq.[43]

Whereas Russia voted against U.N. Resolution 678 authorizing military force against Iraq in March 2003, China abstained, primarily motivated by its desire to gain access to Iraq's future oil flow.[44]

**Sudan.** China, and to a lesser extent Russia, have also been blocking the deployment of U.N. peacekeeping troops to Sudan's Darfur region, where black Arab-Muslim militia, the Janjaweed, are accused of genocide against non-Arab tribes.

Using its status as a developing nation unencumbered by colonial baggage in Africa, and playing on suspicions that the West is trying to break up Sudan, China has spearheaded an investment boom in Khartoum and has "become Sudan's leading trade partner, absorbing almost two-thirds of all Sudanese exports in 2004, and supplying more than 10% of its imports."[45]

CNPC has acquired the largest stake in two of Sudan's most lucrative oil consortiums, the Greater Nile Petroleum Operating Company (GNPOC), and Petrodar.[46] China is also involved in the construction of two hydroelectric plants at Merowe and Kajbar, and provided 75 percent of the financing for the Kajbar dam.[47] According to Kent Calder, the author of *Pacific Destiny* and a distinguished professor of East Asian studies, China has stationed "4,000 non-uniformed forces in the Sudan...closely related to its oil interests."[48]

The Economist Intelligence Unit cites "uncorroborated reports suggesting that Sudan has bought arms [from Russia] in return for oil concessions. Indeed, Russia sees Sudan as one of its top clients in the defense industry";[49] and according to the U.S. State Department, "Sudan now receives most of its military equipment from China and Russia."[50] This must grate on Washington, especially as Sudan had backed Iraq's invasion of Kuwait in 1991 and had provided a safe haven for Osama bin Laden from 1994–1996.

In "The Strategic Implications of China's Energy Needs," a report sponsored by London's International Institute for Strategic Studies, the authors state:

> There is the question of whether China should strengthen its ties to oil-producing states in the region which have antagonistic relations with the US, such as Iran and Iraq, and to continue its policy of promoting arms sales to such states. The more general dilemma is how China should respond to its inevitable dependence on the US for the security of the Persian Gulf and the sea lines of communication and whether it should offer de facto support for US policies or seek to counterbalance US dominance through coalitions with countries such as Russia and Iran.[51]

The evidence suggests that China and Russia have opted to counterbalance U.S. global dominance.

*

While China and Russia have been coordinating their policies toward Iran, Iraq and North Korea, their bilateral relations with the United States have been steadily deteriorating in a global political environment turned decidedly unfavorable for the Americans.

9/11 struck during a triple transition at the apex of power in China, Russia, and the United States. President Jiang—one of China's third generation, "made-in-Russia," leaders—was in the process of shedding his posts to Hu Jintao, who represents China's fourth generation of homegrown technocrats. Putin, born after World War II and twenty-one years younger than his predecessor, had already replaced Yeltsin. And George W. Bush secured the presidency of the United States by a 5-4 decision of the U.S. Supreme Court in one of the most contentious elections ever. The moment was ripe for an historical realignment.

**Russia.** Although President "Yeltsin's personal investment in promoting relations with Beijing is perhaps bigger than any other Russian leader's in the 20th century, from the Czar to Gorbachev,"[52] President Putin paused, and waited until he obtained legitimacy in Russia's March 2000 presidential election,[53] before reassessing Russia's China policy. Only after several postponements that irked the Chinese did Putin travel to Beijing for his first summit with President Jiang in July 2000.

According to the *The Washington Post*, the Bush administration had "promised to remove [Jackson-Vanik] trade restrictions imposed on Russia"[54] (in 1974!) after Putin had agreed to let U.S. forces plant themselves in Russia's (and China's) backyard for the war against Afghanistan's Taliban. Less than a month later, Russia announced another strategic retreat: It was closing its electronic listening post in Lourdes, Cuba, and withdrawing from its naval base at Cam Ranh Bay, Vietnam.

Up until 9/11, the Bush administration had been focusing on China as the primary strategic threat facing America. Even so, the United States responded to Russia's overtures after 9/11—and during this critical period of leadership transitions—by abrogating the *ABM Treaty* with Russia in December 2001, and by foisting a 3-page treaty on President Putin in May 2002. "Russia had given in to virtually every U.S. demand on the *Treaty of Strategic Offensive Reductions*,"[55] and the Jackson-Vanik trade restrictions are still in place.

Even though President Bush looked into President Putin's eyes, got a sense of his soul, and found someone he could trust at their first meeting in Slovenia in June 2001,[56] relations between Russia and the United States have been deteriorating ever since 9/11. In Russia's view, U.S. troops in Central Asia have overstayed their welcome—indeed, the SCO has demanded that the United States set a departure date—and the United States has been meddling in almost every country on Russia's periphery.

Russia suspects U.S. complicity in a string of "colorful" revolutions that have swept through the region: Georgia's Rose Revolution of November 2003 forced Eduard Shevardnadze from office,[57] Ukraine's Orange Revolution of late 2004 catapulted Viktor Yushchenko into the presidency,[58] and Kyrgyzstan's Tulip Revolution of April 2005 deposed Askar Akayev. In July 2005, Uzbekistan gave the United States six months to remove its troops from the Khanabad Air Base in Karshi after accusing the United States of complicity in riots that erupted in Andijan in May 2005. With the death of President Saparmurat Niyazov in December 2006, Turkmenistan has come into play: Its natural gas exports to Russia are critical to Moscow's energy strategy, and its utility as a launching pad into Iran make it an attractive target to both Tehran and Washington.

As if NATO expansion into most of the former eastern European satellites[59] and the Baltic Republics[60] was not enough, Russia now sees NATO nipping away at Ukraine, its linchpin and breadbasket, where the Western-leaning Yushchenko came to power—in Moscow's view—with the connivance of foreign powers. And in March 2007, Georgia's Parliament unanimously passed a declaration expressing a desire to join NATO.

In what was seen as a countermove to influence Ukraine's parliamentary elections in March 2006, Russia's state-controlled monopoly, Gazprom, briefly halted the flow of gas to Ukraine in the dead of winter over a pricing dispute,[61] but since Gazprom supplies about 25 percent of Europe's natural gas, most of which passes through Ukraine, the Kremlin's heavy-handedness backfired. Still, there are concerns that Russia's chokehold on Ukraine may cause "one of the signal democratic breakthroughs of the Bush years to suffer a crippling reverse."[62]

In a throwback to the Cold War era, Russia's foreign intelligence agency, the FSB, accused a British diplomat, Marc Doe, of colluding with nongovernmental organizations (NGOs) active in Russia, after Doe was reportedly filmed in a Moscow park retrieving a fake rock that concealed an electronic listening device. The Kremlin used this incident to justify new licensing restrictions that it had imposed on NGOs, many of which were engaged in the types of activities—that is, advocating a civil society based on the rule of law, a free press, and greater transparency—that had fostered the "color" revolutions in Georgia, Ukraine, and Kyrgyzstan.[63]

In an exchange reminiscent of Cold War rhetoric, Vice President Cheney, in Lithuania for the Vilnius Conference in May 2006, rebuked Russia for backpedaling on its democratic reforms and engaging in energy blackmail. President Putin responded in his annual address to the nation by referring to "Comrade Wolf"—presumably the United States—who "eats without listening" and "wants to tear off a big chunk of our country."[64]

Finally, in another move indicative of the Kremlin's ingathering of Russia's energy resources, Gazprom announced that it would not partner with foreign companies to develop the massive Shtokman gas field in the Barents Sea, a $20 billion project. This is seen as a quid pro quo for what Moscow views as trifling U.S. delays in approving Russia's application for membership in the World Trade Organization—especially as Chevron and ConocoPhillips, two U.S. companies, had been bidding on the Shtokman project.[65]

**China.** On April 1, 2001, a U.S. EP-3 spy plane collided with a Chinese fighter jet that crashed and then perished in the East China Sea. The EP-3, with 24 U.S. service personnel on board, made an emergency landing at Lingshui Airforce Base on China's Hainan Island, where the Chinese government held the U.S. crew for 11 days as senior U.S. diplomats haggled over the wording of an official apology to the Chinese.

As though calibrated to infuriate the Chinese even more, on April 24 "the Bush administration authorized a $5 billion sale of arms to Taiwan, the largest in history,"[66] and the next day, President Bush made his "whatever it takes to help Taiwan defend itself" statement on *Good Morning, America*.[67] The United States then granted Chen Shui-bian, Taiwan's president, a transit visa for a stopover in New York, where he met with a group of U.S. congressional representatives and other notables.[68] A couple of days later, President Bush met with the

Dalai Lama—whom Beijing regards as the leader of the Tibetan separatist movement—in the White House residence.

The EP-3 incident, "the most serious military confrontation between the United States and China in more than three decades,"[69] followed by the arms package for Taiwan, Chen's visa, and the Dalai Lama's visit, set the tone for Sino-American relations in the first one hundred days of George W. Bush's presidency.

Since then, the U.S. government has issued a stream of reports that highlight China's threat to U.S. primacy. For example, the U.S.-China Security Review Commission's first report of July 2002 asserts that China is covertly funding a strategic buildup to challenge U.S. interests in Asia and "spends about $65 billion a year on defense," even though its official defense budget is $20 billion.[70]

The *Quadrennial Defense Review* (QDR), the *National Security Strategy*, the *Nuclear Posture Review*, and the Pentagon's annual report, *Military Power of the People's Republic of China*, all reinforce the same message. The 2006 QDR concludes, "China has the greatest potential to compete militarily with the United States and field disruptive technologies that could over time offset traditional U.S. military advantages." Because China has also supplied missile technology and advanced weaponry to Iran and Pakistan, "the Bush administration has imposed sanctions against Chinese entities 62 times in its first four years in office."[71]

The Chinese have not been silent. In a signed article in *Xinhua*, the official state news agency, a rare personal attack on the U.S. leadership countered, "Some people regard Bush, Cheney, and Rumsfeld as the 'axis of evil.'"[72]

Qian Qichen, China's dean of diplomacy (akin to Kissinger in the United States and Primakov in Russia), issued a harsh critique of Bush's foreign policy on the eve of the November 2004 U.S. presidential election. Qian's article, "U.S. Strategy to Be Blamed," appeared in the Communist Party's English-language *China Daily*, and chastised America for its "cocksureness and arrogance" buttressed "with a Cold War mentality." The piece—described as "stridently anti-American"—attacks the U.S. war of choice in Iraq, and implores the Europeans to recognize the irreparable breach in the Atlantic Alliance.[73]

In the age of globalization, however, economic issues—especially the Chinese economic miracle—dominate the headlines: China has delivered close to 9.4 percent annual GDP growth over the past thirty years, lifting more than 300 million out of poverty; and its trade surplus with the United States reached a whopping $201.6 billion in 2005, up 25 percent from 2004. At the end of 2005, China had amassed more than $1 trillion in foreign exchange reserves, more than four times its reserves in 2001; and as of January 2007, China held $455 billion, or 21.5 percent, of all outstanding U.S. Treasury securities.[74]

Many have linked the loss of U.S. manufacturing jobs and the burgeoning U.S. trade deficit to the undervaluation of China's currency, the yuan, and to the lax enforcement of intellectual property rights in China, making China a convenient scapegoat for America's economic woes. In addition, because China does not allow independent trade unions, workers' pay and benefits are even lower, while state banks provide cheap credit to state companies that are not concerned about repayment. The Chinese government offers tax rebates to local exporters—but does not extend these rebates to foreign companies in China, while lax environmental protection guidelines and the artificially low price of utilities further suppress the true cost of goods. All of these factors act as indirect government subsidies of China's exports.[75]

Protectionist sentiments seem to swell whenever the U.S. economy falters and as U.S. elections approach; two U.S. senators have tried to harness this political dynamic by introducing legislation that would impose a 27.5 percent tariff on Chinese imports.[76] But according to Alan Greenspan, the former chairman of the U.S. Federal Reserve, the real culprit in the trade deficit argument is the low savings rate in the United States: Whereas China boasts a personal savings rate of almost 50 percent, America's savings rate hovers near zero—an all-time post-Depression low.

Because China has also emerged as a major competitive threat to Mexico's low-cost labor force—"since 2003, as many as 500 maquiladora factories and 500,000 jobs have departed for China"[77]—illegal immigration from Mexico also feeds anti-China and protectionist sentiments in the United States.

This has most recently manifested itself in the outcry that greeted CNOOC's $18.5 billion unsolicited cash bid for Unocal, a U.S. oil and gas producer. Even though CNOOC had hired Public Strategies, a public relations firm with ties to President Bush,[78] the takeover bid generated such a negative response in the United States that the Chinese withdrew their offer on August 2, 2005. Chevron, in what must have been an abject lesson in capitalism for the Chinese, succeeded in taking control of Unocal with a less competitive $17 billion cash-and-stock offer.

Less than a year later, even a hint that malicious software code could have been planted in 16,000 desktop computers purchased from Lenovo, the Chinese computer maker, forced the U.S. State Department to keep the computers off its classified computer network. Lenovo had only recently purchased IBM's personal computer division, and these computers had been manufactured, for the most part, in the same U.S. plants built and formerly used by IBM.[79]

\*

In Chapter 6, "When China Meets Russia," emphasis was placed on the Chinese imperial court's focus on form over content, on the primacy of pomp and protocol. Russian emissaries, supplicants before the emperor, repeatedly failed to perform the ritual kowtow and the presentation of tribute. If the "ceremonial was the outward expression of the Confucian world order...the

Russians simply didn't know the drill"[80] after almost two hundred years of contact with their neighbor. And the Americans aren't doing much better.

The April 2006 meeting at the White House between President Bush and President Hu, "plagued by gaffes that upended months of painstaking diplomacy over protocol and staging,"[81] began inauspiciously with the White House designating the Chinese president's visit a working, rather than a state, visit. Since working visits do not qualify for state dinners, a luncheon was held in the East Room rather than in the State Dining Room, and President Bush withheld an invitation to his Crawford, Texas ranch.

The Chinese, exquisitely attuned to these gradations, must have been infuriated when a White House announcer, as a prelude to remarks by President Hu, introduced the Chinese national anthem as the Republic of China's—Taiwan's official name—rather than the PRC's. Just moments after President Hu began to speak, Wanyi Wang, a reporter for Falun Gong's *Epoch Times* who had somehow penetrated White House security, began interrupting and heckling Hu; Secret Service agents removed her only several minutes later. All the while, Vice President Cheney donned his sunglasses during the opening ceremony—and kept them on while President Hu spoke—another breach of diplomatic etiquette. The White House also neglected to fly China's national flag on lampposts in the vicinity, a courtesy typically extended to visiting heads of state.[82]

This wanton failure to observe basic diplomatic protocol when hosting the leader of China's 1.3 billion reveals America's cavalier response to "a country with a liberal economy but an illiberal polity [that] should warrant at least as much concern as the old Soviet Union ever did, since it poses the prospect of economic power without political restraint. The possibility of this combination in China's future, together with the country's size, makes it the great power in the region about which U.S. strategists should worry most over the long term."[83]

# THE BALANCE OF POWER

*What makes a future Chinese threat so worrisome is that it might be far more powerful and dangerous than any of the potential hegemons that the United States confronted in the twentieth century. Neither Wilhelmine Germany, nor imperial Japan, nor Nazi Germany, nor the Soviet Union had nearly as much latent power as the United States had during their confrontations. But if China were to become a giant Hong Kong, it would probably have somewhere on the order of four times as much latent power as the United States does, allowing China to gain a decisive military advantage over the United States in Northeast Asia.*

—John Mearsheimer

Even without a decisive military advantage in traditional terms, China's combination of asymmetric capabilities (especially in cyberwarfare), its continental depth, the overwhelming concentration of its population in rural areas, and the distance to theater across the Pacific could neutralize America's military superiority, while China's strategic partnership with Russia provides a protective outer ring shielding its western and northern periphery. China also has its horde of U.S. dollar reserves and Treasury bonds, Russia and Iran their oil and gas weapons.

At the same time, China has embarked on a global campaign to win the hearts and minds of the world's dispossessed in Africa, Latin America, and the Middle East by brandishing a winning combination, "socialism with Chinese characteristics," that seems to have eliminated the pitfalls of capitalism—unemployment and social exclusion—and the shortages associated with Communism. The Chinese model appears to offer phenomenal economic growth, while retaining a system of one-party, iron-fisted rule that maintains a stranglehold over free expression; Russia's Putin has adopted this approach.

**Europe.** It may be countered that a Sino-Russian alliance will be offset, or balanced, by the Atlantic Alliance—now expanded to include the 27-member European Union (EU). But it is no longer certain that America can rely on its former European allies. Some even suggest that the European Union, a "geopolitical revolution of historic dimensions,"[1] intends to become a counterweight to the United States. This discord in the Atlantic Alliance has been summarized by Robert Kagan, author of the influential *Of Paradise and Power: America and Europe in the New World Order,* who writes, "Americans are from Mars and Europeans are from Venus."[2]

In the European imagination, multilateralism and a predisposition to negotiations, diplomacy, and commercial ties based on international law distinguish Europe from the American preference to go it alone using blunt force. The Europeans think that they inhabit a Kantian universe based on laws of reason, while Americans thrive—and may perish—in a Hobbesian jungle. America's appetite for capital punishment, its super-powerful gun lobby, its boisterous patriotism and hypercompetitiveness, and lately, its ineffectual war mongering, astonish Europeans—in stark contrast to their self-described peaceful intentions.

Recent accounts of Europe's evolution focus on its development in antithesis to America: "the presumptively 'un-American' qualities of Europe were fast becoming the highest common factor in European self-identification.... Europe was—or should strive to be—everything that America wasn't."[3] According to Josef Joffe, one of Germany's most prominent commentators on foreign affairs, a basic theme throughout contemporary Europe is a sense of superiority over a morally deficient, culturally and socially retrograde, yahoo America.[4] This pancontinental anti-American mood is so pervasive that "right now many Europeans are betting that the risks from the 'axis of evil,' from terrorism and tyrants, will never be as great as the risk of an American Leviathan unbound."[5]

This is very difficult for Americans to understand, since the United States saved Europe from the Nazis, rebuilt the continent after the war, and shielded Western Europe from the Soviet menace during the Cold War. But early on Charles De Gaulle responded to the Marshall Plan as a threat to French independence; he "had long been sensitive to France's serial humiliation—less by its German foe in 1940 than at the hands of the Anglo-American alliance ever since."[6] America's stance as the champion of decolonization after WWII must have irked Europe's colonial masters, shorn of empire in succeeding decades. "When President Dwight Eisenhower undermined and humiliated Britain and France at Suez in 1956, it was only the most blatant of many American efforts to cut Europe down to size and reduce its already weakened global influence."[7] Throughout the 1960s, Europe's students rallied against the American war in Vietnam; in the early 1980s, widespread protests erupted against the placement on European soil of U.S. Pershing missiles targeted at the Soviet Union.

Europe's protection under the U.S. nuclear security umbrella during the Cold War, its strategic dependence, was an indirect subsidy, or "free ride," that accounts for the continent's economic rebirth after the war. It also created a technological gap in Europe's military capabilities that is now almost impossible to close because the diversion of scarce resources would undermine the foundation of Europe's welfare states. What is more, the eventual deployment of a U.S. nuclear missile defense shield threatens to leave Europe unprotected and vulnerable, the British and French nuclear arsenal devalued.

While the EU has grown rapidly from six founding members[8] to twenty-seven, with a combined population of more than 460 million and an annual GDP of more than $10 trillion, it is highly unlikely that the Union will be able to serve as a counterweight to the United States any time soon.

The EU has "specifically designed [the euro] to challenge the global hegemony of the U.S. dollar as the world's preferred reserve currency and as the standard unit of exchange for international financial transactions."[9] It also uses its industrial policy—government support for European firms—to counter American predominance, and has enough combined voting power to check and block the United States in international organizations, such as the UN, the World Trade Organization, and the International Monetary Fund. However, many organizational obstacles hamper its overall development and cohesion, and since each member of the Union has the power of veto, unanimity must be attained for progress on major issues. For example, in the spring of 2005, voters in France and the Netherlands—two of the founding members—rejected the proposed EU constitution.

The combined might of the EU and the UN could not stop Bosnian Serbs from slaughtering hundreds of thousands of Muslims and displacing more than 2 million people between 1991 and 1995; instead, Europeans bickered until the Clinton administration reevaluated its Bosnia policy and finally intervened. This scenario repeated itself in Kosovo in 1999, highlighting a major deficiency —the Union has "no instruments of coercion: no EU tax collectors, no EU policemen," and no army.[10] More importantly, would anyone be willing to die for a new Europe that "is fitfully undoing national sovereignty while failing to provide its citizens with a common sense of identity or collective nationhood?"[11] Even if the EU unanimously decided to build a standing army, how will it disentangle itself from NATO, and how will it recruit soldiers, when "the number of military-age young men...is expected...to decline by 22 percent in the EU-25?"[12]

Further, how will the EU finance a standing army when its revenue-raising capabilities are so constrained,[13] and when its members violate the Stability and Growth Pact's 3 percent limit on debt as a percentage of GDP, secure in the knowledge that there are no enforcement mechanisms with which to penalize them?[14] Who amongst Europe's leaders would dare to take on the European system of welfare capitalism—extensive insurance and pension coverage, subsidized health care and housing, and free education—to build an army—just as Europe's baby-boom generation prepares to retire and so will lay claim to an even larger slice of ballooning government entitlements?

The increase in the number of retirees will exacerbate projected labor shortages, particularly in the burgeoning underclass of service workers required to care for the elderly; but increased immigration from the Middle East to address these shortages will no doubt fan the flames of xenophobic nationalism espoused by Europe's right wing parties. At the same time, as traditional Europe is becoming more secular, as Christianity is withering away, Islam's appeal is expanding amongst Europe's approximately 15 million Muslims; that is why the EU is so reluctant to extend membership to Turkey and its 68 million Muslims.

But "the most significant implication of the secularization of Europe is that it deepens the divide between Europeans and Americans,"[15] especially as the prominent strain of religiosity that permeates American foreign policy has now been radicalized, mobilized, and concentrated in Dixie. "Never before has a U.S. political coalition been so dominated by an array of outsider religious denominations caught up in biblical morality, distrust of science, and a global imperative of political and religious evangelism,"[16] led by a "president [who] made it clear that he felt no doubt that a higher authority was looking after and guiding him."[17]

**India.** Finally, in view of recent developments in U.S.-Indian relations—most importantly, the U.S.-India Peaceful Atomic Energy Cooperation Act[18]—it must be asked: Would India, once the standard-bearer of the nonaligned movement and then Moscow's undeclared ally for almost twenty years, now allow itself to be used by the United States as an "India card" to counter the rise of China? Does India's historic animosity toward China outweigh its suspicions of a fickle America that has intermittently supported Pakistan, India's mortal enemy? Or might Sino-Indian rivalry itself act as a check on China's rise—irrespective of America's diplomatic maneuverings?

China, India, Pakistan, and Russia—nuclear neighbors linked by geography—represent the Sinic, Hindu, Islamic, and Orthodox civilizations. China shares a border with India, Pakistan, and Russia, and has gone to war with India in 1962 and with Russia in 1969. India and Pakistan have waged war against each other in 1947, 1965, and 1971, and were on the precipice of a nuclear confrontation after the December 2001 attack on India's parliament by Islamist guerillas based in Pakistan. Russia and India do not share a border and have never fought against each other; indeed, they were unofficial allies during much of the Cold War. China's relationship with Pakistan, however, is "of a truly special character...[and] is arguably *the most* stable and durable element of China's foreign relations."[19]

Paradoxically, America has also supported Pakistan and its periodic military dictatorships rather than India—the world's most populous parliamentary democracy. After the formation of the Baghdad Pact in 1954, the United States began supplying arms to Pakistan that better enabled Pakistan to attack India in 1965; during the ensuing war, the United States stopped "supplying India with critical electronics components,"[20] affecting India's ability to respond.

The United States also supported Pakistan in its unsuccessful bid to prevent Bangladeshi independence in 1971 by deploying the USS Enterprise task force —assumed to be armed with nuclear weapons—to the Bay of Bengal during the Indo-Pakistani War of 1971. There is "clear evidence that U.S.-supplied tanks and aircraft were being used [by Pakistan] against the Bengalis."[21]

"What Richard Nixon and Henry Kissinger intended as a political gesture to an already defeated Pakistan and a new partner, China, lives on in Indian history as a symbolic demonstration of U.S. hostility to India."[22] It also spurred India's naval buildup—with massive Soviet assistance—and played a major role in India's decision to develop its own nuclear capability so that it would never again be subjected to America's "atomic gunboat diplomacy."[23]

A summary of conversations between President Nixon and Henry Kissinger reveals their visceral dislike for the Indians—"bastards"—and their leader, Mrs. Gandhi—a "bitch."[24] President Nixon, who had been using Pakistan as a go-between for his secret opening to China, exploited the 1971 Indo-Pakistani crisis as a way to show China that Washington was a dependable ally.

Although it had been U.S. policy to block Pakistan's acquisition of plutonium, enriched uranium, and related technologies, the United States ignored China's covert support of Pakistan's nuclear ambitions after the Soviet invasion of Afghanistan in 1979 because it needed access to Pakistan as a launching pad into Afghanistan. Pakistan, then ruled by General Zia ul-Huq, used this window of opportunity to embark on a "monumental—and costly—programme of clandestine activity and it worked."[25]

The United States also began to funnel massive amounts of covert aid to Afghanistan through Pakistan's Inter-Services Intelligence (ISI) agency. This hastened an expansion of Indian-Soviet ties, and New Delhi, in turn, "embarked upon the largest conventional arms-buying spree in the Subcontinent's history."[26]

During the 1980s, Washington focused on building up the mujahideen in Afghanistan (who later formed the core of al Qaeda). But not long after the Soviet Union's retreat from Afghanistan, President George H.W. Bush suspended all military and most economic assistance to Pakistan, whose "bitter sense of betrayal after it had served Washington's interests as a frontline state"[27] may have been assuaged by the steadfastness of its reliable ally, China, who readily supplied M-11 ballistic missiles, capable of delivering Pakistan's nuclear warheads. When Pakistan responded to India's nuclear tests with its own tests in May 1998,

"India's conventional military superiority over Pakistan had at a stroke been converted into a level nuclear field. China, meanwhile, which had all but arranged Pakistan's nuclear capability, remains many years—and possibly decades—in advance of India's nuclear capabilities."[28]

After 9/11, another Pakistani military dictatorship—this time under General Pervez Musharraf—made itself indispensible to Washington, and "there was a sense of déjà vu by May of 2002. For not only was the United States back in Pakistan, and, even more self-consciously, in Afghanistan, but the mujahideen armies, the warlords, and tribal chiefs whom Washington had sponsored twenty years ago, to such disastrous effect, had largely been returned to power in Afghanistan—by the United States."[29] What's more, without any forewarning to India, the Bush II administration designated Pakistan a "major non-NATO ally."

With all of this in mind, the historical record suggests that Sino-Pakistani, Russian-Indian, and Sino-Russian relations are by far the strongest bilateral relationships amongst the five nuclear powers under discussion here (China, India, Pakistan, Russia, the United States), while Indian-Pakistani relations are fraught with danger: Kashmir is to Indian-Pakistani relations what Taiwan is to Sino-American relations—a potential nuclear trigger. U.S. relations with both China and Russia have been addressed in other parts of this book, and Pakistani-Russian relations are a wildcard—which leaves the Sino-Indian relationship.

Although this is not the book to examine the history of Sino-Indian relations,[30] for the first time in more than five hundred years, China and India are emerging as aspiring regional hegemons at the same time—China in East Asia and the East and South China Seas, India in South Asia and the Indian Ocean. This historical coincidence is aggravated by global competition for scarce energy resources—especially from the Middle East—to fuel unprecedented economic growth in both countries: China has averaged 9.7 percent annual growth from 1991–2003, India 5.8 percent for the same period. By 2025, China and India will need to import more than 75 percent of their oil.

As a result, China has been establishing a vast network of land and sea lines of communication—a "string of pearls"[31]—that could serve as alternate transport routes from the Middle East. The Sino-Pakistani entente, the linchpin of this strategy, provides China with access to a deepwater seaport at Gwadar, close to the Strait of Hormuz in the Persian Gulf—through which 40 percent of the world's oil passes. From the port of Gwadar, the Makran Coastal Highway provides a direct link to Karachi, an ideal forward logistics base; this landline of communication extends north to the Chinese-built Sino-Pakistani Friendship Highway, leading all the way to China's Xinjiang Province. China has already spent hundreds of millions of dollars on these infrastructure projects; and "Beijing has provided more military assistance to Pakistan than it has to any other state."[32] In the event China's access to Pakistan's ports was blocked by, say, India,

**Table 11.1   China-India Balance Sheet**

| | China (1949) | India (1947) |
|---|---|---|
| Form of government | Chinese Communist Party | Parliamentary federal democracy ruled by fractious coalitions |
| Population (% world total) | Homogenous: 1.3 billion (21%) | Diverse: 1.1 billion (17%) |
| Average age | 33 | 26 |
| Life expectancy | 71 | 63 |
| Sex ratio (men : women) | 118:100 | 108:100 |
| Rural population | 60–70% | 68–72% |
| Muslims | ≤ 35 million (2.6%), concentrated in Xinjiang province | 150 million (13–14%), dispersed; majority Sunni |
| Economic reforms launched | 1978 | 1991 |
| Average annual growth rate | 9.7% (1991–2003) | 5.8% (1991–2003) |
| GDP per head (U.S.$ at PPP, 2005) | 6,292 | 3,492 |
| Agricultural as % of GDP | 15–16% | 22% |
| Defense spending as % of GDP | 2.1% (Western estimate) | 15% (2003) |
| Consumption as % of GDP | 42% | 66% |
| Literacy rate (Female literacy) | >90% (87%) | 65% (45%) |
| Middle Class | ≈ 100 million | 200–300 million |
| % living on $1 per day | 17% | 35% |
| Active workforce | 800–900 million | 470 million |
| Oil imports 2004/2025 | 48% / 77% | 68% / 80% |
| Economic characteristics | Hardware: "sweatshops" Labor-intensive Manufacturing Brawn | Software: "technocoolies" Capital-intensive Service sector Brains |
| Strengths | Nuclear capability, possibly decades ahead of India; seat on UNSC | English-language speakers |

| Weaknesses | Banking system – Nonperforming loans Floating population: 100–150 million Aging population: dependency ratio Corruption | Hierarchical caste system Bureaucracy: remnants of license Raj Infrastructure Elementary education Corruption |
| --- | --- | --- |
| Territorial dispute: a swap? | Aksai Chin (Western sector) | Arunachal Pradesh (Eastern sector) |
| Sore spots | Tibet – the Dalai Lama | Sikkim – Nathu La Pass |
| Nuclear flashpoints | With U.S. over Taiwan | With Pakistan over Kashmir |
| Recent wars | India (1962), USSR (1969), Vietnam (1979) | China (1962), Pakistan (1947, 1965, 1971) |
| Major treaties with Russia | *Treaty of Good Neighborliness, Friendship, and Cooperation* 2001 | *Friendship and Cooperation Treaty* 1993 Declaration of Strategic Partnership 2003 |
| How many in U.S.? | *ABCs = 1.8 million | *PIOs = 2 million |
| Other | East-West divide (coastal vs. inland) | British influence/ Anglophone elites Nehru-Gandhi dynasty North-South divide Bollywood |

*ABC: American-born Chinese; PIO: People of Indian Origins.

*Notes:* Sino-Indian trade grew from $2.6 billion to $20 billion in 2006, and India's population is expected to surpass China's by 2030–2035. If current demographic trends continue, this trade relationship will become the world's largest, leading to speculation that a Sino-Indian Free Trade Agreement may be in the offing.

*Sources:* Economist Intelligence Unit, *Country Profile 2006–China* and *Country Profile 2006–India;* Edward Luce, *In Spite of the Gods: The Strange Rise of Modern India* (New York: Doubleday, 2007); "The Tiger in Front: A Survey of India and China," *The Economist,* March 5, 2005, and The World Bank, *World Development Indicators 2006,* available at http://devdata.worldbank.org/wdi2006/contents/cover.htm, last accessed April 2007.


China has also arranged for access to Iran's naval base, Bandar Beheshti, on the Gulf of Oman.

To India's east in Myanmar, China's "corridor to the sea" and a traditional tributary, the People's Republic has been supplying the country's ruling junta with massive amounts of military assistance. This may have influenced the government of Myanmar to sign a deal with PetroChina in late 2005 to supply natural gas from the Shwe field—an offshore field in the Bay of Bengal—via an eight hundred kilometer pipeline from Sittwe to Kunming, China.[33] Myanmar has also reportedly allowed the PRC to build a naval base on Hainggyi Island and a radar installation/listening post on one of the Coco Islands in the Andaman Sea.[34]

While relations between India and Bangladesh have been more strained since the Bangladeshi Nationalist Party came to power in 2001, China has recently expanded relations with Bangladesh by agreeing to construct a highway linking Chittagong (Bangladesh), Mandalay (Myanmar), and Kunming (China). It has also been reported that Bangladesh "offered China naval access to its prized Chittagong port, which India has long but unsuccessfully sought."[35] China is also "the largest and most important provider of the latter's [Bangladesh's] military hardware and training of its armed forces."[36] This goes a long in explaining how China supplanted India as Bangladesh's largest trading partner in 2005.

Other "pearls" in China's string include plans for a proposed railway line from southern China through Cambodia to the sea; and in Thailand, a $20 billion canal across the Kra Isthmus is under consideration.

India has responded to this perceived encirclement by a Beijing-Islamabad-Yangon-led axis with a "new balancing act [that] combines appeasement of China...with the pursuit of improved ties with China's other potential balancers, especially Vietnam and Russia."[37] India has also been strengthening its ties with the Himalayan buffer states: Sikkim—annexed by India in 1975, Bhutan—an Indian protectorate, and Nepal—although seeking to balance between China and India—closer to India.

India is also seeking to diversify its energy sources and has approached Iran about a $4 billion, 2,775-kilometer gas pipeline that would run from Iran through Pakistan to India. India's state-owned Oil & Natural Gas Corporation (ONGC) regularly goes up against one or another of China's state-owned oil companies, igniting bidding wars for deals all over the world—and China usually trumps India. For example, in 2004, Sinopec nudged aside ONGC for a 50 percent stake in an exploration project in Angola's Block 18 by sweetening its bid with a $2 billion aid offer;[38] in 2005, China National Petroleum Corporation (CNPC) outbid ONGC for Canadian-owned PetroKazakhstan. And China "won" the right to help the Russian oil giant, Rosneft, acquire Yuganskneftegaz —the most productive subsidiary of beleaguered Yukos—by loaning $6 billion to Rosneft in exchange for future crude deliveries.[39]

To provide for their future national security imperatives—which includes secure supply routes—China and India have embarked on long-term programs to develop bluewater naval capabilities. Russia has again maneuvered itself into the position of "swing" player as the leading arms merchant to China and India, and so influences their pace of naval development. By the late 1990s, more than 70 percent of China and India's imported arms came from Russia.[40] Russia is in the enviable position of selling China the arms that Pakistan uses to neutralize the weapons purchased by India from Russia.

China and India are also competing in the United Nations, where India has been angling for a permanent seat on the Security Council since it can no longer depend on Russia to exercise its veto on India's behalf. China, however, is perceived to be blocking India because it wants to protect its status as the only nonwhite and Asian power with a permanent seat.

Vestiges of India's heritage of nonviolence and nonalignment, of its image as a moral and spiritual force, suggest that it may try to balance between the United States and China—thereby strengthening Russia's status as the crucial "swing" player in great power politics; Russia is closer to both India and China than all three are to the United States. In any event, there is no evidence that India would throw its weight behind the United States if a conflict erupted between the United States and China. To the contrary, Stephen P. Cohen, a leading scholar on India and author of *India: Emerging Power,* concludes, India "could side with Beijing (and Russia) to challenge the American-dominated alliance system in East and Southeast Asia."[41]

Russia's influential "India lobby" has been focused on arranging just that outcome. Russia and India conducted several joint military exercises in 2005,[42] and during Prime Minister Singh's visit to Moscow in December 2005, he "reinforced India's military ties with Russia, signing several agreements that will transform the relationship from one of military-technical cooperation to the joint development and production of next-generation weapons systems."[43]

On February 10, 2007, Russia's president, Vladimir Putin, publicly chastised America at a security conference in Munich. Putin, a fluent German speaker from his days in Dresden as a KGB operative, must have reveled in the irony of delivering this landmark speech—compared to Churchill's Iron Curtain Speech of 1946 and Khrushchev's shoe moment at the U.N. in 1960—on NATO turf in a Germany hooked on Russian oil.

Several days later the foreign ministers of Russia, China, and India held another tripartite conference, this time in New Delhi.[44] The next day, Putin elevated Defense Minister Sergei Ivanov—a proponent of triangular defense cooperation between Beijing, Moscow, and New Delhi—to the position of First Deputy Prime Minister. Ivanov, also groomed in the former KGB and a member of Putin's St. Petersburg clique, is one of two favorites touted as Putin's successor in 2008.[45]

All of this smacks of the imprimatur of Yevgeny Primakov—Russia's Kissinger and architect of the Primakov Doctrine espousing a Sino-Russian-Indian alliance against Western unilateralism. Primakov, reputed to be a former KGB field agent in the Middle East, friend of Saddam Hussein, spy chief, prime minister, presidential aspirant, and doyen of Russia's Sinologists—must be delighted that the once-disgraced KGB has infiltrated the key levers of government, brought the oligarchs to heel, seized Russia's energy behemoths, and taken control of the Kremlin. The most sinister and reviled organ of Soviet power has engineered a silent coup and neutered all forms of opposition. But will Primakov's grand design come to pass?

*

Gaddis, in *The Cold War: A New History*, identified three major structural transformations of that epochal conflict: the collapse of the Sino-Soviet alliance, the U.S. opening to China, and the breakup of the Soviet Union.[46]

The United States has proclaimed victory in the Cold War and pundits refer to a post-Cold War era but Asia remains mired in the vestiges of that conflict. Taiwan's ambiguously defined status, a divided Korea, an unresolved territorial dispute between Russia and Japan,[47] and Communist regimes ensconced in the hermit kingdom of North Korea, and in Vietnam, are all remnants of the Cold War.

A rising and resentful China in partnership with a resurgent Russia set amidst this "cauldron of civilizations"[48] may well signal the fourth great transformation of the Cold War and become the key to victory in *The Next Great Clash*.

# NOTES

## CHAPTER 1

1. Dan N. Jacobs, *Borodin: Stalin's Man in China* (Cambridge, MA: Harvard University Press, 1981), viii.
2. Several details have been changed to protect the identity of "Sharon."
3. Zhenya and Natasha are not their real names.
4. Thunderbird School of Global Management, located in Glendale, Arizona, was originally founded in 1946 as the American Institute for Foreign Trade.
5. Michael D. Swaine and Ashley J. Tellis, *Interpreting China's Grand Strategy: Past, Present and Future* (Santa Monica, CA: RAND, 2000), 220n111.

## CHAPTER 2

1. George Modelski and William R. Thompson, *Leading Sectors and World Powers: The Coevolution of Global Politics and Economics* (Columbia: University of South Carolina Press, 1996), 55.
2. Named after Nikolai Kondratieff (1892–1938), founder of the Moscow Business Conditions Institute in 1920; he was arrested in 1930 and executed in 1938 during Stalin's purges.
3. Modelski and Thompson, *Leading Sectors,* 106.
4. Ibid., 106. The authors point out that "the only exception is the 1560s Dutch peak that is one decade off from the generalization."
5. Ibid., 175.
6. Ibid., 222–23.
7. Philip Bobbitt, *The Shield of Achilles: War, Peace and the Course of History* (New York: Knopf, 2002), xxi.
8. Ibid., xxvii.
9. Ibid., xxiv.

10. Ibid., 689–90.

11. John J. Mearsheimer, *The Tragedy of Great Power Politics* (New York: W.W. Norton, 2001).

12. Ibid., 83.

13. With these two exceptions: the U.S. naval blockade of Japan during World War II; and NATO's strategic bombing of Kosovo in 1999. On naval blockades, see Mearsheimer, *Tragedy of Great Power Politics,* 90–96; on strategic bombing, see Mearsheimer, *Tragedy of Great Power Politics,* 99–110.

14. Japan's defeat is attributed to the combined effect of the U.S. naval blockade, the massive strategic fire-bombing of Japanese cities, the use of atomic weapons on Hiroshima and Nagasaki, and the Soviet Union's attack against the Japanese army in Manchuria during the last days of the war. On wars between the great powers, see Mearsheimer, *Tragedy of Great Power Politics,* 110–14.

15. In only one of those instances was a great power, Russia, attacked from the sea (during the Crimean War, Russia was invaded from the Black Sea).

16. Mearsheimer, *Tragedy of Great Power Politics,* 41.

17. Ibid., 356.

18. See Table 9.3, "Summary of European Wars by System Structure," in Mearsheimer, *Tragedy of Great Power Politics,* 357.

19. Ibid., 135.

20. See A. F. K. Organski and Jack Kugler, *The War Ledger* (Chicago: University of Chicago Press, 1980), 19–28.

21. Ibid., 28.

22. Ibid., 61.

23. Organski and Kugler, "David and Goliaths: Predicting the Outcomes of International Wars," in *The War Ledger,* chap. 2.

24. Paul Kennedy, *The Rise and Fall of the Great Powers: Economic Change and Military Conflict from 1500 to 2000* (New York: Random House, 1987), 417.

25. Organski and Kugler, *War Ledger,* 60.

26. Ibid., 164–76.

27. Ibid., 161.

28. Ibid., 177.

29. Ibid., 27.

30. Samuel P. Huntington, *The Clash of Civilizations and the Remaking of the World Order* (New York: Simon & Schuster, 1996), 209.

31. Ibid., 51.

32. David B. Abernethy, *Dynamics of Global Dominance: European Overseas Empires 1415–1980* (New Haven, CT: Yale University Press, 2000). See chap. 10, "The Institutional Basis for the Triple Assault," 225–53.

33. Huntington, *Clash,* 103.

34. In a survey of China's foreign policy crises during the 50-year period from 1929 to 1979. See Jonathan Wilkenfeld, Michael Brecher, and Sheila Moser, eds., *Crises in the Twentieth Century, Volume II: Handbook of Foreign Policy Crises* (Oxford: Pergamon, 1988), 161.

35. Dominic Lieven, *Empire: The Russian Empire and Its Rivals* (London: John Murray, 2000), 70–71.

36. Abernethy, *Global Dominance,* 225–53.

37. Ibid., 12.

38. Ibid., 345.

39. Albania, Bulgaria, Czechoslovakia (later split into the Czech Republic and Slovakia), East Germany, Hungary, Poland, and Romania.

40. To eventually become the independent countries of Bosnia–Herzegovina, Croatia, Macedonia, Serbia–Montenegro, and Slovenia.

41. Lieven, *Empire,* 386.

42. Abernethy, *Global Dominance,* 378.

43. Karl E. Meyer, *The Dust of Empire: The Race for Mastery in the Asian Heartland* (New York: Public Affairs, 2003), 89.

44. Michael T. Klare, *Resource Wars: The New Landscape of Global Conflict* (New York: Metropolitan Books, 2001).

45. See *BP Statistical Review of World Energy June 2005,* 9.

46. See the U.S. Department of Energy, Energy Information Administration (DoE EIA), *International Energy Outlook 2005,* Table A4, "World Oil Consumption by Region, Reference Case," available at http://www.eia.doe.gov/oiaf/ieo/ieorefcase.html (last accessed April 2007).

47. Sadad al-Husseini, formerly Saudi Aramco's most senior executive for exploration and production, has stated, "the world will need...to pump an additional six to eight million barrels a day"—or 2.19 to 2.92 billion barrels annually—to meet replacement needs. See Peter Maass, "The Beginning of the End of Oil," *New York Times Magazine,* August 21, 2005, 56.

48. Robert L. Hirsch, "Peaking of World Oil Production: Impacts, Mitigation, & Risk Management" (aka "The Hirsch Report"), February 2005, 64. This report was commissioned by the U.S. Department of Energy's National Energy Technology Laboratory and produced under the auspices of Science Applications International Corporation (SAIC). Full text available at http://www.energybulletin.net/4638.html (last accessed April 2007).

49. Maass, "Beginning of the End," 33.

50. Charles T. Maxwell, "The Gathering Storm," *Barron's,* November 15, 2004. Full text available at http://www.energybulletin.net/3161.html (last accessed April 2007). This topic is also discussed in Clyde Prestowitz, "Cheap No More," in *Three Billion New Capitalists: The Great Shift of Wealth and Power to the East* (New York: Basic Books, 2005), chap. 8. For a summary of peaking forecasts, see Hirsch, "Peaking of World Oil Production," Table II-1, "Projections of the Peaking of World Oil Production," 19.

51. OPEC currently produces approximately 28 million bpd (36 percent of demand) and by 2025 is expected to increase output to 60 million bpd, or 50 percent of demand.

52. See International Energy Agency (IEA), "Executive Summary," in *World Energy Investment Outlook 2003,* (Paris: IEA, 2003), 33, cited in Michael T. Klare, *Blood and Oil: The Dangers and Consequences of America's Growing Dependency on Imported Petroleum* (New York: Metropolitan Books, 2004), 123n28.

53. Hirsch, "Peaking of World Oil Production," 65.

54. Ibid., 31.

55. According to the U.S. Department of Energy, Energy Information Administration, *Country Analysis Briefs: United States* (last updated November 2005), natural gas comprises 23 percent, coal about 22 percent, nuclear power about 8 percent, hydroelectricity about 3 percent, and other forms about 1 percent.

56. Ibid., 3.

57. Philip Andrews-Speed, Xuanli Liao, and Roland Dannreuther, "The Strategic Implications of China's Energy Needs," in *Adelphi Paper 346* (London: Oxford University Press for The International Institute of Strategic Studies, July 2002), 74–75.

58. Robert A. Manning, *The Asian Energy Factor: Myths and Dilemmas of Energy, Security, and the Pacific Future* (New York: Palgrave/St. Martin's, 2000), 93.

59. Kent E. Calder, *Pacific Destiny: Arms, Energy, and America's Future in Asia* (New York: William Morrow & Company, 1996), 200.

60. Ibid., 127.

## CHAPTER 3

1. Kennedy, *Rise and Fall of the Great Powers,* 515.

2. John Lewis Gaddis, *Surprise, Security, and the American Experience* (Cambridge: Harvard University Press, 2004), 101.

3. Zbigniew Brzezinski, *The Choice: Global Domination or Global Leadership* ( New York: Basic Books, 2004), 17.

4. According to James Mann, *Rise of the Vulcans: The History of Bush's War Cabinet* (New York: Viking, 2004), 252, the original eight foreign policy advisers during George W. Bush's first presidential campaign called themselves Vulcans after a statue in the center of Condoleezza Rice's hometown, Birmingham, Alabama. This group consisted of Richard Armitage, Robert Blackwill, Stephen Hadley, Richard Perle, Rice, Paul Wolfowitz, Dov Zakheim, and Robert Zoellick.

5. Walter Isaacson and Evan Thomas, *The Wise Men: Six Friends and the World They Made: Acheson, Bohlen, Harriman, Kennan, Lovett, McCloy* (New York: Simon & Schuster, 1986).

6. David Halberstam, *The Best and the Brightest* (New York: Random House, 1972), which focuses on the role that Robert McNamara, the Bundy brothers, Dean Rusk, George Ball, William Westmoreland, Maxwell Taylor, John Kennedy, and Lyndon Johnson all played in the formulation of U.S. foreign policy during the Vietnam era.

7. Mann points out the distinction between the "Wise Men," the "Best and the Brightest," and the Vulcans in *Rise of the Vulcans,* "Introduction."

8. Mann, *Rise of the Vulcans,* 52. Secretary Rumsfeld at Defense resigned after the 2006 midterm elections, Secretary of State Powell resigned after the 2004 general election, Paul Wolfowitz was reassigned as president of the World Bank (and as of April 2007 was embroiled in a scandal that led to his resignation), and Richard Armitage resigned from the State Department not long after Secretary Powell.

9. For example, National Security Advisor Henry Kissinger's end-runs around Secretary of State William Rogers and then Kissinger's battle with Melvin Laird and James Schlesinger at Defense; Zbigniew Brzezinski's battles with Cyrus Vance—and Vance's resignation over the U.S. attempt to rescue the American hostages in Iran; and the chronic feud between George Shultz and Casper Weinberger during the Reagan era. The Clinton administration was an exception first with its creation of a National Economic Council (NEC) lead by Robert Rubin and then Rubin's appointment as Secretary of the Treasury during a period in which global economic crises, and Rubin, captured the agenda. George W. Bush's administration downgraded the NEC in favor of the National Security Council (NSC). For the history and evolution of the NSC, see David J. Rothkopf, *Running the World: The Inside Story of the National Security Council and the Architects of American Power* (New York: Public Affairs, 2005).

10. Secretary Powell resigned on January 26, 2005; Donald Rumsfeld was a wrestler in high school and college. David Von Drahle, "Wrestling with History," *Washington Post Magazine,* November 13, 2005.

11. Clark Clifford, Melvin Laird, Elliott Richardson, James Schlesinger (no), Donald Rumsfeld, Harold Brown (no), Casper Weinberger, Frank Carlucci (no), Richard Cheney, Les Aspin, William Perry (no), William Cohen, and Donald Rumsfeld; this observation attributed to Harold Brown in Rothkopf, *Running the World,* 179. Shortly after the November 2006 midterm elections, in which the Democrats regained control of the House and the Senate, Donald Rumsfeld resigned as Secretary of Defense. President George W. Bush nominated Robert M. Gates, a career intelligence officer and former Director of the Central Intelligence Agency, to succeed Rumsfeld; after confirmation hearings, Gates was sworn in on December 18, 2006.

12. It is striking how many of the leading intellectual figures of the neoconservative movement have been succeeded (usurped) by their sons, whom in most cases are more radical than their fathers. For example, Norman and John Podhoretz, Irving and William Kristol, Donald, Robert and Frederick Kagan, Richard and Daniel Pipes. For more details, see Andrew J. Bacevich, "Left, Right, Left," in *The New American Militarism: How Americans Are Seduced by War* (New York: Oxford University Press, 2005), chap. 3.

13. Abba Eban, *Diplomacy for the Next Century* (New Haven, CT: Yale University Press, 1998), 91.

14. For more on Ford's "Halloween Massacre," see Mann, "Combating the Soviets, Détente, and Henry Kissinger," in *Rise of the Vulcans,* chap. 4.

15. See especially Jeffrey Goldberg, "Breaking Ranks: What Turned Brent Scowcroft Against the Bush Administration?" *New Yorker,* October 31, 2005. There are indications that Scowcroft has regained some influence within the Republican elite, especially as his protégé and former Deputy National Security Adviser, Robert M. Gates, was appointed to succeed Rumsfeld at the Department of Defense in December 2006. Scowcroft and Gates served together during the administration of George H. W. Bush.

16. Anne Norton, *Leo Strauss and the Politics of American Empire* (New Haven, CT: Yale University Press, 2004).

17. Bacevich, *New American Militarism,* 146.

18. Norton, *Leo Strauss,* 110.

19. According to comparisons in data presented in International Institute of Strategic Studies, *The Military Balance 2002/2003 and 2003/2004.*

20. According to the U.S. Department of Defense's *Worldwide Manpower Distribution by Geographical Area* of September 2004, of the 458,449 U.S. troops stationed abroad, 170,647 were deployed in Afghanistan, Iraq, and Kuwait.

21. According to the U.S. Department of Defense's *Base Structure Report* of September 2004, almost 79 percent of those bases are concentrated in four countries: Germany (302), Japan (111), South Korea (106), and Italy (61). I am indebted to Chalmers Johnson, *The Sorrows of Empire: Militarism, Secrecy, and the End of the Republic* (New York: Metropolitan Books/Henry Holt, 2004), especially chap. 6, "The Empire of Bases," for referring to these Department of Defense resources.

22. See Paul Kennedy, "The Eagle Has Landed," *Financial Times,* January 31, 2002.

23. According to *The Military Balance 2003/2004,* each of the following countries has one aircraft carrier battle group: Brazil, India, Italy, Russia, Spain, Thailand (serviceability in doubt); the United Kingdom maintains three carrier battle groups, although one is being refitted.

24. Dana Priest, *The Mission: Waging War and Keeping Peace with America's Military* (New York: W. W. Norton, 2003), 17.

25. See Chalmers Johnson, "Stealth Imperialism," in *Blowback: The Costs and Consequences of American Empire* (New York: Henry Holt, 2000), chap. 3 and Johnson, *Sorrows of Empire,* 140.

26. For example, the Egyptian armed services is "propped up by $1.3 billion annually in U.S. military aid," according to *Washington Post,* December 17, 2003, A34. In addition, $8.2 billion for international assistance was requested in the 2004 Defense Department budget for such activities as foreign military financing and economic support to countries such as Afghanistan, Egypt, Israel, Jordan, and Turkey. See *The Military Balance 2003/2004,* 237.

27. *The Military Balance 2003/2004,* 341.

28. Johnson, *Sorrows of Empire,* 137.

29. At least ninety-three SOFAs acknowledged as of September 2001 according to Johnson, *Sorrows of Empire,* 36.

30. *The Military Balance 2003/2004,* 14. Romania and Bulgaria joined NATO in May 2004.

31. Johnson, *Sorrows of Empire,* 146.

32. Bradley Graham, "Rumsfeld Discusses Tighter Military Ties with Azerbaijan," *Washington Post,* December 4, 2003, A23.

33. William D. Hartung, Frida Berrigan, and Michelle Ciarroca, "Operation Endless Deployment," *Nation,* October 21, 2002, 24.

34. Peter Slevin, "Powell Decries Putin's Policies," *Washington Post,* January 27, 2004, A14.

35. Ilham Aliyev, 42, inaugurated in October 2003 as Azerbaijan's president following elections marred by accusations of widespread fraud, succeeded his father Haidar, who recently died in a Cleveland hospital while being treated for heart disease. In Georgia, former President Shevardnadze was forced from office on November 23, 2003. Mikhail Saakashvili, (b. 1967), the leader of Georgia's "Rose Revolution," is a U.S.-trained lawyer educated at George Washington University and Columbia Law School; he was inaugurated as Georgia's new president on January 25, 2004. Secretary of State Colin Powell attended the inauguration ceremony as the guest of honor.

36. *The Military Balance 2003/2004,* 14.

37. Hartung, Berrigan, and Ciarroca, "Operation Endless Deployment," 24.

38. Robert D. Kaplan, *Imperial Grunts: The American Military on the Ground* (New York: Random House, 2005), 289.

39. Economist Intelligence Unit, *Country Profile 2005—Ethiopia,* 16.

40. Economist Intelligence Unit, *Country Profile 2005—Kenya,* 13.

41. Kaplan, *Imperial Grunts,* 293–94.

42. Priest, *Mission,* 180. Nigeria is not officially a part of Centcom's area of responsibility.

43. Hartung, Berrigan, and Ciarroca "Operation Endless Deployment," 23.

44. Kaplan, *Imperial Grunts,* 30.

45. Stratfor, "U.S. Strategic Plan for the 21st Century: The Pacific, Part II," November 19, 2003.

46. See Priest, "The Indonesian Handshake," *Mission,* chap. 10.

47. Stratfor, "When Is 'Not a Base' Still a Base for US?" September 3, 2002.

48. Kaplan, *Imperial Grunts,* 101.

49. Stratfor, "Not a Base."

50. Stratfor, "Strategic Plan."

51. "Our Man in Bangkok," *Washington Post,* December 26, 2003, A34.

52. Priest, *Mission,* 198.

53. Ibid., 205.

54. Ibid., 208.

55. Kaplan, *Imperial Grunts,* 60.

56. Mark Danner, "Abu Ghraib: The Hidden Story," *New York Review of Books* 51, no. 15 (October 7, 2004).

57. Jane Mayer, "Outsourcing Torture," *New Yorker,* February 14, 2005.

58. Michael Ignatieff, "The Burden," *New York Times Magazine,* January 5, 2003, 50.

59. William Perry, Chair, National Security Advisory Group, "An American Security Policy: Challenge, Opportunity, Commitment," July 2003, 42.

60. Jeffrey E. Garten, "A Foreign Policy Harmful to Business," *Business Week,* October 14, 2002, 72–76.

61. Fareed Zakaria, "The Arrogant Empire," *Newsweek,* March 24, 2003, 18–33.

62. Michael Howard, *The Lessons of History* (New Haven, CT: Yale University Press, 1991), 136.

63. Ignatieff, "Burden," 24.

64. Michael Howard, "Smoke on the Horizon," *Financial Times,* September 6, 2002.

65. Based on data in *The Military Balance 2003/2004,* 335, 340.

66. Kennedy, "The Eagle Has Landed."

67. An estimated seventy-nine million baby boomers were born in the United States between 1946 and 1964 and so will most likely enter the ranks of America's retirees from 2011 to 2029.

68. According to *The Military Balance 2003/2004,* 233, total U.S. national defense budget requests (including the Department of Defense, defense-related activities in the Department of Energy and other defense-related activities) for 2004–2008 are as follows: for 2004, $401 billion (does not include anticipated supplemental appropriations for Iraq and Afghanistan); for 2005, $420 billion; for 2006, $440 billion; for 2007, $460 billion; and for 2008, $481 billion. The budget request for 2004 was approved by Congress and was signed into law by President Bush on November 24, 2003.

69. Peter G. Peterson, *Gray Dawn: How the Coming Age Wave Will Transform America—and the World* (New York: Times Books/Random House, 1999), 197.

70. Ibid., 14.

71. Ibid., 100. Note that this book was published in 1999 and so the estimate of $10 trillion has undoubtedly increased.

72. Ibid, 108.

73. China's total includes Hong Kong. Data available on the U.S. Treasury Department Web site at http://www.treas.gov/tic/mfh.txt (last accessed April 2007).

74. David Calleo, *Rethinking Europe's Future* (Princeton, NJ: Princeton University Press, 2001), 367.

75. Peter F. Drucker, *Management Challenges for the 21st Century* (New York: Harper Business, 1999), 44.

76. Peterson, *Gray Dawn,* 228.

77. Ibid., 115, estimates that Social Security outlays will exceed revenues by 2013, but his book was published in 1999. The Social Security Administration estimates that this will occur in 2016.

78. Ibid., 232.

79. Swaine and Tellis, *Interpreting China's Grand Strategy,* 229.

## CHAPTER 4

1. Gari Ledyard, "Yin and Yang in the China–Manchuria–Korea Triangle," in *China among Equals: The Middle Kingdom and Its Neighbors, 10th–14th Centuries,* ed. Morris Rossabi (Berkeley: University of California Press, 1983), 313.

2. Swaine and Tellis, *Interpreting China's Grand Strategy,* 46–47.

3. Ledyard, "Yin and Yang," 339.

4. Mark Mancall, *China at the Center: 300 Years of Foreign Policy* (New York: Free Press, 1984), xiii.

5. Ian Buruma, *Inventing Japan: 1853–1964* (New York: Modern Library, 2003), 28.

6. Michael H. Hunt, "Chinese Foreign Relations in Historical Perspective," in *China's Foreign Relations in the 1980s,* ed. Harry Harding (New Haven, CT: Yale University Press, 1984), 2.

7. John King Fairbank and Merle Goldman, *China: A New History* (Boston, MA: Harvard University Press, 1998), 234.

8. Elizabeth Wishnick, *Mending Fences: The Evolution of Moscow's China Policy from Brezhnev to Yeltsin* (Seattle: University of Washington Press, 2001), 28.

9. Buruma, *Inventing Japan,* 50.

10. Warren I. Cohen, "The Foreign Impact on East Asia," in *Historical Perspectives in Contemporary East Asia,* eds. Merle Goldman and Andrew Gordon (Cambridge, MA: Harvard University Press, 2000), 11.

11. Points I and V, respectively, of Wilson's Fourteen Points.

12. Margaret MacMillan, *Paris 1919: Six Months That Changed the World* (New York: Random House, 2001), 330.

13. Robert A. Pastor, "The United States: Divided by a Revolutionary Vision," in *A Century's Journey: How the Great Powers Shape the World,* ed. Robert A. Pastor (New York: Basic Books, 1999), 214.

14. Cohen, "Foreign Impact," 21.

15. Mancall, *China at the Center,* 297.

16. Alastair Iain Johnston, "China's Militarized Interstate Dispute Behavior 1949–1992: A First Cut at the Data," *China Quarterly,* no. 153 (March 1998): 2.

17. Gerald Segal, "East Asia and the 'Constrainment' of China," *International Security* 20, no. 4 (Spring 1996): 110.

18. On this point, see Andrew J. Nathan and Robert S. Ross, "Policy-Making," in *The Great Wall and the Empty Fortress: China's Search for Security* (New York: W. W. Norton, 1997), chap. 7.

19. Calder, *Pacific Destiny,* 105.

20. Robert S. Ross, "The Geography of the Peace," *International Security* 23, no. 4 (Spring 1999): 103.

21. John King Fairbank, "A Preliminary Framework," in *The Chinese World Order: Traditional China's Foreign Relations,* ed. John King Fairbank (Cambridge, MA: Harvard University Press, 1968), 1–19. See especially Table 2, "Aims and Means in China's Foreign Relations," 13.

22. Mark Mancall, "The Ch'ing Tribute System: An Interpretive Essay," in *The Chinese World Order: Traditional China's Foreign Relations,* ed. John K. Fairbank (Cambridge, MA: Harvard University Press, 1968), 82.

23. Ross, "The Geography of the Peace," 104.

24. "A *foreign policy crisis,* that is, a crisis viewed from the perspective of an individual state, is a situation with three necessary and sufficient conditions deriving from change in a state's

external or internal environment. All three are perceptions held by the highest level decision-makers of the actor concerned: a *threat to basic values,* along with the awareness of *finite time for response* to the external value threat, and a *high probability of involvement in military hostilities.*" See Jonathan Wilkenfeld, Michael Brecher, and Sheila Moser, eds., *Crises in the Twentieth Century, Volume I: Handbook of International Crises* (Oxford: Pergamon, 1988), 3. For an analysis of China's responses to these crises, see Wilkenfeld, Brecher, and Moser, *Crises in the Twentieth Century,* 160–64.

25. India, Japan (all in the 1930s), Taiwan, the Soviet Union, the United States, and Vietnam.

26. Wilkenfeld, Brecher, and Moser, *Crises, Volume II,* 161.

27. Ibid., 162.

28. Ibid., 162.

29. Johnston, "Militarized Interstate Dispute." The group of "leading powers" considered in this study are China, France, India, the Soviet Union, the United Kingdom, and the United States. *Militarized Interstate Disputes* are defined as "united historical cases in which the threat, display or use of military force short of war by one member is explicitly directed towards the government, official representatives, official forces, property, or territory of another state." Johnston, p. 5; in n. 7, attributed to Stuart Bremer, J. David Singer, and Dan Jones, "Militarized Interstate Disputes, 1816–1992: Rationale, Coding Rules and Statistical Findings," mimeo, February 1996, 6.

30. Ibid., 14.

31. Ibid., 2.

32. H. Lyman Miller and Liu Xiaohong, "The Foreign Policy Outlook of China's 'Third Generation' Elite," in *The Making of Chinese Foreign and Security Policy in the Era of Reform,* ed. David Lampton (Stanford, CA: Stanford University Press, 2001), 140.

33. For a lengthier discussion of these events, see chap. 8, "Maotai and Vodka: The Communist Dynasty."

34. Nathan and Ross, *Great Wall,* xiii.

35. See John Shy and Thomas W. Collier, "Revolutionary War," in *Makers of Modern Strategy: From Machiavelli to the Nuclear Age,* ed. Peter Paret (Princeton, NJ: Princeton University Press, 1986), 815–62.

36. Ho later came to resent China's omnipresence in Vietnam's affairs, and said, "it is better to sniff French shit for a while than to eat China's for the rest of our lives." Cited in William Duiker, *Ho Chi Minh* (New York: Hyperion, 2000), 361.

37. See Michael Mandelbaum, "China, 1949–1976: The Strategies of Weakness," in *The Fate of Nations* (New York: Cambridge University Press, 1988), chap. 4.

38. Gerald Segal, *Defending China* (New York: Oxford University Press, 1985), 58.

39. The formal decision was made at a January 15, 1955, meeting of the Central Secretariat of the Chinese Communist Party. See John Wilson Lewis and Xue Litai, "The Strategic Decision and Its Consequences," in *China Builds the Bomb* (Stanford, CA: Stanford University Press, 1988), chap. 3.

40. Evan A. Feigenbaum, "Who's Behind China's High-Technology 'Revolution'?" *International Security* 24, no. 1 (Summer 1999): 98.

41. Gordon H. Chang, *Friends and Enemies: The United States, China, and the Soviet Union, 1948–1972* (Stanford, CA: Stanford University Press, 1990), 245, and Avery Goldstein, *Deterrence and Security in the 21st Century: China, Britain, France and the Enduring Legacy of the Nuclear Revolution* (Stanford, CA: Stanford University Press, 2000), 104–6.

42. Henry Kissinger, *White House Years* (Boston, MA: Little, Brown, 1979), 184–85.

43. Arkady N. Shevchenko, *Breaking with Moscow* (New York: Knopf, 1985), 165.

44. The "Four Modernizations" encompassed the modernization of industry, agriculture, science and technology, and national defense.

45. According to Jose T. Almonte, "Ensuring Security the 'ASEAN Way'," *Survival* 39, no. 4 (Winter 1997–98): 92n16, China's average annual GDP growth rate of 9.4 percent between 1978 and 1995 doubled individual income in less than eight years. During the 150-year period from 1835 to 1985, the United States doubled individual income every forty-seven years. Further, according to the World Bank's *World Development Indicators,* China's average annual GDP growth for the period 1980–1990 was 10.1 percent; for the period 1990–2000, 10.3 percent.

46. Swaine and Tellis, *Interpreting China's Grand Strategy,* 2.

47. Ibid., 169.

48. Ibid., 97–98 and 141 for the authors' definition of China's "calculative security strategy."

49. Reference to a shift from the three norths—north, northwest, and northeast (sanbei)—to the eastern maritime zone is made in Ji You, *The Armed Forces of China* (New York: I.B. Tauris, 1999), xviii.

50. Paul H.B. Godwin, "From Continent to Periphery: PLA Doctrine, Strategy and Capabilities Towards 2000," *China Quarterly,* no. 146 (June 1996): 478.

51. Ibid., 465.

52. Alexander A. Sergounin and Sergey V. Subbotin, *Russian Arms Transfers to East Asia in the 1990s: SIPRI Research Report No. 15* (New York: Oxford University Press for SIPRI, 1999), 76.

53. The transfer agreement deal was signed in February 1996 for approximately U.S. $2 billion. You, *Armed Forces of China,* 156.

54. Michael Mandelbaum, *The Ideas That Conquered the World: Peace, Democracy and Free Markets in the Twenty-First Century* (New York: Public Affairs, 2002), 148.

55. There is speculation that China actually purchased twenty-two submarines from Russia. See You, *Armed Forces of China,* 66.

56. Greg Austin and Alexey D. Muraviev, *The Armed Forces of Russia in Asia* (New York: I.B. Tauris, 2000), 309.

57. *The Military Balance 2001–2002* (London: International Institute for Strategic Studies, 2001), 111.

58. See especially John H. Noer with David Gregory, *Chokepoints: Maritime Economic Concerns in Southeast Asia* (Washington, DC: National Defense University Press, 1996).

59. See Calder, "Asia and the Nuclear Threshold," in *Pacific Destiny,* chap. 4.

60. Alastair Iain Johnston, "China's New 'Old Thinking': The Concept of Limited Deterrence," *International Security* 20, no. 3 (Winter 1995): 5–6.

61. You, *Armed Forces of China,* 112.

62. After all, President Reagan used Star Wars as a bargaining chip against the Soviet Union in "the greatest sting operation in history." Comment attributed to Robert McFarlane, President Reagan's National Security Adviser, in Frances Fitzgerald, *Way Out There in the Blue* (New York: Simon & Schuster, 2000), 195.

# CHAPTER 5

1. William Burr, ed., *The Kissinger Transcripts: The Top Secret Talks with Beijing & Moscow* (New York: The New Press, 1998), 186.

2. Ibid., 392.

3. According to Article 2(b) of the treaty, China ceded "the island of Formosa, together with all islands appertaining or belonging to the said island of Formosa" to Japan.

4. At the Cairo Conference of November 22–26, 1943, the allies declared, "Japan shall be stripped of all the islands in the Pacific which she has seized or occupied since the beginning of the first World War in 1914, and that all the territories Japan has stolen from the Chinese, such as Manchuria, Formosa, and the Pescadores, shall be restored to the Republic of China." At the Potsdam Conference of July 17–August 2, 1945, the allies declared, "The terms of the Cairo Declaration shall be carried out and Japanese sovereignty shall be limited to the islands of Honshu, Hokkaido, Kyushu, Shikoku and such minor islands as we determine." See the *Protocol of the Proceedings,* Annex II (b) (8).

5. Chang, *Friends and Enemies,* 18.

6. Ibid., 12, 117, 161. In addition, according to Philip Short, *Mao: A Life* (London: Hodder and Stoughton, 1999), 413: During the civil war period from 1945 to 1949, the United States provided the Nationalists with "arms and equipment worth, by State Department calculations, some 300 billion dollars." However, the author does not cite any sources for this assertion.

7. James Lilley with Jeffrey Lilley, *China Hands: Nine Decades of Adventure, Espionage and Diplomacy in Asia* (New York: Public Affairs, 2004), 79.

8. Chang, *Friends and Enemies,* 116.

9. Robert S. Norris, William M. Arkin, and William Burr, "Where They Were," *Bulletin of Atomic Scientists* 55, no. 6 (November/December 1999): 26–35.

10. Lilley, *China Hands,* 92.

11. Chang, *Friends and Enemies,* 166.

12. Richard H. Solomon, *Chinese Political Negotiating Behavior, 1967–1984* (Santa Monica, CA: RAND, 1995), 10. Negotiations at Panmunjom lead to the armistice that brought the Korean War to a standstill; Sino-American ambassadorial talks were held for many years in Warsaw.

13. Appointed Vice President under the U.S. Constitution's 25th Amendment—Nixon's first Vice President, Spiro Agnew, resigned after being charged with criminal tax evasion—Ford had later been accused of striking a "corrupt bargain" with Nixon—a presidential pardon in exchange for the highest office in the land.

14. In addition to Jiang Qing, the "Gang of Four" also included Zhang Chunqiao, Yao Wenyuan, and Wang Hongwen.

15. A Soviet–Vietnamese *Treaty of Friendship and Cooperation* was signed on November 4, 1978.

16. Zbigniew Brzezinski, *Power and Principle: Memoirs of the National Security Adviser 1977–1981* (New York: Farrar, Straus and Giroux, 1985), 218.

17. Patrick Tyler, *A Great Wall: Six Presidents and China: An Investigative History* (New York: Public Affairs, 1999), 269.

18. See the Taiwan Relations Act of April 10, 1979, Section 3(a).

19. See the Taiwan Relations Act, Section 2(b) (3).

20. Tyler, *Great Wall,* 274.

21. Burr, *Kissinger Transcripts,* 168, 186.

22. Tyler, *Great Wall,* 316.

23. James Mann, *About Face: A History of America's Curious Relationship with China, from Nixon to Clinton* (New York: Knopf, 1999), 116.

24. Tyler, *Great Wall,* 290.

25. Ibid., 291.

26. Ibid., 304–6.

27. Ibid., 308.

28. Ibid., 299.

29. Ibid., 314.

30. "The United States government states that it does not seek to carry out a long-term policy of arms sales to Taiwan, that its arms sales to Taiwan will not exceed, either in qualitative or quantitative terms, the level of those supplied in recent years since the establishment of diplomatic relations between the United States and China, and that it intends to reduce gradually its sales of arms to Taiwan, leading over a period of time to final resolution."

31. Tyler, *Great Wall,* 327.

32. Lilley, *China Hands,* 252.

33. Lilley served as Director of the American Institute in Taiwan from 1981 to 1984.

34. Lilley, *China Hands,* 247.

35. Mann, *About Face,* 127.

36. Ibid., 127.

37. Tyler, *Great Wall,* 332.

38. Lilley, *China Hands,* 341. Further, "Peace Pearl,...funded solely by the PLAAF through a United States foreign military sales (FMS) program, originally called for selling a fire control package to modernize 50 basic F-8-2 aircraft with a modified Westinghouse AN/APG 66 radar and fire control computer, a Litton LN-39 inertial navigation system and a head-up display. The program, which did not include any technology transfer, also included five spares." See http://www.globalsecurity.org/military/library/report/1991/plaaf-appd.htm (last accessed April 2007).

39. Lilley, *China Hands,* 342–43.

40. Ibid., 344.

41. Arms Control Association, "U.S. Conventional Arms Sales to Taiwan," June 2004. See http://www.armscontrol.org/factsheets/taiwanarms.asp (last accessed April 2007).

42. Richard Bernstein and Ross H. Munro, *The Coming Conflict with China* (New York: Vintage, 1998), 153.

43. Tyler, *Great Wall,* 378.

44. Ibid., 386.

45. Robert L. Suettinger, *Beyond Tiananmen: The Politics of U.S.–China Relations, 1989–2000* (Washington, DC: Brookings Institution Press, 2003), 173.

46. Ted Galen Carpenter, *America's Coming War with China: A Collision Course over Taiwan* (New York: Palgrave Macmillan, 2005), 67. See also Robert G. Kaiser, "From Citizen K Street: How Lobbying Became Washington's Biggest Business," *Washington Post,* March 25, 2007, chap. 15.

47. Lee had succeeded Chiang Ching-Kuo (Chiang Kai-shek's son), who died in 1988, as president. Taiwan's 1996 presidential election was its first presidential election by direct vote; previously, the National Assembly elected the president.

48. According to Charles W. Freeman Jr., in Mann, *About Face,* 334.

49. Tyler, *Great Wall,* 36.

50. Huntington, *Clash of Civilizations,* 223.

51. Calder, *Pacific Destiny,* 74.

52. See Richard F. Grimmett, "U.S. Arms Sales: Agreements with and Deliveries to Major Clients, 1996–2003," (Congressional Research Service, December 8, 2004, Washington, DC), CRS-6. Available at www.fas.org/man/crs/RL32689.pdf (last accessed April 2007).

53. See the Federation of American Scientists' database of pending arms sales to Taiwan at www.fas.org/asmp/profiles/world.html (last accessed April 2007).

54. According to Carpenter, *America's Coming War,* 163, Taiwan's defense budget as a percentage of GDP is 2.5 percent, whereas China's is 3.5–5.0 percent, or $6.6 billion versus $50–70 billion.

55. Mark A. Stokes, "Taiwan's Security: Beyond the Special Budget," *Asian Outlook, an AEI Online Publication,* March 27, 2006, 2. Available at http://www.aei.org/publications/filter.all,pubID.24113/pub_detail.asp (last accessed April 2007). According to Jane Rickards, "Taiwan Rejects Most of U.S. Arms Package Offered in 2001," *Washington Post,* June 16, 2007, A11, Taiwan's legislature "approved the purchase of P-3 Orion anti-submarine reconnaissance aircraft" valued at approximately $300 million, a fraction of the $18 billion arms package recommended by the Bush administration.

56. According to information posted on the Formosan Association for Public Affairs' Web site, www.fapa.org (last accessed April 2007).

57. "PAVE" is a program name for electronic systems; "PAWS" stands for Phased Array Warning System.

58. See Taiwan Country Profile at www.fas.org/asmp/profiles/taiwan.htm (last accessed April 2007).

59. For a better understanding of the issues involved and the formulation of these questions, I relied on Richard K. Betts and Thomas J. Christensen, "China: Getting the Questions Right," *National Interest,* Winter 2000, 17–29; Thomas J. Christensen, "Posing Problems without Catching Up: China and U.S. Security," *International Security* 25, no. 4 (Spring 2001): 5–40; and Thomas J. Christensen, "Theater Missile Defense and Taiwan's Security," *Orbis* 44, no. 1 (Winter 2000): 79–90.

60. See Article 7 of the "Joint Declaration on Security-Alliance for the 21st Century," signed April 17, 1996.

61. Jonathan Mirsky, "The Party Isn't Over," *New York Review of Books* LI, no. 8 (May 13, 2004): 39.

62. In comments made during an interview on an early morning news show on April 25, 2001.

63. Michael D. Swaine, "Trouble in Taiwan," *Foreign Affairs* 83, no. 2 (March–April 2004): 42.

64. Carpenter, *America's Coming War,* 175.

65. Christensen, "Posing Problems without Catching Up," 39. Christensen, on leave from Princeton University, was appointed Deputy Assistant Secretary of State for East Asian and Pacific Affairs on July 16, 2006.

66. Robert S. Ross, "Taiwan's Fading Independence Movement," *Foreign Affairs* 85, no. 2 (March–April 2006): 143.

67. According to the Economist Intelligence Unit, *Country Profile—Taiwan 2005,* 33, "In 2004 exports of goods and services were equivalent to 65.8 percent of GDP on a current-price national-accounts basis." Of total exports, it is difficult to determine accurately what percentage of Taiwan's exports goes to China because an indeterminate amount of goods are shipped

from Taiwan to its plants in China and then reexported as finished products. However, the *EIU Country Profile,* 41, reports that Taiwan's Ministry of Finance estimates that in 2004, 36.4 percent of its exports went to China.

68. According to the Economist Intelligence Unit, *Country Profile—Taiwan 2005,* 32.

69. Carpenter, *America's Coming War,* 94.

70. Ibid., 76.

71. Joseph Kahn, "Taiwan Voters Weighing How Far to Push China," *New York Times,* March 18, 2004, A1. I first came across reference to this article in Carpenter, *America's Coming War,* 90.

72. Mandelbaum, *The Ideas That Conquered the World,* 148.

73. Before the reunification of Germany and the fall of the Soviet Union, the Fulda Gap was a strategic divide between East and West Germany and an obvious attack route for Warsaw Pact forces.

74. Bernstein and Munro, *Coming Conflict,* 150.

75. Attributed to a "former American diplomat" in Bernstein and Munro, *Coming Conflict,* 149.

76. John Lewis Gaddis, *The Cold War: A New History* (New York: Penguin Press, 2005), 131.

77. Suettinger, *Beyond Tiananmen,* 436.

78. Tyler, *Great Wall,* 6.

79. Nathan and Ross, *Great Wall and the Empty Fortress,* 205.

## CHAPTER 6

1. John P. LeDonne, *The Russian Empire and the World 1700–1917: The Geopolitics of Expansion and Containment* (Oxford: Oxford University Press, 1997), 212–13.

2. R.K.I. Quested, *Sino-Russian Relations: A Short History* (Sydney: George Allen & Unwin, 1984), 27.

3. Mancall, *China at the Center,* xiii.

4. Mark Mancall, *Russia and China: Their Diplomatic Relations to 1728* (Cambridge, MA: Harvard University Press, 1971), 18.

5. O. Edmund Clubb, *China and Russia: The Great Game* (New York: Columbia University Press, 1971), 17.

6. Quested, *Sino-Russian Relations,* 32.

7. Clubb, *China and Russia,* 27.

8. Milescu was a Moldovan Greek. Other examples include Izbrant Ides, a Danish merchant, who led Russia's first official trade caravan to China in 1692; Lorents Lange, a Swede who served as Russia's first commercial agent in Peking (1719–22); Sava Vladislavich, a Bosnian-Serb appointed to head a mission to Peking in 1725.

9. Mancall, *Russia and China,* 100.

10. Nixon and Kissinger also relied upon China's, rather than State Department, translators at their first meeting with Chairman Mao.

11. Quested, *Sino-Russian Relations,* 40–41.

12. Clubb, *China and Russia,* 42.

13. Mancall, *Russia and China,* 246.

14. Quested, *Sino-Russian Relations,* 52.

15. In modern day China, the Russians have developed an enclave in Beijing known as Yabaolu, an area located adjacent from the west side of Ritan Park.

16. Also known as the Court for the Administration of the Borderlands.

17. This pattern resumes in the twentieth century with the Sun/Lenin, Mao/Stalin, Deng/Gorbachev pairings.

18. LeDonne, *Russian Empire,* 174.

19. Mancall, *Russia and China,* 34.

20. Clubb, *China and Russia,* 68.

21. LeDonne, *Russian Empire,* 172.

22. Ibid., 18.

23. Clubb, *China and Russia,* 89.

24. LeDonne, *Russian Empire,* 180.

25. Joseph Fletcher, "Sino-Russian Relations, 1800–62," in *Cambridge History of China,* eds. Denis Twitchett and John K. Fairbank, vol. 10, pt. 1 (New York: Cambridge University Press, 1978), 347.

26. Quested, *Sino-Russian Relations,* 74.

27. S.C.M. Paine, *Imperial Rivals: China, Russia, and Their Disputed Frontier* (Armonk, NY: M.E. Sharpe, 1996), 16.

28. Ibid., 8.

29. Fletcher, "Sino-Russian Relations, 1800–62," 346.

30. LeDonne, *Russian Empire,* 172.

31. Clubb, *China and Russia,* 119.

32. Karl E. Meyer and Shareen Blair Brysac, *Tournament of Shadows: The Great Game and the Race for Empire in Central Asia* (Washington, DC: Counterpoint, 1999), 225.

33. Ibid., 230.

34. Paine, *Imperial Rivals,* 163.

35. Clubb, *China and Russia,* 114.

36. LeDonne, *Russian Empire,* 194.

37. Ibid., 193.

38. Ibid., 204.

39. Clubb, *China and Russia,* 119.

40. Abernethy, *Global Dominance,* 90.

41. Clubb, *China and Russia,* 123.

42. Quested, *Sino-Russian Relations,* 82.

43. LeDonne, *Russian Empire,* 212.

44. Quested, *Sino-Russian Relations,* 84.

45. After Captain Aleksandr M. Bezobrazov, appointed state secretary to the tsar in 1903.

46. LeDonne, *Russian Empire,* 213.

47. Buruma, *Inventing Japan,* 58.

48. LeDonne, *Russian Empire,* 217.

## CHAPTER 7

1. Anatoly Dobrynin commenting on Sino-American relations—"trying to pick up caviar with chopsticks"—in Anatoly Dobrynin, *In Confidence: Moscow's Ambassador to America's Six Cold War Presidents* (New York: Times Books, 1995).

2. Mancall, *China at the Center,* 259.

3. Marius B. Jansen, *The Making of Modern Japan* (Cambridge, MA: Belknap Press of Harvard University, 2000), 513.

4. MacMillan, *Paris 1919,* 71.

5. The May Fourth Movement also signaled the formation of an organized student class in China; one of its leaders, Chen Duxiu, along with Li Dazhao, went on to found the Chinese Communist Party (CCP), whose first meeting was held in Shanghai in July 1921. Mao Zedong, during his first visit to Peking in the winter of 1918, had obtained an apprenticeship with Li Dazhao as a library assistant at Peking University. Several years later, in April 1927, the Chinese raided the Soviet Embassy in Peking on the orders of Chang Tso-lin. Li Dazhao was captured, along with "eighteen or nineteen Russians and sixty Chinese...On April 28... twenty-four of the arrested Chinese were put to death [strangled]...[including] Li Ta-chao." See Clubb, *China and Russia,* 224, 226; and Short, *Mao: A Life,* 185. Former U.S. Ambassador to China, James Lilley, refers to this precedent in his memoirs when he was considering whether to offer sanctuary within the embassy compound to the Chinese dissident Fang Li Zhi. See Lilley, *China Hands,* 353–54.

6. Short, *Mao,* 90.

7. MacMillan, *Paris 1919,* 318.

8. Allen S. Whiting, *Soviet Policies in China, 1917–1924* (Stanford, CA: Stanford University Press, 1953), 134.

9. Associated with Chang Tsolin and Wu Pei-fu.

10. Jung Chang and Jon Halliday, *Mao: The Unknown Story* (New York: Knopf, 2005), 16.

11. Ibid., 25.

12. Ibid., 27.

13. Ibid., 34–35.

14. Ibid., 31–32.

15. Ibid., 36.

16. Ibid., 40.

17. Ibid., 44.

18. Whiting, *Soviet Policies,* 245.

19. Short, *Mao,* 160.

20. Chang and Halliday, *Mao,* 175: "This assassination is generally attributed to the Japanese, but Russian intelligence sources have recently claimed that it was in fact organized, on Stalin's orders, by the man later responsible for the death of Trotsky, Naum Eitingon, and dressed up as the work of the Japanese."

21. Ibid., 72.

22. Ibid., 97.

23. Ibid., 135.

24. Ibid., 133.

25. Ibid., 189.

26. Ibid., 190. According to Yu Bin, "End of History? What's Next?" *Pacific Connections* 6, no. 4 (January 2005): 155, during Ching-kuo's captivity in the USSR from 1925 to 1937, he met his future wife, Faina Epatcheva Vahaleva, while working at the Ural Heavy Machinery Plant, a steel factory in Siberia. The couple's first two children were born in Russia. Later, according to Clubb, *China and Russia,* 344, after father and son were reconciled, Chiang Ching-kuo returned to the USSR on several occasions as his father's personal envoy to Stalin. Chiang Ching-kuo followed his father to Taiwan, and succeeded Chiang Kai-shek as president of the Republic from 1978 to 1988. Madame Chiang died in Taiwan on December 15, 2004.

27. Short, *Mao,* 349.

28. Ibid., 193–94: "Stalin...had decided that Chen must go."

29. Ibid., 210.

30. Ibid., 253.

31. Chang and Halliday, *Mao,* 206.

32. Quested, *Sino-Russian Relations,* 104.

33. Short, *Mao,* 299–300.

34. Chang and Halliday, *Mao,* 178; Short, *Mao,* 376.

35. Chang and Halliday, *Mao,* 196–97; Short, *Mao,* 372.

36. Chang and Halliday, *Mao,* 452.

37. Short, *Mao,* 183.

38. Clubb, *China and Russia,* 283.

39. Chang and Halliday, *Mao,* 202.

40. Quested, *Sino-Russian Relations,* 102–3.

41. Chang and Halliday, *Mao,* 273.

42. Mearsheimer, *Tragedy of Great Power Politics,* 196.

43. Chang and Halliday, *Mao,* 201–3.

44. Ibid., 253–56.

45. Ibid., 259.

46. John Lewis Gaddis, *We Now Know: Rethinking Cold War History* (New York: Oxford University Press, 1997), 55.

47. Chang and Halliday, *Mao,* 284.

48. Ibid., 295.

49. Sun Tzu, "Using Spies," in *The Art of Warfare,* chap. 13.

50. According to Short, *Mao,* 413: "The United States poured in arms and equipment worth, by State Department calculations, some 300 billion dollars" in support of Chiang's battle against the Chinese Communists in post–WWII China until the Communists' victory.

51. The situation is reversed today, as Russia provides a measure of security against U.S./ NATO encroachment along China's continental border, although with the fall of the Soviet Union and the U.S. penetration of the Central Asian states, China's western border is now vulnerable.

## CHAPTER 8

1. Kissinger's comment to Nixon—"we should be able to have our maotai and drink our vodka, too"—cited in Lilley, *China Hands,* 159–60. Maotai is a very potent Chinese liquor and national drink, like vodka in Russia.

2. Clubb, *China and Russia,* 421.

3. Richard Reeves, *President Nixon: Alone in the White House* (New York: Simon & Schuster, 2001), 95.

4. Zhisui Li, with the editorial assistance of Anne F. Thurston, *The Private Life of Chairman Mao: The Memoirs of Mao's Personal Physician* (New York: Random House, 1994), 115.

5. Ibid., 117.

6. Sergei N. Goncharov, John Lewis, and Xue Litai, *Uncertain Partners: Stalin, Mao and the Korean War* (Stanford, CA: Stanford University Press, 1993), 81.

7. Ibid., 88.

8. According to Chang and Halliday, *Mao,* 338–39, Mao had raised the idea of a visit to Russia in November 1947, but Stalin stalled. In April 1948, Mao again suggested a visit to Moscow; Stalin agreed, but then postponed the visit. A third departure date in July 1948 was postponed.

9. Harrison E. Salisbury, *The New Emperors: China in the Era of Mao and Deng* (New York: Little, Brown, 1992), 93.

10. Chang and Halliday, *Mao,* 351.

11. See the Cold War International History Project's Virtual Archive 2.0, Sino-Soviet Relations, "Conversation between Stalin and Mao, Moscow—December 16, 1949." Last accessed April 2007 at http://www.wilsoncenter.org/index.cfm?topic_id=1409&fuseaction=va2.browse&sort=Collection&item=Sino%2DSoviet%20Relations.

12. Simon Sebag Montefiore, *Stalin: The Court of the Red Tsar* (New York: Knopf, 2004), 604.

13. Salisbury, *New Emperors,* 96.

14. Chang and Halliday, *Mao,* 352.

15. Ibid., 352. Goncharov, Lewis, and Litai, *Uncertain Partners,* refers to three meetings on December 23 or 24, December 25, and December 30, 91.

16. Chang, *Friends and Enemies,* 64.

17. Goncharov, Lewis, and Litai, *Uncertain Partners,* 92.

18. See the Cold War International History Project's Virtual Archive 2.0, Sino-Soviet Relations, "Telegram, Mao Zedong to CCP CC, January 2, 1950." Last accessed April 2007 at http://www.wilsoncenter.org/index.cfm?topic_id=1409&fuseaction=va2.browse&sort=Collection&item=Sino%2DSoviet%20Relations.

19. Goncharov, Lewis, and Litai, *Uncertain Partners,* 99–100.

20. Chang and Halliday, *Mao,* 353.

21. Goncharov, Lewis, and Litai, *Uncertain Partners,* 104.

22. Ibid.

23. The *Treaty of Friendship, Alliance, and Mutual Assistance* of February 14, 1950.

24. Short, *Mao: A Life,* 425.

25. Goncharov, Lewis, and Litai, *Uncertain Partners,* 121; Chang and Halliday, *Mao,* 354.

26. Goncharov, Lewis, and Litai, *Uncertain Partners,* 122.

27. The Chinese refer to the Korean War as "The Fight America to Assist Korea War" (Kang Mei Yuan Chao).

28. Goncharov, Lewis, and Litai, *Uncertain Partners,* 134.

29. Ibid., 182. China had first intervened in Korea in 1592 to repel an invasion led by Japan's Hideyoshi.

30. Ibid., 174.

31. Ibid., 190.

32. Short, *Mao,* 430.

33. Goncharov, Lewis, and Litai, *Uncertain Partners,* 191.

34. Many of the Chinese troops sent into Korea were former Nationalists, some of whom wanted to repatriate to Taiwan after the war. For more on this, see Ha Jin, *War Trash* (New York: Pantheon Books, 2004).

35. Chang and Halliday, *Mao,* 368.

36. Cohen, "Foreign Impact," 28.

37. The historical record on Yakov's death is unclear: some suggest that he committed suicide by hurling himself against an electrified fence on the camp's perimeter.

38. Short, *Mao,* 282.

39. Ibid., 434.

40. Li, *Private Life,* 115.

41. Gaddis, *We Now Know,* 213.

42. Vladislav Zubok and Constantine Pleshakov, *Inside the Kremlin's Cold War: From Stalin to Khrushchev* (Cambridge, MA: Harvard University Press, 1996), 215.

43. In June 1957, Vyacheslav Molotov, Georgi Malenkov, and Lazar Kaganovich—members of the Soviet Presidium (Politburo)—led an attempt to remove Khrushchev as first secretary of the CPSU. Khrushchev survived this challenge by diverting the vote on his future from the Presidium to the full Central Committee. For a recent account of the Anti-Party Group's attempted coup, see Aleksandr Fursenko and Timothy Naftali, *Khrushchev's Cold War: The Inside Story of an American Adversary* (New York: W. W. Norton, 2006), 144–49.

44. Quested, *Sino-Russian Relations,* 121; Chang and Halliday, *Mao,* 408.

45. Gaddis, *Cold War,* 109. See also William Taubman, *Khrushchev: The Man and His Era* (New York: W. W. Norton, 2003), 339.

46. Li, *Private Life,* 218.

47. Ibid., 221.

48. Taubman, *Khrushchev,* 390.

49. Ibid., 390.

50. Li, *Private Life,* 261.

51. Chang, *Friends and Enemies,* 187.

52. Gaddis, *Cold War,* 141.

53. Zubok and Pleshakov, *Inside the Kremlin's Cold War,* 212.

54. Short, *Mao,* 497; Jonathan D. Spence, *The Search for Modern China* (New York: W. W. Norton, 1990), 582.

55. Short, *Mao,* 500.

56. Chang and Halliday, *Mao,* 536. Peng died of rectal cancer in 1974.

57. Spence, *Search for Modern China,* 588.

58. This description is attributed to John Kenneth Galbraith, in Taubman, *Khrushchev,* 428.

59. Zubok and Pleshakov, *Inside the Kremlin's Cold War,* 201.

60. Ibid., 230.

61. Taubman, *Khrushchev,* 471.

62. Edward Crankshaw and Strobe Talbott, eds., "Mao Tse-tung and the Schism," in *Khrushchev Remembers* (Boston, MA: Little, Brown, 1970), 461.

63. Ibid., 466.

64. Ibid., 471.

65. Chang and Halliday, *Mao,* 464.

66. Ibid., 466–67.

67. Mancall, *China at the Center,* 416.

68. Quested, *Sino-Russian Relations,* 131.

69. Ibid., 132.

70. William Burr and Jeffrey T. Richelson, "Whether to 'Strangle the Baby in the Cradle': The United States and the Chinese Nuclear Program, 1960–64," *International Security* 25, no. 3 (Winter 2001): 87.

71. Khrushchev was ousted on October 14, 1964; China's first nuclear test was conducted on October 16, 1964, at 1500.

72. Chang and Halliday, *Mao,* 489–90.

73. Ibid., 508.

74. Ibid., 509.

75. Ibid., 535.

76. Ibid., 615.

77. Yuri Andropov became head of the KGB in 1967; Andrei Gromyko served as Minister of Foreign Affairs from 1957 to 1985; Mikhail Suslov, a member of the Politburo and Secretariat, was the party's chief ideologist; Dmitri Ustinov, a candidate member of the Politburo, later became Defense Minister.

78. According to http://www.globalsecurity.org/military/world/war/prc-soviet.htm (last accessed April 2007).

79. Tyler, *Great Wall,* 49.

80. Chang, *Friends and Enemies,* 285. See also Shevchenko, *Breaking with Moscow,* 165.

81. Nathan and Ross, *The Great Wall and the Empty Fortress,* 141.

82. Kissinger, *White House Years,* 184–85.

83. Henry Kissinger, *Diplomacy* (New York: Simon & Schuster, 1994), 723.

84. Ho Chi Minh died on September 5, 1969.

85. Tyler, *Great Wall,* 73.

86. Quested, *Sino-Russian Relations,* 139.

87. Ibid., 141.

88. For more on this, see Christopher Van Hollen, "The Tilt Policy Revisited: Nixon–Kissinger Geopolitics and South Asia," *Asian Survey* 20, no. 4 (April 1980): 339–61.

89. Tyler, *Great Wall,* 120.

90. Attributed to K. Subrahmanyam, the dean of India's nuclear strategists.

91. Quested, *Sino-Russian Relations,* 146.

92. Wishnick, *Mending Fences,* 44.

93. Jeanne L. Wilson, *Strategic Partners: Russian–Chinese Relations in the Post-Soviet Era* (Armonk, NY: M.E. Sharpe, 2004), 49, in a quote attributed to Russian ambassador Igor Rogachev during an interview in 1992.

94. Wishnick, *Mending Fences,* 62.

95. Tyler, *Great Wall,* 163.

96. Bob Woodward, *Veil: The Secret Wars of the CIA 1981–87* (New York: Simon & Schuster, 1987), 162.

97. Christopher Andrew and Vasili Mitrokhin, *The World Was Going Our Way: The KGB and the Battle for the Third World* (New York: Basic Books, 2005), 303.

98. Ibid., 287.

99. Fairbank and Goldman, *China,* 406.

100. Robert S. Ross, "U.S. Policy Toward China: the Strategic Context and the Decision-Making Process," in *China, the United States and the Soviet Union: Tripolarity and Policy-Making in the Cold War,* ed. Robert S. Ross (Armonk, NY: M.E. Sharpe, 1993), 162.

101. Mann, *About Face,* 98.

102. Ibid., 99.

103. Segal, *Defending China,* 211.

104. Mann, *About Face,* 100.

105. Ibid., 97.

106. According to Meyer, *The Dust of Empire,* 135, U.S. weapons and aid to the Afghan resistance totaled more than $3 billion.

107. Seweryn Bialer, *The Soviet Paradox: External Expansion, Internal Decline* (New York: Knopf, 1986), 246.

108. According to Wishnick, *Mending Fences,* 79, "the Soviets increased ground forces in the Far Eastern strategic theater from forty-six divisions in 1981 to fifty-three in 1985" and also increased the number of SS-20 missiles deployed in Siberia.

109. The boundary between Xinjiang Province and Afghanistan's Wakhan Corridor is 46 miles wide. A road connecting Afghanistan and China through the Pamir/Himalayan mountain range was completed in 1971.

110. Su Chi, "The Strategic Triangle and China's Soviet Policy," in *China, the United States and the Soviet Union: Tripolarity and Policy-Making in the Cold War,* ed. Robert S. Ross (Armonk, NY: M.E. Sharpe, 1993), 53.

111. For a more detailed analysis of personnel changes, see Wishnick, *Mending Fences,* 99–101.

112. Suettinger, *Beyond Tiananmen,* 45.

113. Jonathan Steele, *Eternal Russia: Yeltsin, Gorbachev and the Mirage of Democracy* (London: Faber and Faber, 1994), 187.

114. Gaddis, *Cold War,* 251.

115. Steele, *Eternal Russia,* 22.

116. David M. Lampton, "China and the Strategic Quadrangle," in *The Strategic Quadrangle: Russia, China, Japan and the United States in East Asia,* ed. Michael Mandelbaum (New York: Council on Foreign Relations Press, 1995), 83.

117. Wishnick, *Mending Fences,* 122.

118. Gaddis, *Cold War,* 239.

119. Ibid., 257.

## CHAPTER 9

1. Steele, *Eternal Russia,* 359.

2. Ibid., 298.

3. Ibid., 396.

4. Ibid., 369.

5. Attributed to Lennart Meri, president of Estonia, in Strobe Talbott, *The Russia Hand* (New York: Random House, 2002), 94.

6. Ibid., 408.

7. Wishnick, *Mending Fences,* 18.

8. Wilson, *Strategic Partners,* 6.

9. Wishnick, *Mending Fences,* 131.

10. Jennifer Anderson, "The Limits of the Sino-Russian Strategic Partnership," in *Adelphi Paper 315* (London: Oxford University Press for The International Institute for Strategic Studies, December 1997), 19.

11. Wilson, *Strategic Partners,* 116.

12. Ibid., 147.

13. William Safire, "Rise of 'The Stepson'," *New York Times,* January 15, 1996, A17.

14. Wilson, *Strategic Partners,* 30.

15. Samuel Huntington, "The Lonely Superpower," *Foreign Affairs* 78, no. 2 (March/April 1999): 44–45.

16. Evgeny Primakov, *Russian Crossroads: Toward the New Millennium* (New Haven, CT: Yale University Press, 2004), 135.

17. Ibid., 129.

18. Ibid., 137.

19. Talbott, *Russia Hand,* 252. The Czech Republic, Hungary, and Poland joined NATO on March 12, 1999. Bulgaria, Estonia, Latvia, Lithuania, Romania, Slovakia, and Slovenia joined on April 2, 2004.

20. Wishnick, *Mending Fences,* 130.

21. Dmitri Trenin, "The China Factor: Challenge and Chance for Russia," in *Rapprochement or Rivalry,* ed. Sherman W. Garnett (Washington, DC: CEIP, 2000), 42.

22. Stated somewhat differently in Wishnick, *Mending Fences,* 133: "Some energy experts argue that oil and gas have replaced Marx and Lenin as the basis for contemporary Russian–Chinese relations."

23. Wishnick, *Mending Fences,* 133.

24. Primakov, *Russian Crossroads,* 203: "For two days Yeltsin urged me to head the government and I flatly refused."

25. Ibid., 246.

26. Ibid., 248.

27. Ibid., 260.

28. Ibid., 255.

29. Talbott, *Russia Hand,* 293.

30. Ibid., 297.

31. Rothkopf, *Running the World,* 303.

32. David Halberstam, *War in a Time of Peace: Bush, Clinton, and the Generals* (New York: Scribner, 2001), 457.

33. Peter Hessler, *Oracle Bones* (New York: HarperCollins, 2006), 30–31. In an exhaustive investigation of the embassy bombing, Steven Lee Myers reports, "The C.I.A. had provided information on scores of targets throughout the war, but it had not previously been asked to propose its own...Mr. Tenet has said that the C.I.A. proposed only one target during the war. Actually, the agency proposed two or three more, but after the embassy bombing, Pentagon officials refused to strike them." Steven Lee Myers, "Chinese Embassy Bombing: A Wide Net of Blame," *New York Times,* April 17, 2000.

34. Suettinger, *Beyond Tiananmen,* 377. The bombing occurred on May 7, 1999.

35. Presidents Jiang and Putin signed the Sino-Russian *Treaty of Good Neighborliness, Friendship, and Cooperation* in Moscow on July 16, 2001.

36. Bin Yu, "Coping with the Post-Kosovo Fallout," in *Comparative Connections, Sino-Russian Relations* (Washington, DC: CSIS, October 1999), 77. According to Bin Yu, "A 'Nice' Treaty in a Precarious World," in *Comparative Connections, Sino-Russian Relations* (Washington, DC: CSIS, October 2001), 126, a purchase agreement was signed on July 19, 2001, for 38 Su-30MKKs.

37. Bin Yu, "Back to the Future," in *Comparative Connections, Sino-Russian Relations* (Washington, DC: CSIS, January 2000), 77.

38. Bin Yu, "Putin's Ostpolitik and Sino-Russian Relations," in *Comparative Connections, Sino-Russian Relations* (Washington, DC: CSIS, October 2000), 121. The author is grateful to Professor Bin Yu of Wittenberg University for pointing out, in an email exchange, that Putin's statement was also reported in Hong Kong's Chinese-language *Sing Tao Jih Pao* on July 8, 2000 (Internet version) and translated by the U.S. Foreign Broadcast Information Service (FBIS) on July 10, 2000.

39. Bin Yu, "Putinism in Its First Year," in *Comparative Connections, Sino-Russian Relations* (Washington, DC: CSIS, January 2001), 98.

40. Bin Yu, "Beautiful Relationship in a Dangerous World," in *Comparative Connections, Sino-Russian Relations* (Washington, DC: CSIS, July 2002), 117, and http://www.global security.org/military/world/russia/877.htm (last accessed April 2007).

41. Bin Yu, "The New World Order According to Moscow and Beijing," in *Comparative Connections, Sino-Russian Relations* (Washington, DC: CSIS, October 2005), 146.

42. Associated Press, "Khristenko Leaving Pipeline Route Open," *Moscow Times,* November 8, 2005, 5; James Brooke, "The Asian Battle for Russia's Oil and Gas," *New York Times,* January 3, 2004; James Brooke, "Disputes at Every Turn of Siberia Pipeline," *New York Times,* January 21, 2005; James Brooke, "Putin Promises Oil Pipeline for Japan," *New York Times,* November 22, 2005; and U.S. Energy Information Administration (EIA), "Country Analysis Briefs—Russia," last updated January 2006, 6–7, available online at http://www.eia.doe.gov/emeu/cabs/Russia/Background.html in the full report, last accessed April 2007.

43. On February 5, 2007, Russian prosecutors presented new charges against Khodorkovsky that guarantee that he will not be released on parole in October 2007, and that he will remain in prison through Russia's presidential election in March 2008.

44. Bin Yu, "The Russian–Chinese Oil Politik," in *Comparative Connections, Sino-Russian Relations* (Washington, DC: CSIS, October 2003), 140.

45. Bin Yu, "Lubricate the Partnership, but with What?" in *Comparative Connections, Sino-Russian Relations* (Washington, DC: CSIS, October 2004), 138.

46. Japan offered $5 billion for the construction of the pipeline and an additional $1 billion for the renovation of cities along the pipeline route to Nakhodka. In addition, according to Bin Yu, "Party Time!" in *Comparative Connections, Sino-Russian Relations* (Washington, DC: CSIS, July 2003), 130, in June 2003, "Russia and Japan signed a $2 billion contract for the construction of the world's largest liquefied natural gas (LNG) plant in Russia's Sakhalin Island with an annual capacity of 9.6 million tons of LNG, mostly earmarked for export to Japan."

47. EIA, "Country Analysis Briefs—Russia," 5.

48. Estimated at 160,000 barrels per day (bpd) for six years, equal to approximately 7 percent of China's 2004 import demand, at $17 per barrel. See Erin E. Arvedlund, "China Helped Oil Company in Russia Buy Yukos Unit," *New York Times,* February 2, 2005, and Catherine Belton, "Chinese Lend Rosneft $6Bln for Yugansk," *Moscow Times,* February 2, 2005.

49. China purchased 66.22 million shares at $7.55 per share. See David Lague, "China Buys Stake in Russian Oil with Eye to Future," *New York Times,* July 19, 2006.

50. Bin Yu, "China's Year of Russia and the Gathering Nuclear Storm," in *Comparative Connections, Sino-Russian Relations* (Washington, DC: CSIS, October 2006), 151.

51. James Brooke, "Russia Catches China Fever," *New York Times,* March 30, 2004.

52. Stephen Boykewich, "Putin Promises to Send Gas to China," *Moscow Times,* March 22, 2006, 1, and Tom Miles, "Russia and China Promise Energy Cooperation," *Reuters,* March 21, 2006.

53. Owen Matthews and Anna Nemtsova, "Fear and Loathing in Siberia," *Newsweek,* March 27, 2006.

54. U.S. Energy Information Administration (EIA), "Country Analysis Briefs—China," last updated August 2006, 6, available online at http://www.eia.doe.gov/emeu/cabs/China/Background.html in the full report, last accessed April 2007.

55. Ibid., 4, and Catherine Belton, "Chinese Buy Udmurtneft for Rosneft," *Moscow Times,* June 21, 2006, 1.

56. Galina Vitkovskaya, Zhanna Zayonchkovskaya, and Kathleen Newland, "Chinese Migration into Russia," in *Rapprochement or Rivalry,* ed. Sherman W. Garnett (Washington, DC: CEIP, 2000), 350.

57. Rajan Menon, "The Sick Man of Asia: Russia's Endangered Far East," *National Interest,* no. 73 (Fall 2003): 102.

58. Tamara Troyakova, "A View from the Russian Far East," in *Rapprochement or Rivalry,* ed. Sherman W. Garnett (Washington, DC: CEIP, 2000), 220.

59. See chap. 6, "When Russia Met China."

60. Gilbert Rozman, "Turning Fortresses into Free Trade Zones," in *Rapprochement or Rivalry,* ed. Sherman Garnett (Washington, DC: CEIP, 2000), 187–88.

61. In February 2001, President Putin "convinced" Nazdratenko to resign and named him head of the State Fisheries Committee in Moscow a few days later.

62. Elizabeth Wishnick, "Chinese Perspectives on Cross-Border Relations," in *Rapprochement or Rivalry,* ed. Sherman Garnett (Washington, DC: CEIP, 2000), 228.

63. Vitkovskaya, Zayonchkovskaya, and Newland, "Chinese Migration," 348.

64. Similar to the outcry in the U.S. Congress that accompanied CNPC's failed bid for Unocal in the summer of 2005.

65. Bin Yu, "Back to Geostrategics," in *Comparative Connections, Sino-Russian Relations* (Washington, DC: CSIS, April 2005), 136.

66. Alexander Petrov, "Russia's 'Spy-Mania'," in *Human Rights Watch Briefing Paper,* October 2003, 8, available at http://www.hrw.org/backgrounder/eca/russia/ (last accessed April 2007).

67. Andrew C. Kuchins, "Will the Authoritarians of the World Unite?" *Moscow Times,* March 28, 2006, 10.

68. Poll cited in Bin Yu, "Putinism in Its First Year," 99.

69. Matthews and Nemtsova, "Fear and Loathing in Siberia".

70. Simon Elegant, "The Great Divide," *Time Asia,* April 16, 2006.

71. According to Paul J. Saunders, "Putin-Up Close, Sans Soul Gazing: Amid a Small Gathering, the Russian President Talks Tough To America," *National Interest Online,* September 11, 2006. Available at http://www.nationalinterest.org/PrinterFriendly.aspx?id=12028 (last accessed April 2007).

72. Sonia Orwell and Ian Angus, eds., *George Orwell: The Collected Essays—Volume 4, In Front of Your Nose* (Boston, MA: D.R. Godine, 2000), 41.

73. Jennifer Lind, "Dangerous Games," *Atlantic Monthly,* March 2006.

## CHAPTER 10

1. The "rotting process," a concept developed by John LeDonne to describe Russia's diplomatic tradition of encouraging "subversion in the name of conservatism," is discussed in Chapter 6, "When Russia Met China." See LeDonne, *Russian Empire,* 180.

2. Bates Gill and Matthew Oresman, *China's New Journey to the West: China's Emergence in Central Asia and Implications for U.S. Interests* (Washington, DC: Center for Strategic and International Studies, August 2003), 20.

3. Ariel Cohen, "After Shanghai: Geopolitical Shifts in Eurasia," *Central Asia Caucasus Institute Analyst,* June 28, 2006, 3.

4. Yu, "Putin's Ostpolitik and Sino-Russian Relations," 117.

5. Bin Yu, "Crouching Missiles, Hidden Alliances," in *Comparative Connections, Sino-Russian Relations* (Washington, DC: CSIS, April 2001), 116.

6. A summary of the Nuclear Posture Review submitted to the U.S. Congress December 31, 2001, by U.S. Secretary of Defense Donald Rumsfeld is available at http://www.global security.org/wmd/library/policy/dod/npr.htm (last accessed April 2007). Reference to the seven countries listed above appears under the heading, "Sizing the Nuclear Force (p. 16)."

7. David Shambaugh, "China and the Korean Peninsula: Playing for the Long Term," *Washington Quarterly* 26, no. 2 (Spring 2003): 46.

8. Chalmers Johnson, "Korea and Our Asia Policy," *National Interest,* no. 41 (Fall 1995): 69.

9. Anne Applebaum, "It's China's Problem," *Washington Post,* October 17, 2006, A21.

10. According to Bruce Cumings, "Tragedy and Hope on the Korean Peninsula," in *The Asia-Pacific in the New Millennium: Geopolitics, Security and Foreign Policy,* ed. Shalendra D. Sharma (Berkeley, CA: Regents of University of California, 2000), 197, 202.

11. Shambaugh, "China and the Korean Peninsula," 45.

12. According to the Economist Intelligence Unit's *South Korea Country Profile 2005,* 39, China is now South Korea's leading trading partner, accounting for 32.8 percent of bilateral trade.

13. Quansheng Zhao, "China and the Dynamics of the Korean Peninsula," in *The Asia-Pacific in the New Millennium: Geopolitics, Security and Foreign Policy,* ed. Shalendra D. Sharma (Berkeley, CA: Regents of University of California, 2000), 106.

14. James Brooke, "China 'Looming Large' in South Korea," *New York Times,* January 3, 2003.

15. This enticing question is raised in Nicholas Eberstadt and Richard J. Ellings, "Assessing Interests and Objectives of Major Actors in the Korean Drama," in *Korea's Future and the Great Powers* (Seattle, WA: National Bureau of Asian Research, 2001), 337.

16. Noah Feldman, "Islam, Terror and the Second Nuclear Age," *New York Times Magazine,* October 29, 2006.

17. Cohen, "After Shanghai," 3.

18. J. Brandon Gentry, "The Dragon and the Magi: Burgeoning Sino-Iranian Relations in the 21st Century," *China and Eurasia Forum Quarterly* 3, no. 3 (November 2005): 116.

19. Vivienne Walt, "Iran Looks East," *Fortune,* February 21, 2005, 56.

20. U.S. Energy Information Agency (EIA), *Country Analysis Briefs—Iran,* last updated August 2006, 8. Available online at http://www.eia.doe.gov/emeu/cabs/Iran/Back ground.html (last accessed April 2007).

21. Ibid., 10.

22. From 1990 to 1996, Russian arms sales to Iran are estimated at $5 billion. Because of the Gore-Chernomyrdin agreements, arms sales were temporarily halted, but promptly resumed after Putin succeeded Yeltsin.

23. Yuri Zarakhovich, "What Putin Hopes to Gain from Iran," *Time,* February 14, 2006. On March 25, 2007, Russia voted with the rest of the U.N. Security Council to impose sanctions on Iran because of its nuclear development program. The next day, Iran reportedly made good on its arrears to Moscow—an instance of Russia using its U.N. vote as a strong-arm tactic to collect a debt. See Yulia Latynina, "The Geopolitics of Accounts Receivable," *Moscow Times,* March 28, 2007, 8.

24. Pavel Felgenhauer, "Proliferation of the Bigwigs," *Moscow Times,* February 22, 2005, 11. The Kh-55 has a range of 1,860 miles.

25. Andrew Kramer, "Russia to Sell Anti-Aircraft Missiles to Iran," *New York Times,* December 3, 2005, and Lyuba Pronina, "Moscow Inks Arms Deal with Tehran," *Moscow Times,* December 5, 2005, 1.

26. Robert O. Freedman, "Russia, Iran, and the Nuclear Record: The Putin Record," *Jerusalem Viewpoints,* no. 544, July 2, 2006. Available online at http://jcpa.org/jl/vp544.htm (last accessed September 2007).

27. Seymour Hersh, "The Iran Plans," *New Yorker,* August 21, 2006, 34.

28. See, for example, L. Carl Brown, "Introduction," in *Diplomacy in the Middle East: The International Relations of Regional and Outside Powers,* ed. L. Carl Brown (New York: I.B. Tauris, 2001), xi.

29. David M. Lampton and Richard Daniel Ewing, *The U.S.–China Relationship Facing International Crises: Three Case Studies in Post-9/11 Bilateral Relations* (Washington, DC: The Nixon Center, 2003), 25.

30. Anthony Alexander Loh, "The Hegemon's Motif: The People's Republic of China and the Middle East, 1949–1998," in *China and Israel, 1948–1998: A Fifty Year Retrospective,* ed. Jonathan Goldstein (Westport, CT: Praeger, 1999), 76.

31. According to the Global Security Organization's summary of the Iran–Iraq War, available at http://www.globalsecurity.org/military/world/war/iran-iraq.htm (last accessed April 2007).

32. Yitzhak Shichor, "The Chinese Factor in the Middle East Security Equation: An Israeli Perspective," in *China and Israel, 1948–1998: A Fifty Year Retrospective,* ed. Jonathan Goldstein (Westport, CT: Praeger, 1999), 175.

33. Peter Baker, "Russian–Iraqi Oil Ties Worry U.S.," *Washington Post,* September 1, 2002, A16, estimates $7–11 billion. Alan B. Krueger, "Economic Scene," *New York Times,* April 3, 2003, estimates $64 billion figure.

34. Stuart D. Goldman, "Russia," Congressional Research Service Issue Brief for Congress, updated May 29, 2003, 15. Available online at http://fpc.state.gov/documents/organization/21351.pdf (last accessed September 2007).

35. According to the private intelligence company, Stratfor, "War in Iraq: What's at Stake for Russia?" issued November 22, 2002, and "Kremlin Tallies Cost of Supporting Hussein," issued April 8, 2003.

36. Baker, "Russian–Iraqi Oil Ties."

37. Mark Kramer, "Did the Russians Aid Saddam Hussein's War Effort?" in *PONARS Policy Memo No. 405* (Washington, DC: CSIS, April 2006), 3.

38. Peter Slevin, "3 Russian Firms' Deals Anger U.S.," *Washington Post,* March 23, 2003, A19.

39. Judith Ingram, "Russia, United States Increasingly at Odds," *Associated Press,* April 4, 2006, and Kramer, "Russians Aid."

40. Ian Johnson, "China Searches for Stable Sources of Energy Abroad," *Wall Street Journal,* June 25, 1997, A18.

41. Tad Szulc, "The New Bigfoot in the Global Oil Market," *Los Angeles Times,* October 5, 1997, M-2.

42. Lampton and Ewing, *U.S.–China Relationship,* 34.

43. Stratfor, "War in Iraq: What's at Stake for China?" issued December 13, 2002.

44. Lampton and Ewing, *U.S.–China Relationship,* 38: "It will be interesting to see whether, over the longer term, China's differentiated policy going into the war leads to favorable treatment to Beijing."

45. Economist Intelligence Unit's *Country Profile Sudan 2006,* 21.

46. According to the U.S. Energy Information Agency's *Country Analysis Briefs—Sudan,* last updated in March 2006, CNPC owned a 40 percent interest in GNPOC and a 41 percent interest in Petrodar.

47. According to Matthias Muindi, "Dam Could Provoke Water Wars," *NewsfromAfrica,* January 2002. Available at http://www.newsfromafrica.org/newsfromafrica/articles/art_609.html (last accessed April 2007).

48. Kent Calder, "East Asia and the Middle East: A Fateful Energy Embrace," *China and Eurasia Forum Quarterly* 3, no. 3 (November 2005), 8.

49. Economist Intelligence Unit, *Country Profile Sudan,* 21.

50. U.S. State Department, "Background Note: Sudan," October 2006, available at http://www.state.gov/r/pa/ei/bgn/5424.htm (last accessed April 2007).

51. Andrews-Speed, Liao, and Dannreuther, *Adelphi Paper 346, 67.*

52. Yu, "Back to the Future," 79.

53. When Yeltsin unexpectedly resigned on December 31, 1999, Putin, who was serving as Russia's Prime Minister, became acting president according to the constitution.

54. Washington Post Foreign Service, "Russia Wondering What it Gets for Backing U.S. Against Iraq," *Washington Post,* October 4, 2002, A22.

55. Wilson, *Strategic Partners,* 170.

56. President Bush made these comments at a press conference that followed the Bush–Putin meeting. Available at http://www.whitehouse.gov/news/releases/2001/06/20010618.html (last accessed April 2007).

57. Mikhail Shaakashvili, a U.S.-trained lawyer, replaced Shevardnadze.

58. The Kremlin-backed candidate, Viktor Yanukovych, initially won Ukraine's 2004 presidential election, but Ukraine's Supreme Court invalidated the results due to widespread voting irregularities. Yushchenko went on to win in the runoff election.

59. The Czech Republic, Hungary, and Poland joined NATO on March 12, 1999; Bulgaria, Romania, and Slovakia joined on March 29, 2004.

60. Estonia, Latvia, and Lithuania joined NATO on March 29, 2004.

61. Gazprom sought to quadruple the price Ukraine paid per cubic meter of gas from $50 to $220–230. In the winter of 2006, Russia doubled the price of its oil exports to Belarus.

62. Jackson Diehl, "An Explosive Gas Deal," *Washington Post,* February 27, 2006, A15.

63. Owen Matthews and Anna Nemtsova, "A Chill in the Moscow Air," *Newsweek,* February 6, 2006.

64. Catherine Belton, "Relations with U.S. Lowest in 20 Years," *Moscow Times,* May 19, 2006, 1.

65. Andrew E. Kramer, "Gazprom Intends to Develop Huge Gas Field on Its Own," *New York Times,* October 10, 2006. On November 10, 2006, the United States and Russia reached a bilateral agreement on accession to the WTO, but Russia still has to reach agreement with Costa Rica, Moldova, and Georgia.

66. Bin Yu, "Treaties Scrapped, Treaties Signed," in *Comparative Connections, Sino-Russian Relations* (Washington, DC: CSIS, July 2001), 112.

67. For more details, see Chapter 5, "Taiwan: The Tripwire."

68. Recall the diplomatic brouhaha that erupted when the Clinton administration granted Lee Teng-hui, the former president of Taiwan, a visa to attend his class reunion at Cornell, discussed in Chapter 5, "Taiwan: The Tripwire."

69. Mann, *Rise of the Vulcans,* 282.

70. The U.S.–China Security Review Commission, "The Defense Budget and the Military Economy," in *The National Security Implications of the Economic Relationship Between the United States and China* (Washington, DC, July 2002), chap. 9. Available at http://www. uscc.gov/annual_report/2002/ch9_02.htm (last accessed April 2007).

71. Bonnie S. Glaser, "Rice Seeks to Caution, Cajole, and Cooperate with Beijing," in *Comparative Connections, U.S.–China Relations* (Washington, DC: CSIS, April 2005), 35.

72. Cited in Bonnie S. Glaser and Jane Skanderup, "Anxiety About Taiwan Hits New Highs," in *Comparative Connections, U.S.–China Relations* (Washington, DC: CSIS, July 2004), 42.

73. Harvey Stockwin, "The Qian Qichen Op-Ed: Official Discontent or Just One Man's Opinion?" in *The Jamestown Foundation's China Brief* 4, no. 24 (December 7, 2004).

74. This figure includes $54.7 billion held by Hong Kong. Data available at http:// www.ustreas.gov/tic/mfh.txt (last accessed September 2007).

75. I am indebted to James Kynge, who reviews these factors in *China Shakes the World: A Titan's Rise and Troubled Future—and the Challenge for America* (New York: Houghton Mifflin, 2006). See especially 109, 127, and 184.

76. Senators Charles Schumer (D-NY) and Lindsey Graham (R-SC) introduced this legislation in February 2005. On July 21, 2005, China revalued the yuan by 2.1 percent and replaced the yuan/dollar peg with a restricted float comprised of a basket of eleven currencies. Schumer and Graham have delayed further action on their bill.

77. Clyde Prestowitz, *Three Billion New Capitalists: The Great Shift of Wealth and Power to the East* (New York: Basic Books, 2005), 199.

78. According to Leslie Wayne and David Barboza, "Unocal Deal: A Lot More than Money is at Issue," *New York Times,* June 24, 2005, C4, Mark McKinnon, Public Strategies' vice chairman, oversaw Bush's 2004 media campaign.

79. Steve Lohr, "State Department Yields on PCs from China," *New York Times,* May 23, 2006.

80. Mancall, *Russia and China,* 34.

81. Joseph Kahn, "Bush and Hu Vow New Cooperation," *New York Times,* April 21, 2006.

82. This account of the Bush/Hu April 2006 meeting at the White House is based on Kahn, "Bush and Hu Vow New Cooperation"; Dana Milbank, "China and Its President Greeted by a Host of Indignities," *Washington Post,* April 21, 2006, A02; and Melinda Liu, "About Face," *Newsweek,* April 21, 2006.

83. Richard K. Betts, "Wealth, Power and Instability," *International Security* 18, no. 3 (Winter 1993/94): 75.

## CHAPTER 11

1. T. R. Reid, *The United States of Europe: The New Superpower and the End of American Supremacy* (New York: Penguin Press, 2004), 1.

2. Robert Kagan, *Of Paradise and Power: America and Europe in the New World Order* (New York: Vintage, 2004), 3.

3. Tony Judt, *Postwar: A History of Europe since 1945* (New York: Penguin Press, 2005), 790.

4. Josef Joffe, *Überpower: The Imperial Temptation of America* (New York: W. W. Norton, 2006), 83–87.

5. Kagan, *Of Paradise and Power,* 158.

6. Judt, *Postwar,* 291.

7. Kagan, *Of Paradise and Power,* 71–72.

8. Belgium, France, Germany, Italy, Luxembourg, and the Netherlands are founding members of the European Union. Norway and Switzerland—with Europe's second- and third-highest per capita income—have not joined the Union; Sweden, a member, has opted to retain its own currency.

9. Reid, *United States of Europe,* 64.

10. Judt, *Postwar,* 733. A European Rapid Reaction Force (ERRF), created in 2003, is comprised of approximately 60,000 soldiers on call/reserve.

11. Joffe, *Überpower,* 123.

12. Ibid., 167.

13. Twenty-one of the EU's twenty-seven members receive more than they contribute to the EU's coffers in Brussels, so Austria, France, Germany, Great Britain, the Netherlands, and Sweden are left to finance the rest.

14. In 2004, France and Germany exceeded the 3 percent limit.

15. Reid, *United States of Europe,* 219.

16. Kevin Phillips, *American Theocracy: The Peril and Politics of Radical Religion, Oil, and Borrowed Money in the 21st Century* (New York: Viking, 2006), 393.

17. Bob Woodward, *State of Denial* (New York: Simon & Schuster, 2006), 334.

18. Signed into law on December 18, 2006, by President Bush—but will the forty-five members of the Nuclear Suppliers Group modify their guidelines to permit cooperation with India?

19. John W. Garver, *Protracted Contest: Sino-Indian Rivalry in the Twentieth Century* (Seattle, WA: University of Washington Press, 2001), 187.

20. Prestowitz, *Three Billion New Capitalists,* 84.

21. Van Hollen, "Tilt Policy," 344.

22. Philip Cohen, *India: Emerging Power* (Washington, DC: Brookings Institution Press, 2001), 136.

23. Van Hollen, "Tilt Policy," 360. The phrase "atomic gunboat diplomacy" is attributed to K. Subrahmanyam, one of India's leading strategic thinkers.

24. National Security Archive, "Nixon/Kissinger Saw India as 'Soviet Stooge' in 1971 South Asia Crisis," June 29, 2005. Available at www.gwu.edu/~nsarchiv/news/20050629/ (last accessed April 2007).

25. Owen Bennett Jones, *Pakistan: Eye of the Storm* (New Haven, CT: Yale University Press, 2002), 200.

26. Cohen, *India,* 170.

27. Mary Anne Weaver, *Pakistan: In the Shadow of Jihad and Afghanistan* (New York: Farrar, Straus and Giroux, 2002), 201.

28. Edward Luce, *In Spite of the Gods: The Strange Rise of Modern India* (New York: Doubleday, 2007), 258.

29. Weaver, *Pakistan,* 222.

30. For a comprehensive treatment of Sino-Indian relations, see Garver, *Protracted Contest.*

31. A phrase reportedly used in a private study, "Energy Futures in Asia," prepared by Booz Allen Hamilton for the U.S. Defense Department. See Bill Gertz, "China Builds Up Strategic Sea Lanes," *Washington Times,* January 18, 2005, and Sudha Ramachandran, "China's Pearl in Pakistan's Waters," *Asia Times Online,* March 4, 2005.

32. Cohen, *India,* 209.

33. Nelly Ming, "China to Buy 10% of Myanmar's Gas Reserves," *Tanker World,* February 1, 2006.

34. See Garver, *Protracted Contest,* Table 10.1, "Chinese Involvement in Myanmar's Maritime Development in the 1990s," 294.

35. Urvashi Aneja, "China–Bangladesh Relations: An Emerging Strategic Partnership?" *IPCS Special Report 33* (New Delhi: Institute of Peace and Conflict Studies, November 2006), 7.

36. Ibid., 4.

37. Cohen, *India,* 56.

38. U.S. Department of Energy, Energy Information Administration, *Country Analysis Briefs—Angola* (last updated January 2007). Available at http://www.eia.doe.gov/emeu/cabs/Angola/Full.html (last accessed April 2007).

39. See Arvedlund, "China Helped Oil Company" and Belton, "Chinese Lend Rosneft $6Bln for Yugansk".

40. U.S. Department of State, Bureau of Verification and Compliance, *World Military Expenditures and Arms Transfers, 1999–2000* (Washington, DC, June 2002), Table III, "Value of Arms Transfer Deliveries, Cumulative 1997–1999," 157.

41. Cohen, *India,* 310.

42. In New Delhi on October 14, 2005, and in Rajasthan on October 16, 2005.

43. *The Military Balance 2006–2007* (London: International Institute of Strategic Studies, 2006), 224.

44. In June 2005, the foreign ministers of Russia, China, and India met in Vladivostok.

45. The other is Dmitri Medvedev, also a First Deputy Prime Minister, CEO of Gazprom, and St. Petersburger. On September 12, 2007, President Putin nominated Viktor Zubkov to be Russia's next prime minister, muddying predictions about who will become Russia's next president.

46. Gaddis, *Cold War,* 131

47. Over the status of the Northern Territories/Kurile Islands.

48. Huntington, *Clash of Civilizations,* 219.

# BIBLIOGRAPHY

Abernethy, David B. *The Dynamics of Global Dominance: European Overseas Empires 1415–1980.* New Haven: Yale University Press, 2000.

Adams, James. *The Next World War.* New York: Simon & Schuster, 1998.

Almonte, Jose T. "Ensuring Security the 'ASEAN Way.'" *Survival* 39, no. 4 (Winter 1997–1998): 80–92.

Anderson, Jennifer. "The Limits of the Sino-Russian Strategic Partnership." *Adelphi Paper 315.* London: Oxford University Press for The International Institute for Strategic Studies, December 1997.

Anderson, Walter. "India's Foreign Policy in the Post-Cold War World: Searching for a New Model." In *The Asia-Pacific in the New Millennium: Geopolitics, Security and Foreign Policy,* edited by Shalendra D. Sharma, 207–23. Berkeley: Regents of University of California, 2000.

Andrew, Christopher, and Vasili Mitrokhin. *The World Was Going Our Way: The KGB and the Battle for the Third World.* New York: Basic Books, 2005.

Andrews-Speed, Philip, Xuanli Liao, and Roland Dannreuther. "The Strategic Implications of China's Energy Needs." *Adelphi Paper 346.* London: Oxford University Press for The International Institute for Strategic Studies, July 2002.

Aneja, Urvashi. "China–Bangladesh Relations: An Emerging Strategic Partnership?" *IPCS Special Report 33.* New Delhi: Institute of Peace and Conflict Studies, November 2006.

Applebaum, Anne. "It's China's Problem." *Washington Post,* October 17, 2006, A21.

Arase, David. "Japan's Post-Cold War Policy Toward China: Attempts at a Broader Relationship." In *The Asia-Pacific in the New Millennium: Geopolitics, Security and Foreign Policy,* edited by Shalendra D. Sharma, 149–64. Berkeley: Regents of University of California, 2000.

Arbatov, Alexei G. "Military Reform in Russia: Dilemmas, Obstacles and Prospects." *International Security* 22, no. 4 (Spring 1998): 83–134.

Arms Control Association. "U.S. Conventional Arms Sales to Taiwan." June 2004.

Aron, Leon. "The Yukos Affair." *Russian Outlook.* Washington, DC: AEI Online, October 2003.

Arvedlund, Erin E. "China Helped Oil Company in Russia Buy Yukos Unit." *New York Times,* February 2, 2005.

Associated Press. "Khristenko Leaving Pipeline Route Open." *Moscow Times,* November 8, 2005, 5.

Austin, Greg, and Alexey D. Muraviev. *The Armed Forces of Russia in Asia.* New York: I. B. Tauris, 2000.

Bacevich, Andrew J. *The New American Militarism: How Americans Are Seduced by War.* New York: Oxford University Press, 2005.

Bachman, David. "Domestic Sources of Chinese Foreign Policy After Deng." In *The Asia-Pacific in the New Millennium: Geopolitics, Security and Foreign Policy,* edited by Shalendra D. Sharma, 33–51. Berkeley: Regents of University of California, 2000.

Baker, Peter. "Russian–Iraqi Oil Ties Worry U.S." *Washington Post,* September 1, 2002, A16.

Baker, Peter, and Susan Glasser. *Kremlin Rising: Vladimir Putin's Russia and the End of Revolution.* New York: Scribner, 2005.

Bakhash, Shaul. "Iran's Foreign Policy Under the Islamic Republic, 1979–2000." In *Diplomacy in the Middle East: The International Relations of Regional and Outside Powers,* edited by L. Carl Brown, 247–58. New York: I. B. Tauris, 2001.

Bakshi, Jyotsna. "Post-Cold War Sino-Russian Relations: An Indian Perspective." *Strategic Analysis.* India: Institute for Defence Studies and Analysis, 26, no. 1, January—March 2002.

Baranovsky, Vladimir G., and Alexei G. Arbatov. "The Changing Security Perspective in Europe." In *Russia and the West: The 21st Century Security Environment,* edited by Robert Legvold, Karl Kaiser, and Alexei Arbatov, 44–73. Armonk, NY: M. E. Sharpe, 1999.

Barnes, Hugh, and Alex Bigham. *Understanding Iran: People, Politics and Power.* London: The Foreign Policy Centre, 2006.

Barnes, Joe. "Slaying the China Dragon: The New China Threat School." Houston: Baker Institute for Public Policy, May 2002.

Bazhanov, Eugene. "Russian Policy Toward China." In *Russian Foreign Policy Since 1990,* edited by Peter Shearman, 159–80. Boulder, CO: Westview Press, 1995.

Bearden, Milt, and James Risen. *The Main Enemy: The Inside Story of the CIA's Final Showdown with the KGB.* New York: Random House, 2003.

Belton, Catherine. "Chinese Buy Udmurtneft for Rosneft." *Moscow Times,* June 21, 2006, 1.

———. "Chinese Lend Rosneft $6Bln for Yugansk." *Moscow Times,* February 2, 2005.

———. "Relations with U.S. Lowest in 20 Years." *Moscow Times,* May 19, 2006, 1.

Benewick, Robert. *State of China Atlas.* New York: Penguin, 1999.

Bennett Jones, Owen. *Pakistan: Eye of the Storm.* New Haven: Yale University Press, 2002.

Bernstein, Richard, and Ross H. Munro. *The Coming Conflict with China.* New York: Vintage, 1998.

Betts, Richard K. "Wealth, Power and Instability." *International Security* 18, no. 3 (Winter 1993–1994): 34–77.

Betts, Richard K., and Thomas J. Christensen. "China: Getting the Questions Right." *National Interest,* Winter 2000, 17–29.

Bialer, Seweryn. *The Soviet Paradox: External Expansion, Internal Decline.* New York: Knopf, 1986.

Blank, Stephen J. "Putin's Twelve-Step Program." *Washington Quarterly* 25, no. 1 (Winter 2002): 147–60.

Bobbitt, Philip. *The Shield of Achilles: War, Peace and the Course of History.* New York: Knopf, 2002.

Boot, Max. *The Savage Wars of Peace: Small Wars and the Rise of American Power.* New York: Basic Books, 2002.

Boykewich, Stephen. "Putin Promises to Send Gas to China." *Moscow Times,* March 22, 2006, 1.

Bracken, Paul. *Fire in the East.* New York: Harper Collins, 1999.

Brecher, Michael, Jonathan Wilkenfeld, and Sheila Moser, eds. *Crises in the Twentieth Century, Volume I: Handbook of International Crises.* Oxford: Pergamon Press, 1988.

Bremmer, Ian. "The Dragon Awakes." *National Interest,* no. 80, Summer 2005, 128–34.

Brill Olcott, Martha. "Russian–Chinese Relations and Central Asia." In *Rapprochement or Rivalry,* edited by Sherman W. Garnett, 371–400. Washington, DC: CEIP, 2000.

British Petroleum. *BP Statistical Review of World Energy.* London: June 2003, 2004, 2005, 2006.

Brooke, James. "The Asian Battle for Russia's Oil and Gas." *New York Times,* January 3, 2004.

———. "China 'Looming Large' in South Korea." *New York Times,* January 3, 2003.

———. "Disputes at Every Turn of Siberia Pipeline." *New York Times,* January 21, 2005.

———. "Putin Promises Oil Pipeline for Japan." *New York Times,* November 22, 2005.

———. "Russia Catches China Fever." *New York Times,* March 30, 2004.

Brown, L. Carl. "Introduction," and "The Foreign Policies of Other Middle Eastern States." In *Diplomacy in the Middle East: The International Relations of Regional and Outside Powers,* edited by L. Carl Brown, ix–xxv and 281–302. New York: I. B. Tauris, 2001.

Brzezinski, Zbigniew. *The Choice: Global Domination or Global Leadership.* New York: Basic Books, 2004.

———. *The Grand Chessboard.* New York: Basic Books, 1997.

———. *Power and Principle: Memoirs of the National Security Adviser 1977–1981.* New York: Farrar, Straus Giroux, 1985.

———. "A Sorry Foreign Policy Own Goal." *Australian,* October 14, 2005.

Burles, Mark. *China Policy Toward Russia and the Central Asian Republics.* Santa Monica: RAND, 1999.

Burr, William, ed. *The Kissinger Transcripts: The Top Secret Talks with Beijing & Moscow.* New York: The New Press, 1998.

Burr, William, and Jeffrey T. Richelson. "Whether to 'Strangle the Baby in the Cradle': The United States and the Chinese Nuclear Program, 1960–64." *International Security* 25, no. 3 (Winter 2001): 54–99.

Buruma, Ian. *Inventing Japan: 1853–1964.* New York: Modern Library, 2003.

———. *Murder in Amsterdam: The Death of Theo van Gogh and the Limits of Tolerance.* New York: The Penguin Press, 2006.

Buzan, Barry, and Gerald Segal. *Anticipating the Future.* New York: Simon & Schuster, 1998.

Calder, Kent E. "East Asia and the Middle East: A Fateful Energy Embrace." *China and Eurasia Forum Quarterly* 3, no. 3 (November 2005): 5–9.

———. *Pacific Destiny: Arms, Energy, and America's Future in Asia.* New York: William Morrow & Company, 1996.

Calleo, David. *Rethinking Europe's Future.* Princeton: Princeton University Press, 2001.

Carpenter, Ted Galen. *America's Coming War with China: A Collision Course over Taiwan.* New York: Palgrave Macmillan, 2005.

Central Intelligence Agency. *The Worldwide Threat in 2003: Evolving Dangers in a Complex World.* Washington, DC: Delivered by Director of Central Intelligence to Senate Foreign Relations Committee, February 11, 2003.

Central Intelligence Agency. *World Factbook 2003.*

Chang, Gordon H. *Friends and Enemies: The United States, China, and the Soviet Union, 1948–1972.* Stanford, CA: Stanford University Press, 1990.

Chang, Jung, and Jon Halliday. *Mao: The Unknown Story.* New York: Knopf, 2005.

Chase, Robert, Emily Hill, and Paul Kennedy, eds. *The Pivotal States: A New Framework for U.S. Policy in the Developing World.* New York: W.W. Norton & Company, 1999.

Cheung, Tai Ming. "The Influence of the Gun: China's Central Military Commission and Its Relationship with the Military, Party and State Decision-Making Systems." In *The Making of Chinese Foreign and Security Policy in the Era of Reform 1978–2000,* edited by David M. Lampton, 61–90. Stanford, CA: Stanford University Press, 2001.

Chi, Su. "The Strategic Triangle and China's Soviet Policy." In *China, the United States and the Soviet Union: Tripolarity and Policy-Making in the Cold War,* edited by Robert S. Ross, 39–61. Armonk, NY: M.E. Sharpe, 1993.

Christensen, Thomas J. "China." In *Strategic Asia: Power and Purpose 2001–2002,* edited by Richard J. Ellings and Aaron L. Friedberg, 27–69. Seattle: National Bureau of Asian Research, 2001.

———. "China, the U.S.–Japan Alliance, and the Security Dilemma in East Asia." *International Security* 23, no. 4 (Spring 1999): 49–80.

———. "Posing Problems Without Catching Up: China and U.S. Security." *International Security* 25, no. 4 (Spring 2001): 5–40.

———. "Theater Missile Defense and Taiwan's Security." *Orbis* 44, no. 1 (Winter 2000): 79–90.

Clubb, O. Edmund. *China and Russia: The Great Game.* New York: Columbia University Press, 1971.

Cohen, Ariel. "After Shanghai: Geopolitical Shifts in Eurasia." *Central Asia Caucasus Institute Analyst,* June 28, 2006.

Cohen, Eliot. "A Revolution in Warfare." *Foreign Affairs* 75, no. 2 (March/April 1996): 37–54.

Cohen, Stephen Philip. *India: Emerging Power.* Washington: Brookings Institution Press, 2001.

Cohen, Warren I. "The Foreign Impact on East Asia." In *Historical Perspectives in Contemporary East Asia,* edited by Merle Goldman and Andrew Gordon, 1–41. Cambridge, MA: Harvard University Press, 2000.

Cold War International History Project's Virtual Archive 2.0, Sino-Soviet Relations, "Conversation Between Stalin and Mao, Moscow—December 16, 1949."

Conboy, Kenneth, and James Morrison. *The CIA's Secret War in Tibet.* Lawrence: University Press of Kansas, 2002.

Craig Harris, Lillian. "The People's Republic of China and the Arab Middle East, 1948–1996: Arab Perspectives." In *China and Israel, 1948–1998: A Fifty Year Retrospective,* edited by Jonathan Goldstein, 47–63. Westport, CT: Praeger, 1999.

Crankshaw, Edward, and Strobe Talbott, eds. *Khrushchev Remembers.* Boston: Little, Brown and Company, 1970.

Crowl, Philip A. "Alfred Thayer Mahan: The Naval Historian." In *Makers of Modern Strategy: From Machiavelli to the Nuclear Age,* edited by Peter Paret, 445–77. Princeton: Princeton University Press, 1986.

Crowley, Monica. *Nixon in Winter.* New York: Random House, 1998.

Cumings, Bruce. "Tragedy and Hope on the Korean Peninsula." In *The Asia-Pacific in the New Millennium: Geopolitics, Security and Foreign Policy,* edited by Shalendra D. Sharma, 192–204. Berkeley: Regents of University of California, 2000.

Danner, Mark. "Abu Ghraib: The Hidden Story." *New York Review of Books* 51, no. 15 (October 7): 2004.

Das, Gurchuran. *India Unbound.* New York: Anchor Books, 2000.

Dawisha, Karen, and Bruce Parrott. *Russia and the New States of Eurasia: The Politics of Upheaval.* New York: Cambridge University Press, 1994.

Dibb, Paul. "The Revolution in Military Affairs and Asian Security." *Survival* 39, no. 4 (Winter 1997–1998): 93–116.

Diehl, Jackson. "An Explosive Gas Deal." *Washington Post,* February 27, 2006, A15.

Dittmer, Lowell. "China and Russia Approach the Millennium." In *The Asia-Pacific in the New Millennium: Geopolitics, Security and Foreign Policy,* edited by Shalendra D. Sharma, 165–91. Berkeley: Regents of University of California, 2000.

Dobrynin, Anatoly. *In Confidence: Moscow's Ambassador to America's Six Cold War Presidents.* New York: Times Books, 1995.

Doran, Charles F. "Economics, Philosophy of History, and the 'Single Dynamic' of Power Cycle Theory: Expectations, Competition, and Statecraft." *International Political Science Review* 24, no. 1 (2003): 13–49.

Doran, Charles F., and Wes Parsons. "War and the Cycle of Relative Power," *American Political Science Review* 74 (1980): 947–65.

Downs, Erica Strecker, and Phillip C. Saunders. "Legitimacy and the Limits of Nationalism: China and the Diaoyu Islands." *International Security* 23, no. 3 (Winter 1998–1999): 114–46.

Drahle, David Von. "Wrestling with History." *Washington Post,* November 13, 2005.

Drucker, Peter F. *Management Challenges for the 21st Century.* New York: Harper Business, 1999.

Duiker, William. *Ho Chi Minh.* New York: Hyperion, 2000.

Eban, Abba. *Diplomacy for the Next Century.* New Haven, CT: Yale University Press, 1998.

Eberstadt, Nicholas. "The Future of AIDS: Grim Toll in Russia, China and India." *Foreign Affairs* 81, no. 6 (November/December 2002): 22–45.

———. "Korea." In *Strategic Asia: Power and Purpose 2001–2002,* edited by Richard J. Ellings and Aaron L. Friedberg, 129–71. Seattle: National Bureau of Asian Research, 2001.

Eberstadt, Nicholas, and Richard J. Ellings. *Korea's Future and the Great Powers.* Seattle: National Bureau of Asian Research, 2001.

Economist Intelligence Unit. *Country Profile 2005* for Ethiopia, Kenya, South Korea, Taiwan, *Country Profile 2006* for China, India, Sudan.

Eilts, Hermann Frederick. "Saudi Arabia's Foreign Policy." In *Diplomacy in the Middle East: The International Relations of Regional and Outside Powers,* edited by L. Carl Brown, 219–44. New York: I.B. Tauris, 2001.

Elegant, Simon. "The Great Divide." *Time Asia,* April 16, 2006.

Elleman, Bruce. "Russian Foreign Policy in the Chinese Context." In *Imperial Decline: Russia's Changing Role in Asia,* edited by Stephen J. Blank and Alvin Z. Rubinstein, 99–126. Durham: Duke University Press, 1997.

Ellison, Herbert J. "Soviet–Chinese Relations: The Experience of Two Decades." In *China, the United States and the Soviet Union: Tripolarity and Policy-Making in the Cold War,* edited by Robert S. Ross, 93–121. Armonk, NY: M.E. Sharpe, 1993.

Elvin, Mark. *The Pattern of the Chinese Past.* Stanford, CA: Stanford University Press, 1973.

Fairbank, John King. "The Early Treaty System in the Chinese World Order." In *The Chinese World Order: Traditional China's Foreign Relations,* edited by John King Fairbank, 257–75. Cambridge, MA: Harvard University Press, 1968.

———. "A Preliminary Framework." In *The Chinese World Order: Traditional China's Foreign Relations,* edited by John King Fairbank, 1–19. Cambridge, MA: Harvard University Press, 1968.

Fairbank, John King, and Merle Goldman. *China: A New History.* Boston: Harvard University Press, 1998.

Faison, Seth. *South of the Clouds: Exploring the Hidden Realms of China.* New York: St. Martin's Press, 2004.

Feigenbaum, Evan A. "China's Challenge to *Pax Americana.*" *Washington Quarterly* 24, no. 3 (Summer 2001): 31–43.

———. "China's Military Posture and the New Economic Geopolitics." *Survival* 41, no. 2 (Summer 1999): 71–88.

———. "Who's Behind China's High-Technology 'Revolution'?" *International Security* 24, no. 1 (Summer 1999): 95–126.

Feldman, Noah. "Islam, Terror and the Second Nuclear Age." *New York Times Magazine,* October 29, 2006.

Felgenhauer, Pavel. "Proliferation of the Bigwigs." *Moscow Times,* February 22, 2005, 11.

Finkelstein, David M. *China Reconsiders Its National Security: "The Great Peace and Development Debate of 1999."* Alexandria, Virginia: CNA Corporation, December 2000.

Fitzgerald, Frances. *Way Out There in the Blue.* New York: Simon & Schuster 2000.

Fletcher, Joseph. "Sino-Russian Relations, 1800–62." In *Cambridge History of China,* edited by Denis Twitchet and John K. Fairbank, Vol. 10, pt. 1, 318–50. New York: Cambridge University Press, 1978.

Foust, Clifford M. *Muscovite and Mandarin: Russia's Trade with China and its Setting, 1727–1805.* Chapel Hill: The University of North Carolina Press, 1969.

Freedman, Lawrence. "The First Two Generations of Nuclear Strategists." In *Makers of Modern Strategy,* edited by Peter Paret, 735–78. Princeton: Princeton University Press, 1986.

———. "The New Great Power Politics." In *Russia and the West: The 21st Century Security Environment,* edited by Robert Legvold, Karl Kaiser, and Alexei Arbatov, 21–43. Armonk, NY: M.E. Sharpe, 1999.

———. "The Revolution in Strategic Affairs." *Adelphi Paper 318.* London: Oxford University Press for The International Institute for Strategic Studies, 1998.

Freedman, Robert O. "Russia, Iran, and the Nuclear Record: The Putin Record." *Jerusalem Viewpoints,* no. 544, July 2, 2006. Available online at http://jcpa.org/jl/vp544.htm (last accessed September 2007).

Friedberg, Aaron L. "The Future of U.S.–China Relations: Is Conflict Inevitable?" *International Security* 30, no. 2 (Fall 2005): 7–45.

———. "Introduction." In *Strategic Asia: Power and Purpose 2001–2002,* edited by Richard J. Ellings and Aaron L. Friedberg, 1–25. Seattle: National Bureau of Asian Research, 2001.

Friedman, George. *America's Secret War: Inside the Hidden Worldwide Struggle Between America and Its Enemies.* New York: Doubleday, 2004.

Friedman, Thomas. *The Lexus and the Olive Tree.* New York: Farrar, Straus and Giroux, 1999.

Fromkin, David. *A Peace to End All Peace.* New York: Avon Books, 1989.

Fu, Jun. *Institutions and Investments: FDI in China During an Era of Reforms.* Ann Arbor: University of Michigan Press, 2000, Table IV-3: FDI Inflows in China, 1978–98, 127.

Fuller, Graham E., and S. Frederick Starr. *The Xinjiang Problem.* Washington, DC: Central Asia Caucasus Institute, 2004.

Fuller, William C., Jr. *Strategy and Power in Russia 1600–1914.* New York: The Free Press, 1992.

Fursenko, Aleksandr, and Timothy Naftali. *Khrushchev's Cold War: The Inside Story of an American Adversary.* New York: W.W. Norton, 2006.

Gaddis, John Lewis. *The Cold War: A New History.* New York: Penguin Press, 2005.

———. *Surprise, Security, and the American Experience.* Cambridge: Harvard University Press, 2004.

———. *We Now Know: Rethinking Cold War History.* New York: Oxford University Press, 1997.

Garnett, Sherman W. "Challenges of the Sino-Russian Strategic Partnership." *Washington Quarterly* 24, no. 4 (Autumn 2001): 41–54.

Garten, Jeffrey E. "A Foreign Policy Harmful to Business." *Business Week,* October 14, 2002, 72–76.

Garver, John W. "The Indian Factor in Recent Sino-Soviet Relations." *China Quarterly* 125 (March 1991): 55–85.

———. *Protracted Contest: Sino-Indian Rivalry in the Twentieth Century.* Seattle: University of Washington Press, 2001.

Gelman, Harry. "Implications for the United States of Russia's Far East Policy." In *Imperial Decline: Russia's Changing Role in Asia,* edited by Stephen J. Blank and Alvin Z. Rubinstein, 213–43. Durham: Duke University Press, 1997.

Gentry, J. Brandon. "The Dragon and the Magi: Burgeoning Sino-Iranian Relations in the 21st Century." *China and Eurasia Forum Quarterly* 3, no. 3 (November 2005): 111–25.

Gertz, Bill. "China Builds Up Strategic Sea Lanes." *Washington Times,* January 18, 2005.

Gill, Bates, and Matthew Oresman. *China's New Journey to the West: China's Emergence in Central Asia and Implications for U.S. Interests.* Washington, DC: Center for Strategic and International Studies, August, 2003.

Glaser, Bonnie S. "Rice Seeks to Caution, Cajole, and Cooperate with Beijing." In *Comparative Connections, U.S.–China Relations.* Washington, DC: CSIS, April 2005.

Glaser, Bonnie S., and Jane Skanderup. "Anxiety About Taiwan Hits New Highs." In *Comparative Connections, U.S.–China Relations.* Washington, DC: CSIS, July 2004.

Godwin, Paul H.B. "From Continent to Periphery: PLA Doctrine, Strategy and Capabilities Towards 2000." *China Quarterly,* no. 146 (June 1996): 464–87.

Goldberg, Jeffrey. "Breaking Ranks: What Turned Brent Scowcroft Against the Bush Administration?" *New Yorker,* October 31, 2005.

Goldman, Stuart D. "Russia." *Congressional Research Service Issue Brief for Congress,* updated May 29, 2003. Available online at http://fpc.state.gov/documents/organization/21351.pdf (last accessed September 2007).

Goldstein, Avery. *Deterrence and Security in the 21st Century: China, Britain, France and the Enduring Legacy of the Nuclear Revolution.* Stanford, CA: Stanford University Press, 2000.

———. "Great Expectations: Interpreting China's Arrival." *International Security* 22, no. 2 (Autumn 1997): 36–73.

Goldstein, Melvyn C. *The Snow Lion and the Dragon: China, Tibet and the Dalai Lama.* Berkeley: University of California Press, 1997.

Goncharev, Sergei N., John Lewis, and Xue Litai. *Uncertain Partners: Stalin, Mao and the Korean War.* Stanford, CA: Stanford University Press, 1993.

Gorbachev, Mikhail. *Memoirs.* New York: Doubleday, 1995.

Graham, Bradley. "Rumsfeld Discusses Tighter Military Ties with Azerbaijan." *Washington Post,* December 4, 2003, A23.

Gray, Colin S. *The Geopolitics of Super Power.* Lexington: University Press of Kentucky, 1988.

Grimmett, Richard F. "U.S. Arms Sales: Agreements with and Deliveries to Major Clients, 1996–2003." Washington, DC: Congressional Research Service, December 8, 2004.

Halberstam, David. *The Best and the Brightest.* New York: Random House, 1972.

———. *War in a Time of Peace: Bush, Clinton, and the Generals.* New York: Scribner, 2001.

Harris, George S. "Turkey's Foreign Policy: Independent or Reactive?" In *Diplomacy in the Middle East: The International Relations of Regional and Outside Powers,* edited by L. Carl Brown, 259–77. New York: I.B. Tauris, 2001.

Hartung, William D., Frida Berrigan, and Michelle Ciarroca. "Operation Endless Deployment." *Nation,* October 21, 2002.

Haselkorn, Avigdor. *Continuing Storm.* New Haven: Yale University Press, 1999.

Hersh, Seymour. "The Iran Plans." *New Yorker,* August 21, 2006.

Herspring, Dale R., and Jacob Kipp. "Understanding the Elusive Mr. Putin." *Problems of Post-Communism* 48, no. 5 (September/October 2001): 3–17.

Hessler, Peter. *Oracle Bones: A Journey Between China's Past and Present.* New York: Harper Collins, 2006.

———. *River Town: Two Years on the Yangtze.* New York: Harper Collins, 2001.

Hirsch, Robert L. "Peaking of World Oil Production: Impacts, Mitigation, & Risk Management" (aka "The Hirsch Report") February 2005. This report was commissioned by the U.S. Department of Energy's National Energy Technology Laboratory and produced under the auspices of Science Applications International Corporation (SAIC). Full text available at http://www.energybulletin.net/4638.html (last accessed April 2007).

Hoffman, David E. *The Oligarchs: Wealth and Power in the New Russia.* New York: Public Affairs, 2002.

Horner, Charles. "China and the Historians." *National Interest,* Spring 2001, 86–96.

———. "The Other Orientalism: China's Islamist Problem." *National Interest,* Spring 2002, 37–45.

Howard, Michael. *Lessons of History.* New Haven: Yale University Press, 1991.

———. "Smoke on the Horizon." *Financial Times,* September 6, 2002.

Hunt, Michael H. "Chinese Foreign Relations in Historical Perspective." In *China's Foreign Relations in the 1980s,* edited by Harry Harding, 1–42. New Haven: Yale University Press, 1984.

Huntington, Samuel P. *The Clash of Civilizations and the Remaking of the World Order.* New York: Simon & Schuster, 1996.

———. "The Lonely Superpower." *Foreign Affairs* 78, no. 2 (March/April 1999): 35–49.

Ignatieff, Michael. "The Burden." *New York Times,* January 5, 2003, 50.

Iklé, Fred C. "The Next Lenin: On the Cusp of Truly Revolutionary Warfare." *National Interest,* no. 47, Spring 1997, 9–19.

Ingram, Judith. "Russia, United States Increasingly at Odds." *The Associated Press,* April 4, 2006.

International Institute of Strategic Studies (IISS). *Military Balance* 2002–2003, 2003–2004, 2004–2005, 2005–2006. London: IISS.

International Monetary Fund. *Direction of Trade Statistics Yearbook* 2000, 2001, 2002, 2003, 2004, 2005.

Isaacson, Walter, and Evan Thomas. *The Wise Men: Six Friends and the World They Made: Acheson, Bohlen, Harriman, Kennan, Lovett, McCloy.* New York: Simon & Schuster, 1986.

Jacobs, Dan N. *Borodin: Stalin's Man in China.* Cambridge: Harvard University Press, 1981.

Jaffe, Amy Myers, and Robert A. Manning. "Russia, Energy and the West." *Survival* 43, no. 2 (Summer 2001): 133–52.

Jansen, Marius B. *The Making of Modern Japan.* Cambridge, MA: Belknap Press of Harvard University, 2000.

Jin, Ha. *Ocean of Words: Stories.* New York: Vintage, 1998.

———. *War Trash.* New York: Pantheon Books, 2004.

Joffe, Josef. *Überpower: The Imperial Temptation of America.* New York: Norton, 2006.

Johnson, Chalmers. *Blowback: The Costs and Consequences of American Empire.* New York: Henry Holt, 2000.

———. "Korea and Our Asia Policy." *National Interest,* no. 41, Fall 1995, 66–77.

———. *The Sorrows of Empire: Militarism, Secrecy, and the End of the Republic.* New York: Metropolitan Books/Henry Holt, 2004.

Johnson, Ian. *Wild Grass: Three Stories of Change in Modern China.* New York: Pantheon, 2004.

———. "China Searches for Stable Sources of Energy Abroad." *Wall Street Journal,* June 25, 1997: A18.

Johnston, Alastair Iain. "China's Militarized Interstate Dispute Behavior 1949–1992: A First Cut at the Data." *China Quarterly,* no. 153 (March 1998): 1–30.

———. "China's New 'Old Thinking': The Concept of Limited Deterrence." *International Security* 20, no. 3 (Winter 1995): 5–42.

Judis, John B., and Ruy Teixeira. *The Emerging Democratic Majority.* New York: Scribner, 2002.

Judt, Tony. *Postwar: A History of Europe Since 1945.* New York: The Penguin Press, 2005.

Kagan, Robert. *Of Paradise and Power: America and Europe in the New World Order.* New York: Vintage, 2004.

Kahn, Joseph. "Bush and Hu Vow New Cooperation." *New York Times,* April 21, 2006.

———. "Taiwan Voters Weighing How Far to Push China." *New York Times,* March 18, 2004, A1.

Kaiser, Robert G. "From Citizen K Street: How Lobbying Became Washington's Biggest Business." Chap. 15. *Washington Post,* March 25, 2007.

Kan, Shirley. "Taiwan: Major U.S. Arms Sales Since 1990." Washington, DC: Congressional Research Service, March 2005.

Kaplan, Robert D. *Imperial Grunts: The American Military on the Ground.* New York: Random House, 2005.

Karny, Yo'av. *Highlanders: A Journey to the Caucasus in Quest of Memory.* New York: Farrar, Straus and Giroux, 2000.

Karpin, Michael. *The Bomb in the Basement: How Israel Went Nuclear and What That Means for the World.* New York: Simon & Schuster, 2006.

Keegan, Nicholas M. "From Chancery to Cloister: The Chinese Diplomat who Became a Benedictine Monk." *Diplomacy and Statecraft* 10, no. 1 (March 1999): 172–85.

Kennedy, Paul. "The Eagle Has Landed." *Financial Times,* January 31, 2002.

———. *The Rise and Fall of the Great Powers: Economic Change and Military Conflict from 1500 to 2000.* New York: Random house, 1987.

Khalilzad, Zalmay, Abram N. Shulsky, Daniel Byman, Roger Cliff, David T. Orletsky, David A. Shlapak, and Ashley J. Tellis. *The United States and a Rising China.* Santa Monica, CA: RAND, 1999.

Khrushchev, Nikita S. *Khrushchev Remembers: The Last Testament.* Boston: Little, Brown and Company, 1974.

Kim, Samuel S. "The Making of China's Korea Policy in the Era of Reform." In *The Making of Chinese Foreign and Security Policy in the Era of Reform 1978–2000,* edited by David M. Lampton, 371–408. Stanford, CA: Stanford University Press, 2001.

King, Ralph. "The Iran–Iraq War: The Political Implications." *Adelphi Paper 219.* London: Oxford University Press for The International Institute for Strategic Studies, 1987.

Kinzer, Stephen. *Overthrow: America's Century of Regime Change from Hawaii to Iraq.* New York: Henry Holt, 2006.

Kissinger, Henry. *Diplomacy.* New York: Simon & Schuster, 1994.

———. *Does America Need a Foreign Policy?* New York: Simon & Schuster, 2001.

———. *Ending the Vietnam War.* New York: Simon & Schuster, 2003.

———. *White House Years.* Boston: Little, Brown and Company, 1979.

———. *Years of Renewal.* New York: Simon & Schuster, 1999.

———. *Years of Upheaval.* Boston: Little, Brown and Company, 1982.

Klare, Michael T. *Blood and Oil: The Dangers and Consequences of America's Growing Dependency on Imported Petroleum.* New York: Metropolitan Books, 2004.

———. *Resource Wars: The New Landscape of Global Conflict.* New York: Metropolitan Books, 2001.

———. "Revving Up the China Threat." *Nation,* October 24, 2005.

Kotkin, Stephen, and Bruce A. Elleman. *Mongolia in the Twentieth Century: Landlocked Cosmopolitan.* Armonk, NY: M.E. Sharpe, 1999.

Kramer, Andrew. "Gazprom Intends to Develop Huge Gas Field on Its Own." *New York Times,* October 10, 2006.

———. "Russia to Sell Anti-Aircraft Missiles to Iran." *New York Times,* December 3, 2005.

Kramer, Mark. "Did the Russians Aid Saddam Hussein's War Effort?" *PONARS Policy Memo No. 405.* Washington, DC: CSIS, April 2006.

Krepinivich, Andrew F. "Cavalry to Computers: The Pattern of Military Revolutions." *National Interest,* Fall 1994, 30–42.

Kristof, Nicholas D., and Sheryl Wu Dunn. *Thunder from the East.* New York: Knopf, 2000.

Krueger, Alan B. "Economic Scene." *New York Times,* April 3, 2003.

Kruze, Uldis. "China–Japan Relations." In *The Asia-Pacific in the New Millennium: Geopolitics, Security and Foreign Policy,* edited by Shalendra D. Sharma, 135–48. Berkeley: Regents of University of California, 2000.

Kuchins, Andrew C. "Will the Authoritarians of the World Unite?" *Moscow Times,* March 28, 2006, 10.

Kumaraswamy, P.R. "The Limitations of Indo-Israeli Military Cooperation." *Contemporary South Asia* 5, no. 1 (March 1996): 75–84.

———. "South Asia and People's Republic of China–Israeli Diplomatic Relations." In *China and Israel, 1948–1998: A Fifty Year Retrospective,* edited by Jonathan Goldstein, 131–52. Westport, CT: Praeger, 1999.

———. "The Strangely Parallel Careers of Israel and Pakistan." *Middle East Quarterly* 4, no. 2 (June 1997): 31–39.

Kynge, James. *China Shakes the World: A Titan's Rise and Troubled Future—and the Challenge for America.* New York: Houghton Mifflin, 2006.

Lague, David. "China Buys Stake in Russian Oil with Eye to Future." *New York Times,* July 19, 2006.

Lampton, David M. "China and the Strategic Quadrangle." In *The Strategic Quadrangle: Russia, China, Japan and the United States in East Asia,* edited by Michael Mandelbaum, 63–106. New York: Council on Foreign Relations Press, 1995.

———. "China's Foreign and National Security Policy-Making Process: Is It Changing, and Does It Matter?" In *The Making of Chinese Foreign and Security Policy in the Era of Reform 1978–2000,* edited by David M. Lampton, 1–36. Stanford, CA: Stanford University Press, 2001.

———. "Paradigm Lost." *National Interest,* no. 81, Fall 2005, 73–80.

Lampton, David M., and Richard Daniel Ewing. *The U.S.–China Relationship Facing International Crises: Three Case Studies in Post-9/11 Bilateral Relations.* Washington, DC: The Nixon Center, 2003.

Landes, David. *The Wealth and Poverty of Nations.* London: Little, Brown and Company, 1998.

Latynina, Yulia. "The Geopolitics of Accounts Receivable." *Moscow Times,* March 28, 2007, 8.

LeDonne, John P. *The Russian Empire and the World 1700–1917: The Geopolitics of Expansion and Containment.* Oxford: Oxford University Press, 1997.

Ledyard, Gari. "Yin and Yang in the China–Manchuria–Korea Triangle." In *China Among Equals: The Middle Kingdom and Its Neighbors, 10th–14th Centuries,* edited by Morris Rossabi, 313–53. Berkeley: University of California Press, 1983.

Legvold, Robert. "Sino-Soviet Relations: The American Factor." In *China, the United States and the Soviet Union: Tripolarity and Policy-Making in the Cold War,* edited by Robert S. Ross, 65–92. Armonk, NY: M.E. Sharpe, 1993.

Lewis, John Wilson, and Xue Litai. *China Builds the Bomb.* Stanford, CA: Stanford University Press, 1988.

Li, Zhisui, with the editorial assistance of Anne F. Thurston. *The Private Life of Chairman Mao: The Memoirs of Mao's Personal Physician.* New York: Random House, 1994.

Lieberthal, Kenneth. *Governing China: From Revolution Through Reform.* New York: W.W. Norton, 1995.

Lieven, Anatol. *Chechnya: Tombstone of Russian Power.* New Haven: Yale University Press, 1998.

Lieven, Dominic. *Empire: The Russian Empire and Its Rivals.* London: John Murray, 2000.

Lilley, James, with Jeffrey Lilley. *China Hands: Nine Decades of Adventure, Espionage and Diplomacy in Asia.* New York: Public Affairs, 2004.

Lind, Jennifer. "Dangerous Games." *Atlantic Monthly,* March 2006.

Lind, Jennifer, and Thomas J. Christensen. "Spirals, Security and Stability in East Asia." *International Security* 24, no. 4 (Spring 2000): 190–200.

Liu, Melinda. "About Face." *Newsweek,* April 21, 2006.

Loh, Anthony Alexander. "The Hegemon's Motif: The People's Republic of China and the Middle East, 1949–1998." In *China and Israel, 1948–1998: A Fifty Year Retrospective,* edited by Jonathan Goldstein, 65–81. Westport, CT: Praeger, 1999.

Lohr, Steve. "State Department Yields on PCs From China." *New York Times,* May 23, 2006.

Lu, Nanquan. "Chinese Views of the New Russia." In *Rapprochement or Rivalry,* edited by Sherman W. Garnett, 99–116. Washington, DC: CEIP, 2000.

Lu, Ning. "The Central Leadership, Supraministry Coordinating Bodies, State Council Ministries and Party Departments." In *The Making of Chinese Foreign and Security Policy in the Era of Reform 1978–2000,* edited by David M. Lampton, 39–60. Stanford, CA: Stanford University Press, 2001.

Luce, Edward. *In Spite of the Gods: The Strange Rise of Modern India.* New York: Doubleday, 2007.

Luft, Gal. "Hizballahland." *Commentary,* July–August 2003, 56–60.

Lukin, Alexander. *The Bear Watches the Dragon: Russia's Perceptions of China and the Evolution of Russian–Chinese Relations Since the Eighteenth Century.* Armonk, NY: M.E. Sharpe 2003.

———. "Russia's Image of China and Russian–Chinese Relations." *CNAPS Working Paper* May 2001, Washington, DC: The Brookings Institution, 2001. Available online at http://www.brookings.edu/fp/cnaps/papers/lukinwp_01.pdf (last accessed April 2007).

Luttwak, Edward. *The Grand Strategy of the Soviet Union.* New York: St. Martin's Press, 1983.

———. "Three Reasons Not to Bomb Iran—Yet." *Commentary,* May 2006, 21–28.

Maass, Peter. "The Beginning of the End of Oil." *New York Times,* August 21, 2005.

Mackinder, H.J. "The Geographical Pivot of History." *Geographical Journal* 23, no. 4 (April 1904): 422–37.

MacMillan, Margaret. *Paris 1919: Six Months That Changed the World.* New York: Random House, 2001.

Mahbubani, Kishore. *Can Asians Think? Understanding the Divide Between East and West.* South Royalton, VT: Steerforth Press, 2002.

Mancall, Mark. *China at the Center: 300 Years of Foreign Policy.* New York: The Free Press, 1984.

———. "The Ch'ing Tribute System: An Interpretive Essay." In *The Chinese World Order: Traditional China's Foreign Relations,* edited by John K. Fairbank, 63–89. Cambridge, MA: Harvard University Press, 1968.

———. *Russia and China: Their Diplomatic Relations to 1728.* Cambridge, MA: Harvard University Press, 1971.

Mandelbaum, Michael. *The Fate of Nations.* New York: Cambridge University Press, 1988.

————. *The Ideas That Conquered the World: Peace, Democracy and Free Markets in the Twenty-First Century.* New York: Public Affairs, 2002.

————, eds. *The Strategic Quadrangle: Russia, China, Japan and the United States in East Asia.* New York: Council on Foreign Relations Press, 1995.

Mann, James. *About Face: A History of America's Curious Relationship with China, From Nixon to Clinton.* New York: Knopf, 1999.

————. *Rise of the Vulcans: The History of Bush's War Cabinet.* New York: Viking, 2004.

Manning, Robert A. *The Asian Energy Factor: Myths and Dilemmas of Energy, Security and the Pacific Future.* New York: Palgrave/St. Martins, 2000.

Matthews, Owen, and Anna Nemtsova. "A Chill in the Moscow Air." *Newsweek,* February 6, 2006.

————. "Fear and Loathing in Siberia." *Newsweek,* March 27, 2006.

Maxwell, Charles T. *Barron's,* "The Gathering Storm," November 15, 2004. Full text available online at http://www.energybulletin.net/3161.html (last accessed April 2007).

Mayer, Jane. "Outsourcing Torture." *New Yorker,* February 14, 2005.

McNeill, William H. *The Pursuit of Power: Technology, Armed Force, and Society Since A.D. 1000.* Chicago: University of Chicago Press, 1982, esp. chap. 2, "The Era of Chinese Predominance 1000–1500," 24–62.

Mearsheimer, John J. *The Tragedy of Great Power Politics.* New York: W.W. Norton, 2001.

Medvedev, Roy. *China and the Superpowers.* New York: Basil Blackwell, 1986.

Meier, Andrew. *Black Earth: A Journey Through Russia After the Fall.* New York: W.W. Norton, 2003.

Menon, Rajan. "The Sick Man of Asia: Russia's Endangered Far East." *National Interest,* no. 73, Fall 2003, 93–105.

————. "The Strategic Convergence Between Russia and China." *Survival* 39, no. 2 (Summer 1997): 101–25.

————. "Structural Constraints on Russian Diplomacy." *Orbis* 45, no. 2 (Fall 2001): 579–96.

————. "Russia." In *Strategic Asia: Power and Purpose 2001–2002,* edited by Richard J. Ellings and Aaron L. Friedberg, 173–221. Seattle: National Bureau of Asian Research, 2001.

————. "Russo-Japanese Relations: Implications for Northeast Asian Security." In *Imperial Decline: Russia's Changing Role in Asia,* edited by Stephen J. Blank and Alvin Z. Rubinstein, 129–52. Durham: Duke University Press, 1997.

Menon, Rajan, and Charles E. Ziegler. "The Balance of Power and U.S. Foreign Policy Interests in the Russian Far East." *NBR Analysis* 11, no. 5, December 2000.

Menon, Rajan, and S. Enders Wimbush. "Asia in the 21st Century." *National Interest,* April 2000, 78–86.

Meyer, Karl E. *The Dust of Empire: The Race for Mastery in the Asian Heartland.* New York: Public Affairs, 2003.

Meyer, Karl E., and Shareen Blair Brysac. *Tournament of Shadows: The Great Game and the Race for Empire in Central Asia.* Washington, DC: Counterpoint, 1999.

Milbank, Dana. "China and Its President Greeted by a Host of Indignities." *Washington Post,* April 21, 2006, A02.

Miles, Tom. "Russia and China Promise Energy Cooperation." *Reuters,* March 21, 2006.

Miller, H. Lyman, and Liu Xiaohong. "The Foreign Policy Outlook of China's 'Third Generation' Elite." In *The Making of Chinese Foreign and Security Policy in the Era of Reform*

*1978–2000,* edited by David M. Lampton, 123–50. Stanford, CA: Stanford University Press, 2001.

Ming, Nelly. "China to Buy 10% of Myanmar's Gas Reserves." *Tanker World,* February 1, 2006.

Mirsky, Jonathan. "The Party Isn't Over." *New York Review of Books* LI, no. 8, May 13, 2004.

Modelski, George, and William R. Thompson. *Leading Sectors and World Powers: The Coevolution of Global Politics and Economics.* Columbia, SC: University of South Carolina Press, 1996.

Montefiore, Simon Sebag. *Stalin: The Court of the Red Tsar.* New York: Knopf, 2004.

Moore, James, and Wayne Slater. *Bush's Brain: How Karl Rove Made George W. Bush Presidential.* New Jersey: John Wiley & Sons, 2003.

Moore, Thomas G., and Dixia Yang. "Empowered and Restrained: Chinese Foreign Policy in the Age of Economic Interdependence." In *The Making of Chinese Foreign and Security Policy in the Era of Reform 1978–2000,* edited by David M. Lampton, 191–229. Stanford, CA: Stanford University Press, 2001.

Morris, Edmund. *Theodore Rex.* New York: Random House, 2001.

Morse, Edward L., and James Richard. "The Battle for Energy Dominance." *Foreign Affairs* 81, no. 2 (March/April 2002): 16–31.

Mrozinski, Lawrence G., Thomas Williams, Roman H. Kent, and Robin D. Tyner. "Countering China's Threat to the Western Hemisphere." *International Journal of Intelligence and Counterintelligence* 15, no. 2 (Spring 2002): 195–210.

Muindi, Matthias. "Dam Could Provoke Water Wars." *NewsfromAfrica,* January 2002.

Myers, Steven Lee. "Chinese Embassy Bombing: A Wide Net of Blame." *New York Times,* April 17, 2000.

Nathan, Andrew J., and Robert S. Ross. *The Great Wall and the Empty Fortress: China's Search for Security.* New York: W. W. Norton, 1997.

National Intelligence Council. *Global Trends 2015: A Dialogue About the Future with Nongovernment Experts.* Washington, DC: Central Intelligence Agency, December 2000.

National Security Archive. *"Nixon/Kissinger Saw India as 'Soviet Stooge' in 1971 South Asia Crisis."* June, 29, 2005.

Noer, John H., with David Gregory. *Chokepoints: Maritime Economic Concerns in Southeast Asia.* Washington, DC: National Defense University Press, 1996.

Norris, Robert S., William M. Arkin, and William Burr. "Where They Were." *Bulletin of Atomic Scientists* 55, no. 6 (November/December 1999): 26–35.

Norton, Anne. *Leo Strauss and the Politics of American Empire.* New Haven: Yale University Press, 2004.

O'Hanlon, Michael. "Why China Cannot Conquer Taiwan." *International Security* 25, no. 2 (Fall 2000): 51–86.

Oberdorfer, Don. *The Two Koreas: A Contemporary History.* Rev. ed. New York: Basic Books, 2001, esp. chap. 13, "Showdown over Nuclear Weapons," 305–36.

Ogilvy, James, and Peter Schwartz. *China's Future.* San Francisco: Jossey-Bass Publishers, 2000.

Olson, Robert. "The Kurdish Question and Chechnya: Turkish and Russian Foreign Policies Since the Gulf War." *Middle East Policy* IV, no. 3 (March 1996): 106–18.

Organski, A. F. K., and Jacek Kugler. *The War Ledger.* Chicago: University of Chicago Press, 1980.

Orwell, Sonia, and Ian Angus, eds. *George Orwell: The Collected Essays—Volume 4, In Front of Your Nose.* Boston: D.R. Godine, 2000.

Paine, S.C.M. *Imperial Rivals: China, Russia, and Their Disputed Frontier.* Armonk, NY: M.E. Sharpe, 1996.

Pape, Robert A. "The True Worth of Air Power." *Foreign Affairs* 83, no. 2 (March/April 2004): 116–30.

Paret, Peter. "Revolutions in Warfare: An Earlier Generation of Interpreters." In *National Security and International Stability,* edited by Bernard Brodie, Michael D. Intriligator, and Roman Kolkowicz, 157–69. Cambridge, MA: Oelgeschlager, Gunn & Hain, 1983.

Pastor, Robert A., ed. *A Century's Journey: How the Great Powers Shape the World.* New York: Basic Books, 1999.

Pavliatenko, Viktor N. "Russian Security in the Pacific Asian Region: The Dangers of Isolation." In *Russia and East Asia: The 21st Century Security Environment,* edited by Gilbert Rozman, Mikhail G. Nosov, and Koji Watanabe, 13–44. Armonk, NY: M.E. Sharpe, 1999.

Perry, William, Chair. National Security Advisory Group. "An American Security Policy: Challenge, Opportunity, Commitment," July 2003.

Peterson, Peter G. *Gray Dawn: How the Coming Age Wave Will Transform America—and the World.* New York: Times Books/Random House, 1999.

Petrov, Alexander. "Russia's 'Spy-Mania.'" *Human Rights Watch Briefing Paper,* October 2003.

Phillips, Kevin. *American Theocracy: The Peril and Politics of Radical Religion, Oil, and Borrowed Money in the 21st Century.* New York: Viking, 2006.

Politkovskaya, Anna. *Putin's Russia: Life in a Failing Democracy.* New York: Metropolitan Books, 2005.

Pomfret, John. "China Raises Defense Budget Again." *Washington Post,* March 5, 2002, A10.

———. *Chinese Lessons: Five Classmates and the Story of the New China.* New York: Henry Holt, 2006.

Pope, Nicole, and Hugh Pope. *Turkey Unveiled: A History of Modern Turkey.* New York: Overlook Press, 1997.

Powers, Thomas. *Intelligence Wars: American Secret History From Hitler to al-Qaeda.* New York: New York Review Books, 2002.

Prestowitz, Clyde. *Three Billion New Capitalists: The Great Shift of Wealth and Power to the East.* New York: Basic Books, 2005.

Priest, Dana. *The Mission: Waging War and Keeping Peace with America's Military.* New York: W.W. Norton, 2003.

Primakov, Evgeny. *Russian Crossroads: Toward the New Millennium.* New Haven: Yale University Press, 2004.

Pronina, Lyuba. "Moscow Inks Arms Deal with Tehran." *Moscow Times,* December 5, 2005, 1.

Pyle, Kenneth B., and Eric Heginbotham. "Japan." In *Strategic Asia: Power and Purpose 2001–2002,* edited by Richard J. Ellings and Aaron L. Friedberg, 71–126. Seattle: National Bureau of Asian Research, 2001.

Quested, Rosemary K.I. *Sino-Russian Relations: A Short History.* Sydney: George Allen & Unwin, 1984.

Ramachandran, Sudha. "China's Pearl in Pakistan's Waters." *Asia Times Online,* March 4, 2005.

Rashid, Ahmed. *Jihad: The Rise of Militant Islam in Central Asia*. New York: Penguin Books, 2002.

Reddaway, Peter. "Is Putin's Power More Formal Than Real?" *Post-Soviet Affairs* 18, no. 1 (2002): 31–40.

Reeves, Richard. *President Nixon: Alone in the White House*. New York: Simon & Schuster, 2001.

———. *President Reagan: The Triumph of Imagination*. New York: Simon & Schuster, 2005.

Reich, Bernard. "Israeli Foreign Policy." In *Diplomacy in the Middle East: The International Relations of Regional and Outside Powers*, edited by L. Carl Brown, 121–37. New York: I.B. Tauris, 2001.

Reid, Anna. *The Shaman's Coat: A Native History of Siberia*. New York: Walker & Company, 2002.

Reid, T. R. *The United States of Europe: The New Superpower and the End of American Supremacy*. New York: The Penguin Press, 2004.

Rickards, Jane. "Taiwan Rejects Most of U.S. Arms Package Offered in 2001." *Washington Post*, June 16, 2007, A11.

Rose, Leo E. "India and China: Forging a New Relationship." In *The Asia-Pacific in the New Millennium: Geopolitics, Security and Foreign Policy*, edited by Shalendra D. Sharma, 224–38. Berkeley: Regents of University of California, 2000.

Ross, Robert S. "Conclusion: Tripolarity and Policy-Making." In *China, the United States and the Soviet Union: Tripolarity and Policy-Making in the Cold War*, edited by Robert S. Ross, 179–95. Armonk, NY: M.E. Sharpe, 1993.

———. "The Geography of the Peace." *International Security* 23, no. 4 (Spring 1999): 81–118.

———. "The Stability of Deterrence in the Taiwan Strait." *National Interest*, Fall 2001, 67–76.

———. "Taiwan's Fading Independence Movement." *Foreign Affairs* 85, no. 2 (March/April 2006), 141–48.

———. "U.S. Policy Toward China: The Strategic Context and the Decision-Making Process." In *China, the United States and the Soviet Union: Tripolarity and Policy-Making in the Cold War*, edited by Robert S. Ross, 149–77, Armonk, NY: M.E. Sharpe, 1993.

Rossabi, Morris. "Introduction." In *China Among Equals: The Middle Kingdom and Its Neighbors, 10th–14th Centuries*, edited by Morris Rossabi, 1–13. Berkeley: University of California Press, 1983.

Rothkopf, David J. *Running the World: The Inside Story of the National Security Council and the Architects of American Power*. New York: Public Affairs, 2005.

Roy, Denny. *China's Foreign Relations*. Latham, MD: Rowman & Littlefield Publishers, 1998.

———. "The 'China' Threat Issue." *Asian Survey* 36, no. 8 (August 1996): 758–71.

Roy, Olivier. *The New Central Asia: The Creation of Nations*. New York: New York University Press, 2000.

Rozman, Gilbert. "Turning Fortresses into Free Trade Zones." In *Rapprochement or Rivalry*, edited by Sherman W. Garnett, 177–202. Washington, DC: CEIP, 2000.

Rubin, Barry. *Paved with Good Intentions: The American Experience and Iran*. New York: Oxford University Press, 1980.

Rubinstein, Alvin Z. "The Middle East in Russia's Strategic Prism." In *Diplomacy in the Middle East: The International Relations of Regional and Outside Powers*, edited by L. Carl Brown, 75–94. New York: I.B. Tauris, 2001.

————. *Soviet Policy Toward Turkey, Iran and Afghanistan.* New York: Praeger, 1982.

Safire, William. "Rise of the Stepson." *New York Times,* January 15, 1996, A17.

Salisbury, Harrison E. *The New Emperors: China in the Era of Mao and Deng.* New York: Little, Brown and Company, 1992.

Saunders, Paul J. "Putin-Up Close, Sans Soul Gazing: Amid a Small Gathering, the Russian President Talks Tough To America." *National Interest Online,* September 11, 2006.

Scalapino, Robert A. "The Asia-Pacific in the New Millennium." In *The Asia-Pacific in the New Millennium: Geopolitics, Security and Foreign Policy,* edited by Shalendra D. Sharma, 15–30. Berkeley: Regents of University of California, 2000.

Schlesinger Jr., Arthur M. "America and Empire." In *The Cycles of American History,* edited by Arthur M. Schlesinger Jr., 118–62. Boston: Houghton Mifflin Company, 1986.

————. "The Cycles of American Politics." In *The Cycles of American History,* edited by Arthur M. Schlesinger Jr., 23–48. Boston: Houghton Mifflin Company, 1986.

Schwartz, Benjamin I. "The Chinese Perception of World Order, Past and Present." In *The Chinese World Order: Traditional China's Foreign Relations,* edited by John Fairbank, 276–88. Cambridge, MA: Harvard University Press, 1968.

Segal, Gerald. "China Changes Shape: Regionalism and Foreign Policy." *Adelphi Paper 287.* London: Oxford University Press for The International Institute for Strategic Studies, 1994.

————. *Defending China.* New York: Oxford University Press, 1985.

————. "East Asia and the 'Constrainment' of China." *International Security* 20, no. 4 (Spring 1996): 107–35.

Sergounin, Alexander A., and Sergey V. Subbotin. *Russian Arms Transfers to East Asia in the 1990s: SIPRI Research Report No. 15.* New York: Oxford University Press for SIPRI, 1999.

Sestanovich, Stephen. "The Third World in Soviet Foreign Policy, 1955–1985." In *The Soviet Union and the Third World: The Last Three Decades,* edited by Andrzej Korbonski and Francis Fukuyama, 1–29. Ithaca, NY: Cornell University Press, 1987.

————. "U.S. Policy Toward the Soviet Union, 1970–90: The Impact of China." In *China, the United States and the Soviet Union: Tripolarity and Policy-Making in the Cold War,* edited by Robert S. Ross, 125–47. Armonk, NY: M.E. Sharpe, 1993.

Shambaugh, David. "China and the Korean Peninsula: Playing for the Long Term." *Washington Quarterly* 26, no. 2 (Spring 2003): 43–56.

Sheridan, James E. "The Warlord Era: Politics and Militarism Under the Peking Government, 1916–28." In *The Cambridge History of China,* edited by John K. Fairbank, Vol. 12, *Republican China 1912–1949,* pt. I, 284–321. New York: Cambridge University Press, 1983.

Shevchenko, Arkady N. *Breaking with Moscow.* New York: Knopf, 1985.

Shichor, Yitzhak. "The Chinese Factor in the Middle East Security Equation: An Israeli Perspective." In *China and Israel, 1948–1998: A Fifty Year Retrospective,* edited by Jonathan Goldstein, 153–78. Westport, CT: Praeger, 1999.

Shkuropat, Anna V. "New Dynamics in Northeast Asia: The Russian Factor." *CNAPS Working Paper,* June 2002, Washington, DC: The Brookings Institution, 2002. Available online at http://www.brookings.edu/fp/cnaps/papers/2002_shkuropat.pdf (last accessed April 2007).

Short, Philip. *Mao: A Life.* London: Hodder and Stoughton, 1999.

Shy, John, and Thomas W. Collier. "Revolutionary War." In *Makers of Modern Strategy: From Machiavelli to the Nuclear Age,* edited by Peter Paret, 815–62. Princeton: Princeton University Press, 1986.

Simon, Sheldon W. "Southeast Asia." In *Strategic Asia: Power and Purpose 2001–2002,* edited by Richard J. Ellings and Aaron L. Friedberg, 269–97. Seattle: National Bureau of Asian Research, 2001.

Slevin, Peter. "Powell Decries Putin's Policies." *Washington Post,* January 27, 2004, A14.

———. "3 Russian Firms' Deals Anger U.S." *Washington Post,* March 23, 2003, A19.

Smolansky, Oles M. "Russia and the Asia-Pacific Region: Policies and Polemics." In *Imperial Decline: Russia's Changing Role in Asia,* edited by Stephen J. Blank and Alvin Z. Rubenstein, 7–39. Durham: Duke University Press, 1997.

Solomon, Richard H. *Chinese Political Negotiating Behavior, 1967–1984.* Santa Monica, CA: RAND, 1995.

Spence, Jonathan D. *The Search for Modern China.* New York: W.W. Norton & Company, 1990.

Steele, Jonathan. *Eternal Russia: Yeltsin, Gorbachev and the Mirage of Democracy.* London: Faber and Faber, 1994.

Stent, Angela. *Russia and Germany Reborn: Unification, The Soviet Collapse, and the New Europe.* Princeton: Princeton University Press, 1999.

Stiglitz, Joseph. *Globalization and Its Discontents.* New York: W.W. Norton, 2002.

Stockwin, Harvey. "The Qian Qichen Op-Ed: Official Discontent or Just One Man's Opinion?" *The Jamestown Foundation's China Brief* 4, no. 24 (December 7): 2004.

Stokes, Mark A. "Taiwan's Security: Beyond the Special Budget." *Asian Outlook, an AEI Online Publication,* March 27, 2006: 2. Available online at http://www.aei.org/publications/filter.all,pubID.24113/pub_detail.asp (last accessed April 2007).

Stratfor. "Kremlin Tallies Cost of Supporting Hussein." April 8, 2003.

———. "U.S. Strategic Plan for the 21st Century: The Pacific, Part II." November 19, 2003.

———. "War in Iraq: What's at Stake for China?" December 13, 2002.

———. "War in Iraq: What's at Stake for Russia?" November 22, 2002.

———. "When Is 'Not a Base' Still a Base for US?" September 3, 2002.

Strode, Dan L. "Arms Control and Sino-Soviet Relations." *Orbis* 28, no. 1 (Spring 1984): 163–88.

Suettinger, Robert L. *Beyond Tiananmen: The Politics of U.S.–China Relations, 1989–2000* Washington, DC: Brookings Institution Press, 2003.

Swaine, Michael D. "Trouble in Taiwan." *Foreign Affairs* 83, no. 2 (March/April 2004): 39–49.

Swaine, Michael D., and Ashley J. Tellis. *Interpreting China's Grand Strategy: Past, Present and Future.* Santa Monica, CA: RAND, 2000.

Swaine, Michael D., with Lauren H. Runyon. "Ballistic Missile Development." In *Strategic Asia: Power and Purpose 2001–2002,* edited by Richard J. Ellings and Aaron L. Friedberg, 299–360. Seattle: National Bureau of Asian Research, 2001.

Szulc, Tad. "The New Bigfoot in the Global Oil Market." *Los Angeles Times,* October 5, 1997, M-2.

Talbott, Strobe. *Engaging India: Diplomacy, Democracy, and the Bomb.* Washington, DC: Brookings, 2004.

———. *The Russia Hand.* New York: Random House, 2002.

Taubman, William. *Khrushchev: The Man and His Era.* New York: W.W. Norton & Company, 2003.

Tellis, Ashley J. "South Asia." In *Strategic Asia: Power and Purpose 2001–2002,* edited by Richard J. Ellings and Aaron L. Friedberg, 223–67. Seattle: National Bureau of Asian Research, 2001.

Tellis, Ashley J., Chung Min Lee, James Mulvenon, Courtney Purrington, and Michael D. Swaine. "Sources of Conflict in Asia." In *Sources of Conflict in the 21st Century,* edited by Zalmay Khalilzad, 43–170. Santa Monica: RAND, 1997.

Trenin, Dmitri. "The China Factor: Challenge and Chance for Russia." In *Rapprochement or Rivalry,* edited by Sherman W. Garnett, 39–70. Washington, DC: CEIP, 2000.

Troyakova, Tamara. "A View from the Russian Far East." In *Rapprochement or Rivalry,* edited by Sherman W. Garnett, 203–25. Washington, DC: CEIP, 2000.

Tyler, Patrick. *A Great Wall: Six Presidents and China: An Investigative History.* New York: Public Affairs, 1999.

Ulam, Adam B. *Expansion and Coexistence: The History of Soviet Foreign Policy, 1917–67.* New York: Praeger, 1968.

U.S.–China Security Review Commission. "The Defense Budget and the Military Economy." Chap. 9 in *The National Security Implications of the Economic Relationship Between the United States and China,* Washington, DC, July 2002.

U.S. Department of Defense. *Base Structure Report,* September 2004.

U.S. Department of Defense. *Worldwide Manpower Distribution by Geographical Area,* September 2004.

U.S. Department of Energy, Energy Information Administration. *International Energy Outlook 2005.* Table A4, "World Oil Consumption by Region, Reference Case," available at http://www.eia.doe.gov/oiaf/ieo/ieorefcase.html (last accessed April 2007).

U.S. Department of Energy, Energy Information Agency. *Country Analysis Briefs* (Angola, China, Iran, Russia, Sudan, United States).

U.S. Department of State, Bureau of Verification and Compliance. *World Military Expenditures and Arms Transfers, 1999–2000.* Washington, DC, June 2002.

Van Hollen, Christopher. "The Tilt Policy Revisited: Nixon–Kissinger Geopolitics and South Asia." *Asian Survey* XX, no. 4 (April 1980): 339–61.

Victor, David G., and Nadejda M. Victor. "Axis of Oil?" *Foreign Affairs* 82, no. 2 (March/April 2003): 47–61.

Vitkovskaya, Galina, Zhanna Zayonchkovskaya, and Kathleen Newland. "Chinese Migration into Russia." In *Rapprochement or Rivalry,* edited by Sherman W. Garnett, 347–68. Washington, DC: CEIP, 2000.

Voskressenski, Alexei D. "Russia's Evolving Grand Strategy Toward China." In *Rapprochement or Rivalry,* edited by Sherman W. Garnett, 117–45. Washington, DC: CEIP, 2000.

Walt, Vivienne. "Iran Looks East." *Fortune,* February 21, 2005.

Washington Post Foreign Service. "Russia Wondering What It Gets for Backing U.S. Against Iraq." *Washington Post* October 4, 2002, A22.

Wayne, Leslie, and David Barboza. "Unocal Deal: A Lot More Than Money Is At Issue." *New York Times,* June 24, 2005.

Weaver, Mary Anne. *Pakistan: In the Shadow of Jihad and Afghanistan.* New York: Farrar, Straus and Giroux, 2002.

Whiting, Allen S. "Chinese Foreign Policy Entering the Twenty-First Century." In *The Asia-Pacific in the New Millennium: Geopolitics, Security and Foreign Policy,* edited by Shalendra D. Sharma, 108–32. Berkeley: Regents of University of California, 2000.

———. *Soviet Policies in China, 1917–1924.* Stanford, CA: Stanford University Press, 1953.

Wilkenfeld, Jonathan, Michael Brecher, and Sheila Moser, eds. *Crises in the Twentieth Century, Volume II, Handbook of Foreign Policy Crises.* Oxford: Pergamon Press, 1988.

Wilson, Jeanne L. *Strategic Partners: Russian–Chinese Relations in the Post-Soviet Era.* Armonk, NY: M.E. Sharpe, 2004.

Wishnick, Elizabeth. "Chinese Perspectives on Cross-Border Relations." In *Rapprochement or Rivalry,* edited by Sherman W. Garnett, 227–56. Washington, DC: CEIP, 2000.

———. *Mending Fences: The Evolution of Moscow's China Policy from Brezhnev to Yeltsin.* Seattle: University of Washington Press, 2001.

———. "One Asia Policy or Two? Moscow and the Russian Far East Debate Russia's Engagement in Asia." *NBR Analysis* 13, no. 1, March 2002.

Woodward, Bob. *Plan of Attack.* New York: Simon & Schuster, 2004.

———. *State of Denial.* New York: Simon & Schuster, 2006.

———. *Veil: The Secret Wars of the CIA 1981–87.* New York: Simon & Schuster, 1987.

World Bank. *World Development Indicators.* Available online at www.worldbank.org/data.

You, Ji. *The Armed Forces of China.* New York: I.B. Tauris, 1999.

Yu, Bin. *Comparative Connections, Sino-Russian Relations.* Washington, DC: Center for Strategic & International Studies. *Comparative Connections* is a quarterly e-journal on East Asian bilateral relations available online at http://www.csis.org/pacfor/.

Zakaria, Fareed. "The Arrogant Empire." *Newsweek,* March 24, 2003, 18–33.

Zarakhovich, Yuri. "What Putin Hopes to Gain from Iran." *Time,* February 14, 2006.

Zhao, Quansheng. "China and the Dynamics of the Korean Peninsula." In *The Asia-Pacific in the New Millennium: Geopolitics, Security and Foreign Policy,* edited by Shalendra D. Sharma, 83–107. Berkeley: Regents of University of California, 2000.

Zimmermann, Warren. *First Great Triumph: How Five Americans Made Their Country a World Power.* New York: Farrar, Straus and Giroux, 2002.

Zubok, Vladislav, and Constantine Pleshakov. *Inside the Kremlin's Cold War: From Stalin to Khrushchev.* Cambridge: Harvard University Press, 1996.

# INDEX

# ABOUT THE AUTHOR

**MICHAEL L. LEVIN** is an Executive-in-Residence at the Thunderbird School of Global Management, where he has provided international consulting, research, and advising for both the school and its clients—multinational corporations. Levin has lived and worked in Hong Kong, Jerusalem, Moscow, Shanghai, and Washington, D.C. He currently resides in Chicago, where he is at work on his next book, the first English-language biography of Yevgeny Primakov, one of Russia's foremost diplomats and politicians.